A Comparison of Eastern and Western Parenting

Parenting adolescents is a challenging task for parents. Professionals offer a range of support and parenting programmes to support parents. However, the importance of culturally adapting parenting programmes to benefit parents and their adolescent children hasn't always been understood. This book provides a comparison of East and West parenting approaches and parenting programmes to show how vital a culturally sensitive approach is to the positive development of the parent–adolescent relationship. It offers a comprehensive overview of current theories and research on parenting adolescents. It focuses on comparing the differences in parenting style and practice between Chinese parents and their Western counterparts and the policy context in Chinese culture with that in the West. It also offers guidance on how to conduct an evaluation of parenting programmes and how to adapt them for the right cultural setting.

Postgraduate students studying parenting, developmental psychology or social work will find this work particularly useful, as will researchers in any of these areas.

Low Yiu Tsang Andrew is Assistant Professor at Department of Social and Behavioural Sciences, City University of Hong Kong. Before moving into social work education in 2010, he worked for 17 years as a registered social worker. His main research interests lie in the evaluation of preventive interventions like indigenous parenting programmes in Chinese culture, positive youth development programmes in school settings and suicide prevention programmes in school settings among others.

Routledge Studies in Asian Behavioural Sciences
Series Editor: T. Wing Lo
City University of Hong Kong

Archaeology of Psychotherapy in Korea
A Study of Korean Therapeutic Work and Professional Growth
Haeyoung Jeong

Hidden Youth and the Virtual World
The Process of Social Censure and Empowerment
Gloria Hongyee Chan

Psychoanalysis in Hong Kong
The Absent, the Present, and the Reinvented
Diego Busiol

Psycho-Criminological Perspective of Criminal Justice in Asia
Research and Practices in Hong Kong, Singapore, and Beyond
Edited by Heng Choon (Oliver) Chan and Samuel M.Y. Ho

Humour and Chinese Culture
A Psychological Perspective
Yue Xiao Dong

Idol Worship in Chinese Society
A Psychological Approach
Xiaodong Yue and Chau-kiu Cheung

A Comparison of Eastern and Western Parenting
Programmes, Policies and Approaches
Low Yiu Tsang Andrew

For the full list of titles in the series visit: www.routledge.com/Routledge-Studies-in-Asian-Behavioural-Sciences/book-series/RABS

A Comparison of Eastern and Western Parenting

Programmes, Policies and Approaches

Low Yiu Tsang Andrew

Routledge
Taylor & Francis Group
LONDON AND NEW YORK

First published 2019 by Routledge

2 Park Square, Milton Park, Abingdon, Oxfordshire OX14 4RN
52 Vanderbilt Avenue, New York, NY 10017

Routledge is an imprint of the Taylor & Francis Group, an informa business

First issued in paperback 2020

British Library Cataloguing-in-Publication Data
A catalogue record for this book is available from the British Library

Library of Congress Cataloging-in-Publication Data
Names: Low, Yiu Tsang Andrew, author
Title: A comparison of Eastern and Western parenting: programmes, policies and approaches/Low Yiu Tsang Andrew.
Description: Abingdon, Oxon; New York, NY: Routledge, 2019. | Series: Routledge studies in Asian behavioural sciences | Includes bibliographical references and index.
Identifiers: LCCN 2018045792 | ISBN 9781138574069 (hardback) | ISBN 9780203701317 (e-book)
Subjects: LCSH: Parenting—Cross-cultural studies. | Parenting—Western countries. | Parenting—Orient.
Classification: LCC HQ755.8.L6865 2019 | DDC 306.87409182/1—dc23
LC record available at https://lccn.loc.gov/2018045792

ISBN: 978-1-138-57406-9 (hbk)
ISBN: 978-0-367-66214-1 (pbk)

Typeset in Galliard
by Apex CoVantage, LLC

Contents

Acknowledgements

This book is based on my PhD dissertation submitted to the University of Bristol and on three articles that I have published in the *Journal of Social Work* and *Revista de Cercetare şi Intervenţie Socială*. It would not have been possible without the support of Professor T.W. Lo, head of the Department of Social and Behavioural Sciences, City University of Hong Kong, who has given me the opportunity to publish in his series. The original PhD dissertation would not have succeeded without the guidance and support of my PhD supervisors, Professor Elaine Farmer and Professor David Berridge, from the School for Policy Studies, University of Bristol. Their help, guidance, advice and patience in supervising my work has allowed me to develop skills and knowledge essential for the completion of this study. They also offered invaluable emotional support throughout the process, especially when I faced obstacles in my work. Their advice and teaching have enhanced my confidence in becoming a competent researcher.

I would also like to express my gratitude to Professor D. Shek of the Hong Kong Polytechnic University, who has given his approval for my use of the Chinese version of parent–adolescent conflict scales. My gratitude is also due to Dr E. Lieber of UCLA/NPI, who kindly allowed my use and modification of the Chinese Parenting Beliefs Questionnaire in this study.

I would like to offer my thanks to Dr T.Y. Lee, Dr John Bola, and Dr Ben Li from the City University of Hong Kong who kindly commented on the draft of my dissertation. They provided me with valuable help.

I would like to thank my wife Michelle, who has given me so much support over these past few years when we were facing many life challenges as well as my completion of this book. Her patience and emotional support have helped me greatly in its completion. I would like to thank my daughters, Grace and Eunice, who inspired me in how to become a father and awakened my interest in research related to parenting. And I would like to thank one above us all, the omnipresent God, for giving me an opportunity to study. He has given me the best supervisors, a supportive and warm family and the strength to complete this study. All glory, honour and praise be to our almighty heavenly Father.

Preface

Parenting adolescents is a challenge to parents worldwide. With changing family structures around the world, divorced and reconstituted families are now more common. Adolescents are normally brought up in non-intact families. Research informs us that there are many negative outcomes associated with adolescents growing up in non-intact families. These include adolescents' behavioural problems, like anti-social behaviour, and emotional problems such as anxiety, depression and suicidal acts. Parenting adolescents has become increasingly stressful for parents from non-intact families. Nevertheless, there is strong evidence that there are many positive outcomes for adolescents if their parents adopt positive parenting practices. Parenting programmes organised by both public and private sectors provide support for parents when they are in difficult situations. Studies have indicated that parents benefit from parenting programmes through improvements in their parenting skills and parenting attitudes, and that these programmes also improve outcomes for their adolescents. Nevertheless, there is little evidence available for helping professionals in Hong Kong to determine the effective elements in these programmes that could benefit parents. There is also a lack of interest among researchers to research the effectiveness of parenting programmes. This book fills this gap and provides a resource for university students who are interested in knowing more about parenting and parenting programmes and how to use them in their interventions. The first chapter introduces the concept of parenting and discusses the current policy and social contexts that currently make parenting a particularly hard job for parents of adolescents. The second chapter compares parenting and parenting styles in the West and in the local Hong Kong context. How parenting practices affect adolescents' behavioural and emotional outcomes is also discussed in detail in this chapter. It further argues that positive parenting practices are a promise for positive development in adolescents. Specifically, this chapter compares the Chinese and Euro–American parenting styles and how the differences between them determine research and practice in these cultures. Chapter 3 first discusses the historical development of parenting programmes, taking into consideration these programmes' roots in early childhood education and parents' participation in education in the early stages. Next, it looks at how, with the professionalisation of education and social welfare, parenting programmes are now conducted more often by professionals.

These intervention programmes are also based on different theoretical and research focuses. Chapter 4 examines our approach to evaluating parenting programmes. Despite the proliferation of parenting programmes in Hong Kong, researchers and interventionists have shown a lack of interest in evaluating the effectiveness of such programmes. Much of the previous research has depended on surveys of participants' opinions, with little use of scientific questionnaires or research tools. This chapter provides an overview of the paradigms and methodology used in programme evaluation. It covers both quantitative and qualitative approaches. It also covers the research design method and the data analysis strategies used in programme evaluation. Chapter 5 is based on my research to provide an example of adapting a Western programme for the Chinese culture. The cultural issues that interventionists need to take into consideration when adapting a programme and how to effectively implement a social learning programme are also illustrated in this chapter. The final chapter focuses on future development in parenting programmes. Culturally sensitive practice is becoming more important in Hong Kong as Hong Kongers are living in a diverse city with people from different parts of the world. In addition, changing family structures present challenges to policy makers and interventionists regarding the possible evidence-based interventions that could be provided to parents of adolescents. This chapter focuses on current changes in family structures and current parenting practices to consider future trends in the design and evaluation of parenting programmes. I hope this book will provide help for university students who are interested in knowing more about the theory, practice and evaluation of parenting programmes, for the benefit of parent participants as well as their adolescent children. In addition, I hope this book can enhance professional interest in evidence-based practice in delivering parenting programmes.

1 Introduction

Introduction

Parenting programmes are widely accepted as a means of supporting parents in modern society. Different programmes for parents of infants, children and adolescents, organised by healthcare professionals (Leung *et al.*, 2003), psychologists and social workers (Tsang, 2004), are available on a daily basis in Hong Kong. This proliferation reflects parents' need for support (Coleman, 2001), particularly in modern society, as more diverse family structures emerge (Wilson *et al.*, 2003). Rapid social and economic changes also pose additional challenges to parents. Furthermore, numerous studies indicate that ineffective parenting is related to anti-social behaviour in adolescents (Loeber & Stouthamer-Leober, 1986; Farrington & West, 1990), as is conflict between parents and adolescents (Shek & Ma, 2001). In contrast to this, positive parenting, which provides warmth, praise and encouragement, is correlated with outcomes such as higher self-esteem, less anti-social behaviour and better academic achievement for children and adolescents. Nevertheless, studies of parenting programmes have not always been able to help scholars and practitioners to form consistent conclusions with regard to the outcomes of parenting programmes, nor the essential elements required to achieve desired outcomes for parents, children and adolescents.

In particular, recent developments in evaluation research have encouraged a stronger focus on what works and in what context (Pawson & Tilley, 1997). As researchers, we need to focus more on which elements of parenting support are particularly useful to which types of client. Furthermore, parenting practices are culturally specific (Ogbu, 1981; Rubin, Bornstein & Cheah, 2006). There are numerous differences in the beliefs generally held about parenting in Euro–American and Chinese cultures. Nevertheless, the majority of parenting programmes have been designed with special attention to Euro–American culture, under the influence of parenting theories developed in the West, such as Baumrind's parenting styles (Baumrind, 1968), Carl Roger's humanistic theories (Thorne, 2003) or behavioural approaches (Skinner, 1965). It is therefore of great importance to understand how useful it is to adapt Western programmes to the local Chinese context.

Parenting

Parenting can be defined as

> the entrusted and abiding task of parents to prepare their offspring for the physical, psychosocial and economic conditions in which they will eventually fare, and it is hoped, flourish. . . . Parents are the "final common pathway" to children's development and stature, adjustment and success.
>
> (Bornstein, 2002: ix)

Other literature suggests that parenting is composed of purposeful activities aimed at ensuring children's survival and development (Hoghughi, 2004: 5).

The word parenting itself is more concerned with the development and education of children than with who does it. Parenting is also a process, an activity and an interaction, usually performed by adults with children, but not necessarily or exclusively with their own biological offspring. The connotation of parenting is related to a positive, nurturing activity.

These definitions relate to parents' responsibility for their children in general, for example, in regard to the provision of care to meet their children's physical and emotional needs. Nevertheless, there is no agreed definition of what constitutes effective parenting or what contributes to positive outcomes for children, nor are suggested definitions able to address the bi-directional nature of parenting practices (Belsky & Vondra, 1989).

Quinton (2004) suggests that parenting is

> something that parents do. It is not something they have. It involves tasks such as giving physical care, boundary setting and teaching social behaviour; behaviours such as responsiveness, affection and positive regard; relationship qualities such as giving emotional security and secure attachment.
>
> (Quinton, 2004: 27)

This definition presents a more concrete idea of what people actually do that is considered to be parenting. Quinton further indicates that what parents do is subject to different influences. These include genetics, such as whether or not children are born with any disabilities or other difficulties, and the parents' own childhood experiences, such as their experience of abuse or family violence. Other aspects that affect parenting include parents' present circumstances, such as their own mental health status and whether or not they are living in poverty (Quinton, 2004).

Holden (2010) notes that "the word parenting is derived from the Latin verb *parere* which was defined as 'to bring forth or produce'" (Holden, 2010: x). Purohit proposes that

> parenting is the process of nurturing and guiding the children. It also means catering to the basic needs – physical, psychological and emotional needs of the children. Parenting is the process of teaching and training your children to earn their own living.
>
> (2005: 3)

It is also through parenting that personal, religious or cultural values are transmitted (Alvy, 1988).

Pugh, De'Ath and Smith (1994) propose a list of tasks, which forms a very good illustration of what constitutes parenting. The list of tasks includes giving physical care to a child and providing emotional security, as well as demonstrating affection. It also includes setting boundaries for a child, while allowing room for the child to develop. Parenting also includes teaching behaviours that facilitate social skills for a child, as well as helping the child to develop skills that promote cognitive development (Pugh, De'Ath & Smith, 1994). It can be seen from this that parenting practices are very important not only in giving physical care but also in setting boundaries and providing emotional support.

Parenting nowadays is not provided solely by biological parents. With the growing diversity in family patterns, some tasks may be carried out by institutions, step-parents, grandparents or other relatives of the biological parents.

Conceptual framework of parenting

Some theorists have posited important elements of positive or optimal parenting when considering what constitutes effective parenting practice. Early work in behavioural and psychoanalytic traditions describes the relationship between parents and their children (Maccoby, 1998). Behaviourism sees the parent–child relationship as one of teacher and learner. Parents help their children to learn expected behaviour and impose rewards and punishments with which to reinforce these lessons and eliminate undesirable actions (Darling, 1999). According to this theory, habits learned can be unlearned once the reinforcement ceases to be received.

Some psychoanalytic theorists (e.g., Strean, 1979; Elliott, 2002) propose that the characteristics acquired during early childhood are irreversible and will affect a child's development into adulthood. According to this view, intra-psychic forces dominate our development through some of the pre-determined psychosexual stages during our early years of life, especially the first four to five years. Parenting practices are important when they involve the imposition of restrictions, which may not be wanted by the child, against a child's free expression of wishes and impulses, and the need to direct children's sexual impulses away from their parents themselves. Children then experience a dilemma in which they need their parents to provide love and care but also fear parental rejection and the lack of parental care and acceptance when they direct their anger and sexuality toward their parents. This conflict is resolved through identifying with the same-sex parent by adopting sex-typed behaviour and attitudes. This theory has been subjected to strong criticism, in particular on the basis that the source of energy and drive in children's behaviour is not sexual (Maccoby, 1992).

Behavioural and psychoanalytic theories constitute early attempts to understand parenting and were subject to significant limitations. For example, behavioural theory lacks any consideration of factors other than stimulation and response. Psychoanalytic theory is in turn limited by the idea that characteristics developed in early childhood will be determinative of someone's whole life thereafter.

Attachment theory consists of another set of concepts that informs us about the importance of emotional bonding between parents and children. There is a strong argument that the secure attachment of children is a crucial outcome of good parenting (Hoghughi, 2004). Attachment theory is based on the work of John Bowlby, who observed interactions between infants and their mothers. It suggests that the person caring for an infant gives strong emotional support and is a source of security and protection (Brooks, 2004), which are important for the child's healthy development. Bowlby (1969) proposes that proximity to an attachment figure is initially accomplished through relating to the mother via infant patterns of behaviour and is very important to the survival of human beings. The resulting sense of security provides a safe foundation for infants to explore the world and learn how to regulate their emotions (Masten & Coatsworth, 1998). There are three forms of insecure attachment. The first is anxious-avoidant; infants in the study who displayed this pattern were unconcerned when their mothers left the room and had no interest in their return. The second form is anxious-resistant attachment, wherein infants protested strongly when their mothers left and found it difficult to re-establish closeness after their return. The third form of insecure attachment is disorganised attachment, in which infants demonstrated unpredictable behaviour with their parents. Sometimes they showed happiness when approaching their parents and sometimes they avoided them (Brooks, 2004).

Other studies indicate that rejected children are aggressive (Coie & Jacobs, 1993). Young children begin to develop ways to control their own behaviour when interacting with their adult caregivers. A link has been established between difficulty regulating one's own behaviour, such as attention span, and anti-social behaviour and academic problems later in life (Eisenberg *et al.*, 1997).

Another influential perspective that describes optimal parenting comes from other work on parenting styles. Parenting style refers to parents' attitudes, beliefs and ways of reasoning about their own and their children's behaviour (Brooks, 2004). Darling and Steinberg define it as

> a constellation of attitudes toward the child that are communicated to the child and that, taken together, create an emotional climate in which the parent's behaviours are expressed. These behaviours include both the specific, goal-directed behaviours through which parents perform their parental duties (to be referred to as parenting practices) and non-goal directed parental behaviours, such as gestures, changes in tone of voice, or the spontaneous expression of emotion.
>
> (1993: 488)

According to Maccoby and Martin (1983), parenting style consists of two important elements: parental responsiveness and parental demandingness. The former refers to "the extent to which parents intentionally foster individuality, self-regulation, and self-assertion by being attuned, supportive, and acquiescent to children's special needs and demands" (Baumrind, 1991: 62). Parental demandingness refers to "the claims parents make on children to become integrated into the family whole, by their maturity demands, supervision, disciplinary efforts and willingness to confront the child who disobeys" (Baumrind, 1991: 61–62).

Four categories of parenting style can be defined according to high or low levels of parental demandingness and the responsiveness of a parent. The categories are made up of indulgent, authoritarian, authoritative and uninvolved parenting styles (Maccoby & Martin, 1983). These styles reflect parents' values and behaviours (Baumrind, 1991). Indulgent (also known as permissive) parents adopt a nondirective approach. They do not require their children to demonstrate mature behaviour or allow their children to self-regulate their own behaviour. They also avoid confrontation with their children (Baumrind, 1991). They are more permissive and more responsive to children's needs and adopt a more lenient approach to discipline.

Authoritarian parents are demanding and directive but they are not responsive to their children's needs. They expect their ideas to be absolutely obeyed and do not need to explain their own decisions or behaviour to their children (Baumrind, 1991). The authoritarian parenting style can be further subdivided into two types. The first is nonauthoritarian–directive, in which parents are directive but are not intrusive in their children's lives. They also do not demonstrate autocratic behaviour in the use of their power. The second is authoritarian–directive, in which the parents have all the features of authoritative parents but are also highly intrusive in their children's lives and activities (Darling, 1999).

Authoritative parenting is regarded by Baumrind (1973) as the optimal parenting style. It provides clear requirements for responsible and pro-social behaviour for children. It also provides affection and responsiveness to children's needs. Such parents "monitor and impart clear standards for their children's conduct. Their disciplinary methods are supportive rather than punitive. They want their children to be assertive as well as socially responsible; self-regulating as well as cooperative" (Baumrind, 1991: 62). Parents need to be firm in regard to helping their children maintain the required standards of behaviour and may even need to confront their children in order to impose this pattern. However, the parents also need to be kind and understanding in order to impose developmentally appropriate requirements on their children (Maccoby, 1992).

The fourth style is uninvolved. Parents displaying this style demonstrate low levels of both responsiveness and demandingness (Darling, 1999). Such parents usually have very low levels of sensitivity to their children's needs. In addition to this, some may even reject or neglect their children. Children and adolescents who are under the influence of an uninvolved parenting style have been found to perform poorly in all domains examined, such as social skills, self-regulation, academic performance and so on (Baumrind, 1991).

The Baumrind typology of parenting style has become a base for research into the optimal approach to parenting. In Euro–American culture, numerous studies confirm that the authoritative parenting style is effective in producing socially adaptable children and adolescents. For example, Steinberg and colleagues (1992) conducted a study based on Maccoby and Martin's classification in order to understand adolescent competence. Their results indicate that the authoritative parenting style is related to adolescent self-confidence, less delinquent activity, good emotional control and general competence, as well as self-reliance, regardless of the adolescents' gender and socio-economic status (Brooks, 2004). Nevertheless, these studies are usually based on Western, middle-class samples.

Less attention has been paid to optimal Chinese parenting. Studies indicate difficulty exists in regard to categorising Chinese parenting according to Baumrind's parenting styles (McBride-Chang & Chang, 1998).

Another influential theory of parenting behaviour is Bronfenbrenner's ecological perspective. Bronfenbrenner (1979) proposes that the whole ecology in which a child is living affects this child's development. This includes parenting practices, marital relationships, relatives and friends and the availability of resources (Quinton, 2004). From an ecological perspective, parenting is seen as a bi-directional process in which the child's behaviour affects and is affected by parenting practices. Adults' behaviour is also influenced by their own experiences of childhood, their physical status, mental wellness and so on. Furthermore, the process is bi-directional, as the way in which children and adolescents react to what their parents do to them will have an impact on the parenting subsequently provided to them. This concept is based on the ecological perspective (Bronfenbrenner, 1979), which provides a frame of reference for the complicated and reciprocal nature of parenting (Quinton, 2004).

The effectiveness of parenting practice, as seen from the ecological perspective, also depends on the parents' relationship with one another and/or with current partners, their economic circumstances, the cultural context in which they are situated and the wider social and political structures that affect the whole family (Hoghughi, 2004). Parenting practices are also affected by the parents' own value systems and their approaches to managing their children.

Recent developments in understanding parenting behaviour have involved coining a new term: 'over parenting'. This term is used to denote those behaviours that demonstrate excessive involvement in children's lives. These behaviours include being over-protective of children in regard to the children's autonomy in the face of age-appropriate life challenges (Segrin *et al.*, 2012). These parents attempt to keep their children out of harm's way (Segrin *et al.*, 2013). They also assume themselves to be highly responsible for their children's success and happiness. Studies have indicated that over parenting is associated with children's anxiety and insecurity (Gar & Hudson, 2008), greater narcissistic traits in children (Cramer, 2011) and lower levels of self efficacy in children when compared with children who are not over parented (Givertz & Segrin, 2014). Recent research findings indicate that over parenting is also highly correlated with parental anxiety and parenting regret (Segrin *et al.*, 2013). The same study also indicates that over parenting is highly related to children's ineffective coping strategies, such as internalising and distancing, as well as higher levels of narcissism.

Another wave of recent developments in describing parenting behaviour is through the lens of positive psychology. Positive psychology is a scientific discipline developed by psychologist Martin Seligman (1998). Positive psychology is defined as "the scientific study of positive experiences and positive individual traits, and the institutions that facilitate their development" (Duckworth, Steen & Seligman, 2005: 630).

Positive emotions described by positive psychology and seen as useful when applied to parenting practices include optimism, hope and faith. This includes placing hope in children and adolescents by not focusing on their current state of behaviour. It also involves faith that, in parenting children and adolescents, they will be successful in the future, rather than focusing on what they have done wrong or not done well enough in the past. It also entails a perspective in which parents are encouraged to focus on the strengths of their children and adolescents, rather than on their weaknesses. Although no systematic package of parenting strategies backed by scientific research has yet been identified, parenting with positive psychology is definitely a trend to watch in coming research and clinical practice.

Based on the above discussion, we can conclude that parenting practices have several important characteristics. The first, and of the utmost importance, is the development of proper attachments with children. From an ecological perspective, children's behaviour is determined by different systems that affect and are affected by children themselves. Furthermore, behavioural approaches and social learning theories help us to understand the importance of how parenting practices affect children's behaviour through appropriate reinforcement and setting a proper example for children to follow. These theories build on early conceptions of what constitutes positive parenting. Furthermore, Baumrind's typology of style has had a significant influence on thinking about parenting, in particular in relation to the importance of an authoritative style in which parents are able to communicate with their children and set appropriate boundaries, which help to bring about appropriate behaviour.

Changing family structures

Changing family structures affect family life and parenting practices. Parents in certain situations sometimes have more difficulties than others in regard to their parenting and their relationships with their children (Charles, Martinez & Forgatch, 2002). More extreme examples of difficulties in parenting are child abuse, family violence and anti-social behaviour. This section considers examples from the UK and Hong Kong, in order to examine how changing family structures affect parenting practice.

In the UK, young people are living with their parents for longer than before (Social Issues Research Centre, 2008). Many adolescents now do not leave their parents' home until they are well into their mid-twenties. In 2006, 60% of British men aged 20–24 still lived with their parents, compared with just 50% in 1991. In addition to this, the growing number of divorces have increased the number of single-parent families in the UK, partly due to the Divorce Reform Act of 1967, which made the irretrievable breakdown of the marriage grounds for divorce (Allan, Hawker & Crow, 2001). As a result, divorce became an individual or joint option. With this change in legislation and an increasingly open attitude toward divorce, single-parent households in the UK increased from 570,000 in 1971 to 1,600,000 in 1996 (Allan, Hawker & Crow, 2001). In

2007, the number of single-parent families was three times higher than in 1977 (Social Issues Research Centre, 2008). In addition to this, the proportion of single-parent households headed by women in the UK also increased. For example, one study indicated that almost 90% of teenage mothers are unmarried (Allan, Hawker & Crow, 2001). Through the formation of new partnerships, single-parent families often become step-families. Lone parents have among the highest rates of unemployment and poverty in the UK. In 2001, the heads of almost 43% of single-parent households with dependent children were unemployed. This is much higher than the overall household rate of 16%, as found in the 2001 UK General Household Survey (Social Issues Research Centre, 2008). Diversified family patterns place extra pressure on parents, especially as far as their relationships with step-children are concerned. High levels of stress and tensions in couples' relationships may result in lower-quality parenting and difficulties in parent–child relationships.

Similar patterns have been observed in Hong Kong, where changes in family structure and the continuous rise of women's status are the two major factors that scholars regard as having led to an increase in divorce (Lam, Lam & Leung, 2005). High divorce rates, together with the growing frequency of remarriage, lead to more diverse family patterns, which in turn lead to parents facing greater challenges than before. More and more women are now involved in the work force and so are unable to take care of their children directly. Parenting tasks are not necessarily performed by parents themselves but may be in the hands of nursery or day-care centre staff, grandparents or other relatives. These more complicated situations have, in some cases, had undesirable effects on children's and adolescents' development (Leung *et al.*, 2005). Reconstituted families are also becoming more and more common, as is parenting by step-parents and single parents. Diverse family structures and the need for parents to work outside the home at the same time as bringing up their children has made this situation more and more difficult and means that parents in modern society increasingly need help from outside sources.

Since the sovereignty of Hong Kong returned to Mainland China in 1997, Chinese immigrants have entered Hong Kong at a rate of 150 per day (Cheung & Law, 2003). This large increase in the population has placed extra pressure on family services in Hong Kong. The majority of immigrants have come to Hong Kong for the purpose of family reunification. Some of them have few skills and are poorly educated. Families composed of a husband and wife who were brought up in different cultures (e.g., one is from Hong Kong and the other is from Mainland China) also face difficulties in regard to adjusting to each other's lives. Many divorces have arisen from adjustment difficulties stemming from cultural differences.

The diversification of family structures in Hong Kong has also shown a pressing need to provide sufficient support and education for families who are experiencing parenting difficulties. There is increasing evidence that some parenting practices are a risk factor for adolescent anti-social behaviour (Loeber & Stouthamer-Loeber, 1986; Farrington & West, 1990). More and more evidence indicates that harsh approaches to parenting, such as the use of excessive physical punishment or even abusive behaviour on the part of parents, have adverse effects on the emotional well-being of young people (Coleman, 2001; Farrington, 1994). The results of these studies suggest that governments need to focus on developing policies that will provide more education in regard to parenting skills, as well as financial support for parents who are facing difficulties. One such approach is the provision of parenting programmes. The following section considers the policy context in both the UK and Hong Kong in this respect.

Policy context

In England, the principles of the Children's Act of 1989 place emphasis on the care of children within their own family. Service planners are required by the Act to focus not just on children who may be 'at risk', but also to plan services at the community level for families 'in need'. This widening of policy to deploy resources for prevention and early intervention called for a specific policy on family-support interventions in the UK. The election of the Labour government in 1997, together with an increased understanding of the risk factors of offending and anti-social behaviour, saw more attention paid to the role of parenting in prevention interventions. The need for a policy focusing on the relationship between parenting behaviour and children's outcomes was acknowledged. These aspects, together with the possibility of including Parenting Orders in the Crime and Disorder Act of 1998, which mandates that the parents of young offenders must receive education and support, highlighted the need for more evidence on the effectiveness of parenting programmes. It also suggested the need to develop an understanding of how parenting programmes lead to improved outcomes for young people.

The recognition of the positive effects of good parenting practice supported an increased emphasis on parenting and the family in the UK government's policy agenda (Barlow, Shaw & Stewart-Brown, 2004). A range of different approaches in parenting programmes was thus developed, aiming to support parents in need and provide them with parenting knowledge. Parenting support is the term used to describe a range of activities, including training programmes, that provide information and empower parents to be more effective.

In the UK, a number of new initiatives were done to support parents. For example, the establishment of the National Family and Parenting Institute and the expansion of a telephone helpline, renamed 'Parenting Plus'. Other new initiatives to support the parents of teenagers through the Family Policy Unit were set up. Furthermore, the inclusion of provisions in the Crime and Disorder Act of 1998, covering the responsibilities of parents, and the introduction of Parenting Orders, evidenced the trend in government policy in the area of youth justice focusing attention on support for parents (Colemen & Roker, 2001). The 1996 Smith Review of parenting programmes in the UK also documented growing interest in group-based parenting support initiatives.

In contrast to this, policy development concerning parenting support in Hong Kong has been very different. Most social care in Hong Kong is provided by non-governmental organisations (NGOs), except social security and social work services needed to fulfil statutory requirements. Those services, such as the probation service, child abuse protection, child custody services and so on, are provided by the Social Welfare Department of the Hong Kong government (Wilding, 1997; Shek, Lam & Tsoi, 2004). A number of initiatives related to family policy have been implemented in Hong Kong. Nevertheless, there is no sign of a coherent picture emerging in regard to what specifically has been provided and the consequences of these initiatives (Kamerman, 2009). Most social policy discussion in Hong Kong does not consider it to be a welfare state, despite the fact that the government spends a great deal of money on public housing and the majority of citizens are able to enjoy government-subsidised healthcare services. In the field of social care, there is no distinct and explicit 'family policy' in Hong Kong. One of the arguments put forward for this situation in regard to analysing social policy development in Hong Kong has been the existence of strong inter-familial help networks within families (Wilding, 1997). Parents are offered a lot of financial as well as practical help within their extended family (e.g., during times of illness). Furthermore, inter-familial help is common in Hong Kong Chinese culture in terms of activities such as purchasing a new flat. However, this has created a situation in which the government does very little to provide its citizens with welfare services. There has been growing concern about whether or not such a pattern of inter-familial help will continue as the traditional social support network in Hong Kong diminishes (Ng, Philips & Lee, 2002). Therefore, more social policy and welfare services are needed.

On the other hand, Hong Kong Chinese culture values and encourages independence, self-reliance and competitiveness, and this supports the "positive non-intervention approach" of the government. These values, together with the fear that providing more social welfare services could increase the burden on the government and create a dependency among service recipients (Wilding, 1997), means that the government plays a minimal role in providing social welfare services. One example of this is the provision of family services. The overall objective of family services is to support the well-being of family members and strengthen family functioning (Cheung & Law, 2003). Family service centres have been in place since the 1970s in Hong Kong and are one of the means of providing such services to the general community. The overall objectives of these family services were most recently set out in the White Paper *Social Welfare*, in regard to the 1990s and beyond, to preserve and strengthen the family as a unit, to develop caring interpersonal relationships, to enable individuals and family members to prevent personal and family problems and deal with them when they arise and to provide for needs which cannot be met from within the family. With these objectives in mind, support services have been developed to assist families when they are unable to discharge their caring and protective functions satisfactorily (Hong Kong Government, 1991: 19).

This indicates that the objectives of family service centres in Hong Kong are very general; their underlying rationale is to support families as a last resort. Society will therefore only provide support to families when the families' own members are unable to provide these functions themselves.

Following the recognition that parenting is one of the factors associated with the anti-social behaviour of children and adolescents in Hong Kong (Ng, 1975), in 1977 the government started funding the "Family Life Education" programme, which aims to help parents adopt more positive practices (Cheung & Law, 2003). This includes providing promotional programmes, such as promotion of life tasks for parents and educational materials on handling family life issues. In line with these services, parenting programmes that aim to promote positive parenting practices are also provided. In addition to this, demand from parents to develop skills and improve their knowledge of how to raise children successfully has led to considerable interest in parenting programmes among both government and non-governmental organisations, as well as in private sectors. Nowadays, it is estimated that there are more than 500 parenting programmes run by different professionals in Hong Kong each year (Tsang, 2004).

The Family Council was established in Hong Kong in 2007 to provide a platform for different sectors and government bureaux to study family-related problems and provide high-level advice and guidance (Hong Kong Family Council, 2012). The Council also set out to inspire policy makers to include 'family factors' in their policy formulation processes. It has initiated some publicity campaigns for the promotion of family core values (such as filial piety in traditional Chinese culture), facilitated parental education and advised the government on ways to support families in need. A number of policy initiatives have developed as a result, such as the development of services for new immigrant families or financial assistance to low-income families. Despite these initiatives, existing policies are fragmented, unsystematic and lacking in a clear ideology. As Kamerman (2009: 121) comments, there is no "coherent, holistic and comprehensive picture of child and family policy measures and assessment of what works", despite an increasing emphasis in social work on evidence-based practice. We need to be more aware of which interventions are effective when providing services to families.

Conclusion

The present study investigates the outcomes of parenting programmes in reducing parent–adolescent conflict in the context of Hong Kong Chinese culture. Changing family structures, with increasing numbers of single-parent families, together with rising unemployment and poverty, are putting pressure on parents. Research evidence helps us to understand the importance of parenting in children's and young people's development and its association with anti-social behaviour in adolescents. Such an understanding, together with the requirement for social work practice to be evidence-based in order to be accountable to funders and service users, makes it essential to investigate the effectiveness of such interventions. Furthermore, the parenting programmes offered in Hong Kong have not been well researched; they are not evidence-based or theory-driven, nor have any studies been conducted on parenting programmes that aim to reduce parent–adolescent conflict in Hong Kong. There has also been no study on the experiences of parents involved in a parenting programme. This study set out to fill these gaps by studying the outcomes of a school-based parenting programme that aimed to reduce parent–adolescent conflict. Particular attention is paid to the extent to which this programme is culturally sensitive to the Hong Kong context.

2 Parenting, parenting styles and adolescent development in Hong Kong and Euro–American culture

Introduction

Parents are the first teachers of their children. Their beliefs and actions have a significant influence on children's development and behaviour (Bornstein & Cheah, 2006). Parenting practices provide experiences within a specific time and context, which exert an influence on children's development. Children's experiences are responses to how they interpret the situations created by these interactions. Children and parents both experience some changes as a result of their interactions. Parenting practices, therefore, are a bi-directional process, with each aspect affecting the other (Stafford & Dainton, 1995). In addition, they are at least partially culturally constructed (Bornstein & Cheah, 2006). Some parenting practices are universal, such as the impulse to nurture and protect children. On the other hand, some parenting beliefs, such as when and how to care for children and how to resolve conflict, are more culturally specific. In a collectivist culture such as Hong Kong, parenting practices place emphasis on preserving harmony among family members, highlighting discipline, filial piety, respect for elders and family obligations (Lin & Fu, 1990). In contrast to this, parenting practices in Euro–American culture have been described as placing more emphasis on children's autonomy and independence. Such cultural differences need to be taken into consideration in regard to understanding parent–adolescent conflict in specific cultures.

Likewise, when considering which parenting styles are preferable to others, several studies indicate that, in white European culture, an authoritative parenting style (Baumrind, 1971) brings about optimal outcomes for children (Barlow, Shaw & Stewart-Brown, 2004). Nevertheless, little is known about optimal parenting beliefs and styles in Chinese society, despite extensive discussions and descriptions of parenting in this culture (Chao, 1994a). For example, one study of Hong Kong Chinese parents shows that Baumrind's typology of parenting styles may not be a sufficient description in this context (McBride-Chang & Chang, 1998). Further exploration of optimal parenting styles in Chinese culture and descriptions of their culturally specific elements are needed.

Adolescence

The onset of puberty marks the beginning of adolescence, a period in which young people experience a range of significant developmental changes. Physical and hormonal changes affect their behaviour (Hamner & Turner, 1996). As Coleman (1990) explains, it is very difficult to ascertain when adolescence begins and ends. The term is usually regarded as applying to young people aged 11 to 19 years. Some parents and teachers may consider puberty to start around 10 or 11 years, in which case, this age defines the start of adolescence. The dominant theme of research on adolescence is that it is a difficult period (Steinberg & Morris, 2001). Traditionally, adolescence is described as a time of transition, wherein the individual is subject to both internal and external pressures from peers, parents and society in general (Coleman, 1990). Early work from a psychoanalytic approach emphasises the importance of internal processes in which the growth of the sex drive leads teenagers to look outside the family for objects of love. This begins the disengagement process, which is manifests in greater associations with peers, rather than family. In addition, the psychoanalytic approach regards ambivalence as another reason for the sometimes incomprehensible behaviour seen in adolescence. This includes fluctuations in mood, bad behaviour and relationship problems, all of which arise from the difficulty the adolescent experiences in regard to coping with inner conflict. The concept of ambivalence leads us to consider teenagers' non-conformity and rebellion as a universal feature of adolescence. It can be seen as an important process that the adolescent has to go through in order to establish relationships outside the home (Coleman, 1990).

Sociological views of adolescence concentrate on socialisation and roles, augmenting the psychoanalytic view of inner conflict by considering the influence of society. Socialisation is a process in which an individual absorbs the current values, standards and beliefs of society (Coleman, 1990). A person learns about the role expectations of a particular society. A child will usually take up the role ascribed to them by their parents, school or society in general. However, adolescents have more opportunities to question these roles and choose how they are to be interpreted. They have more independence from authority figures and more involvement with their peers. Adolescents have been perceived as having problems managing all these changing role expectations, sometimes leading to role conflict when they face demands from parents, peers, schools and the mass media, as well as society in general. These all cause stress and difficulty for adolescents in establishing a bridge toward their adult roles. Insights from early psychoanalytic work and the sociological point of view both indicate that adolescence is a period of stress (Freud, 1958).

Nevertheless, such a view of adolescence is not supported by research from the previous decade (Dornbusch, 1989; Coleman, 1990). This is because the majority of psychoanalytic models of adolescence are based on clinical studies (Dornbusch, 1989). Another possible reason is that adolescent anti-social behaviour, such as vandalism, drug addiction and participation in large-scale riots, is normally perceived as threatening by adults (Coleman, 1990). However, there is no research evidence that the majority of adolescence face a significant identity crisis (Coleman, 1990). In addition, the majority of adolescents have positive and constructive relationships with their parents and share most of their values. Further evidence also indicates that the majority of teenagers make it through this challenging period without suffering significant social, emotional or behavioural difficulties (Steinberg & Morris, 2001).

What, then, does research tell us about adolescence? Steinberg and Morris' (2001) overview draws on empirical studies to highlight some significant aspects of adolescence that differ from the traditional concepts discussed above. This indicates that adolescents mature earlier and faster in homes in which family relationships are less close and more conflicted (Kim & Smith, 1998). In addition, studies indicated that boys mature later than their counterparts and have lower self-esteem when compared with boys who mature earlier. Nevertheless, those who mature earlier indicated in the study that they have a higher risk for delinquency and anti-social behaviour than boys who mature later. Girls who mature earlier than others demonstrated a higher level of emotional problems and depression and have poorer self-image than their peers (Ge, Conger & Elder, 1996). Similar to boys, girls are at a higher risk than those who mature later of becoming involved in delinquent activities and have better interpersonal relationships. Nevertheless, studies indicated that young people whose behaviour is problematic in their adolescence will have had a history of difficulties during their childhood. Adolescence itself is therefore not the cause of these problems but rather a manifestation of issues that originated in childhood (Coleman, 1990).

Steinberg and Morris (2001) also indicate that the popular conception of turmoil associated with puberty has been exaggerated (see, for example, Brooks-Gunn & Reiter, 1990; Petersen, 1985). For example, differences in hormone levels actually account for very little variation in adolescents' negative affect

(Brooks-Gunn, Graber & Paikoff, 1994). Richards and Larson (1993) find no association between mood changes and puberty in girls. These findings suggest popular perceptions about adolescence (which are normally negative) may be inaccurate and help to provide a clearer picture of reality.

Erikson (1968) also significantly influenced how we understand adolescence. Erickson's theory of psychosocial development proposed an 'identity crisis' among adolescents. It suggested a consideration of adolescence as a time in which young people begin to explore their own personal characteristics. They need to discover who they are and how they develop and adjust themselves to the social system to which they are attached (Steinberg & Morris, 2001). Adolescence is considered as a time of disturbance, during which young people search for their own identity, which may be different from that ascribed to them by their parents or society. The non-conformist behaviour of adolescents can be considered as an expression of their efforts to discover their own identities. From this perspective, studies of self-esteem have emerged, indicating that self-esteem becomes more stable as age increases and fluctuates more in early adolescence. Another study indicated that adolescents' self-conceptions also differ depending on whether they are more attached to their peers, parents or teachers (Harter, Whitesell & Junkin, 1998), so are dependent on context (Steinberg & Morris, 2001).

Other popular perceptions about adolescence focus on teenagers' relationships with their peers. The general view is usually that adolescent culture is opposed to that of adults. Nevertheless, Steinberg and Morris' (2001) study indicates that adolescents whose parents are supportive and demonstrate warmth have more positive friendships than adolescents whose parents are less supportive (Lieberman, Doyle & Markiewicz, 1999). In addition, parents who perform authoritative parenting could help to reduce the effects of negative peer influences. Nevertheless, adolescents who are brought up in less cohesive and less adaptive families are less influenced by their parents and more influenced by their friends and peers (Steinberg & Morris, 2001). These findings indicate that the traditional description of adolescence as a period of stress needs to be given careful consideration in light of research evidence. It is also important to consider whether or not these findings are capable of describing the experiences of adolescence in other cultures.

Parenting styles in Chinese and Euro-American culture

Chinese culture is usually characterised as collectivist, in contrast to Western individualism (Fuligni, 1998; Peterson *et al.*, 2004). The Chinese are described as more focused on families' collective values, while Western societies, such as in the US, place more emphasis on personal values and autonomy. Being loyal to family, responsiveness to family and relatives' expectations, and conformity with elders and those in authority are considered important elements of a collectivist society such as China (Ho, 1994; Peterson *et al.*, 2004). Such descriptions of Chinese parenting are based on Confucian ideas about family hierarchy and structure.

However, given the British occupation of Hong Kong and the resulting Westernisation of its people, Hong Kong Chinese parents tend to be more accepting of Western parenting ideologies, while at the same time preserving their distinctive, traditional beliefs. In addition, Chinese adolescents have taken on board elements of Western culture and strive for more autonomy and independence, while adopting some traditional Chinese beliefs.

Another important issue is that Hong Kong Chinese scholars have a long tradition of borrowing from Western theories to understand and explain adolescent behaviour in Hong Kong (Lau & Yeung, 1996). Culturally sensitive concepts and theories have received minimal attention (Leung & Fan, 1996). Such a tradition overlooks the culturally specific nature of adolescence in Hong Kong. Another approach that has often been taken is to explain the behaviour of Chinese adolescents solely with reference to the influence of Confucianism. Such a monolithic view over-generalises the influence of Confucian philosophy in modern Chinese society. It also leads to misconceptions about the process of investigating Chinese culture (Lau & Yeung, 1996). Nevertheless, because of the lack of culturally specific research to explain adolescence in Hong Kong, we have to rely on studies looking at the parenting of American immigrants by Chinese parents, together with literature dating back to the 1990s, which examines the nature of adolescence in Hong Kong. This body of work includes studies that borrow and translate tools and measurement instruments that have already been validated in the West and those based on survey and observations.

Chinese parenting beliefs and practices

Confucian traditions have long been recognised by researchers as dominant in the formation of Chinese cultural beliefs (Wu, 1981; Lieber, Fung & Leung, 2006). Chinese child-rearing practices have also been affected by Confucian ideology (Ho, 1987). The guiding principle of this is filial piety, in which children are taught to obey and honour the family (Ho, 1994). One important concept of Confucian beliefs considers that a person is defined or perceived by other people by his or her relationship with others. Relationships are dependent upon the hierarchy a person experiences within his or her family. In addition, social order and harmony are maintained through each person loyally fulfilling the requirements and responsibilities of their roles in relationships. Accordingly, the main characteristics of the Confucian tradition are maintaining interpersonal harmony, abiding by moral values, fulfilling social expectations and bringing honour to the family through achievements. Building on this, Chinese children are expected to self-monitor, be sensitive to other people's expectations, follow the rules and obey their seniors as well as other adults (Lin & Wang, 1995).

Chinese family structures and interactions emphasise filial piety and hierarchical relationships (Chan & Leong, 1994). Chinese people's orientation toward children tends to be moralistic, rather than psychological. This covers children's obedience to their parents, their obligation to respect their parents and the responsibility of adults taking care of their young children while caring for their elderly parents (Chao, 1995; Ho, 1989). Such an ideology influences Chinese parenting with regard to paying less attention to the psychological development of an individual. Chinese families also discourage their children from expressing angry or aggressive emotions. Children are supposed to honour their family through moral acts, rather than bringing shame and dishonour to their families. Behaviours that are not accepted include aggression, anti-social activities and disobedience. Chinese young people are expected to do well in school and bring honour to the family through achievements such as this. They need to be obedient and fulfil their obligations to their parents. Personal achievement is regarded as increasing the family's honour, rather than as an individual accomplishment. In addition, Chinese families are child-centred. Taking care of young children becomes the focus of the family. More attention is paid to parent–child relationships than to the marital bond (Lim & Lim, 2005). It should be noted that traditional Confucian ideology still influences Chinese families today, but the extent and nature of its effects will depend upon different families in modern society. Relying solely on a Confucian analysis without addressing other ideologies, such as Taoism and Buddhism, may lead to over-generalisations of Chinese family behaviour (Lau & Yeung, 1996).

Another dimension that is important to Chinese parenting beliefs is the concept of 'training', as articulated by Chao (1994b). This has its origin in Confucian traditions and is developed from the indigenous concepts of '*chiao shun*' and '*guan*'. The term '*chiao shun*' has the meaning of teaching or training a child to behave in a socially acceptable way. '*Guan*' literally means 'to govern'. For Chinese people, this is a very positive term, the meaning of which connotes loving and caring for a person. It strongly denotes expecting children to do well in school and helping them to perform socially and culturally desirable behaviours. One of the aims of 'training' is to expose children to explicit examples of positive behaviour and restrict their exposure to undesirable behaviour. The concept also includes a set of standards of conduct that both families and society enforce. The motivation for imposing these ideas is to further the familial and societal goals of building a harmonious relationship with others in society and to preserve family integrity (Chao, 1994a). When applied to adolescents, '*guan*' includes guiding young people by setting expectations for their obeience, explaining the reasons for such expectations and monitoring their whereabouts (Padmawidjaja & Chao, 2010).

Chinese parenting differs from that of Western families in a number of ways. Hsu (1971) discusses the Chinese concept of '*jen*', whereby an individual's interpersonal interactions are emphasised above internal qualities in regard to understanding his or her personality. That is, American Chinese parents are more concerned about how their children behave and interact with their peers than with their personal qualities (Chao, 1995). This is different from the orientation of mainstream Western society, wherein individuality is emphasised.

Chinese parents also regard education as a means for social mobility. Chinese people believe in the value of education for the nation's well-being (Chen, Lee & Stevenson, 1996). They place emphasis on hard work and value the resulting achievements, regardless of their children's innate abilities. This is in line with Confucian teachings. Chinese parents highly value their children's achievements with regard to their academic results and are highly involved in their learning through both their academic work and extracurricular activities, such as learning to play the piano, ballet dancing and so on. This involves requiring their children to attend extra lessons after school. The majority of Chinese children spend their after-school time doing homework (Chen & Stevenson, 1989).

Chao (1994b) posits a culturally specific concept of 'training' to distinguish the parenting style of Chinese parents from authoritative and authoritarian styles. The concept of training in this context means an emphasis on helping children to be hardworking and obedient, to achieve self-discipline and academic success. As a result, the family will be honoured through their children's good behaviour (Sorkhabi, 2005). The expression of warmth by Chinese parents tends to be more implicit and expressed in terms of supporting children's achievements, rather than the demonstrative expression of affection favoured by Western parents. Chao (2000), using a regression analysis to test the relationship between 'training' and other dimensions of parenting style, suggested that training is consistent with the parenting dimension of warmth (i.e., the demonstration of affection, love, interest and involvement in children's activities, etc.), which is part of the definition of an authoritative parenting style. Nevertheless, Sorkhabi's (2005) study shows that there is no direct relationship between training style and academic achievement.

McBride-Chang and Chang (1998) discuss the proposition that Baumrind's typology of parenting styles may not be applicable in Hong Kong Chinese culture. Their study involved four different phases with different participants. A total of 180 adolescents were invited to complete a questionnaire with one of their parents. The first phase of the study compared parents and adolescents' rating of parenting style. The second measured emotional autonomy and parenting style. The third phase measured emotional autonomy and the fathers' responses to Chao's (1994b) concept of training. In the fourth phase, the measure of parenting style was compared to the banding of the young people's schools.[1] This study suggests that an emphasis on the Western typology of parenting style may not be appropriate in Hong Kong Chinese culture. We may need different ways of describing how Chinese parents and adolescents interact, necessitating further research.

Unlike most studies carried out in a Euro–American context, in which parents usually rate themselves as more authoritative than they are rated by adolescents, the Chinese adolescents studied by McBride-Chang and Chang (1998) rated their parents as less authoritarian, more permissive and more authoritative than their parents self-rated themselves. In summary, there are some culturally specific parenting styles within Chinese culture that are additional to those defined by Baumrind. On the other hand, in one study, a sample of Chinese parents scored significantly higher than their Euro–American compatriots in measures of parental control and authoritarian parenting style (Chao, 1995). Nevertheless, the meaning of the term authoritarian in the Chinese context may be different from that in Western society. In general, the Western term 'authoritarian' carries a meaning of harsh treatment. However, for the Chinese, this concept includes the setting of standards for children. It also carries the suggestion of parental concern and care behind the harsh demands made regarding children's behaviour.

Moreover, Lam (1997) argues that Western views of the developmental tasks of adolescents may not be applicable in Chinese society, in which collectivism is emphasised. Western ideas of searching for the self, which originate from Freudian theory, are not applicable in the Chinese context, since Chinese adolescents are encouraged to be both physically and emotionally close to their parents by sharing their social activities (Lam, 1997). Such encouragement may cause Chinese adolescents to expect to achieve autonomy at a later stage than their Euro–American counterparts (Russell, Crockett & Chao, 2010). This belief may also make Chinese adolescents less able to achieve autonomy at a younger age.

A study of Chinese-American families sheds light on the parenting behaviours of contemporary Chinese parents who have been acculturated in the West. These parents endorsed Confucian values as more important than child-centred values (Padmawidjaja & Chao, 2010). Nevertheless, they tended to adapt their parenting style to show more warmth and to have more child-centred goals (Padmawidjaja & Chao, 2010). This may be a sign of the influence of American acculturation. There was a strong positive association between parental warmth and having child-centred goals. In contrast to this, the parents who had strong beliefs based on Confucian values showed less warmth toward their children. The same study indicates that Chinese-American parents value Confucian goals more than child-centred values. The Chinese-American adolescents in this study reported less parental warmth than European-American adolescents (Padmawidjaja & Chao, 2010). This shows that, relative to European Americans, Chinese-American parents showed less warmth toward their adolescent children. Furthermore, the Chinese Americans were found to adopt more behavioural control than European Americans. Although this study was based on a sample of Chinese-American parents, similar results may be expected from Hong Kong Chinese parents, given that they are also exposed to Western influences in regard to their beliefs and parenting practices. A similar pattern may therefore emerge, in that they hold traditional parenting beliefs but may start to adopt more Western ideas related to showing warmth and giving autonomy to their adolescents.

It may therefore be concluded that Chinese parenting beliefs include some culturally specific and some universal components. This can best be conceptualised based on the work of Lieber, Fung and Leung (2006), who derive four key dimensions of Chinese child-rearing beliefs: training and shame (both part of the indigenous Chinese concept of parenting), autonomy and authoritativeness (Baumrind, 1971; Maccoby & Martin, 1983). Such a conceptualisation includes both universal and culturally specific dimensions in the parenting beliefs of contemporary Chinese parents and so seems to make sense of their diverse nature.

The parent–adolescent relationship in Chinese families

Studies in this area share a common view that the Chinese parent–adolescent relationship is different from that found in Western societies. Cultural factors affecting such differences must be acknowledged. There are also differences in the perceptions of parenting styles among adolescents in Chinese society when compared with their Western counterparts. The following review is based on literature describing the parenting relationships of Chinese Americans, as well as Hong Kong Chinese people.

Chinese adolescents have a different interpretation of parental warmth and responsiveness to their Western counterparts. Shek (1999) attempts to study the Chinese perception of global parenting style and specific parenting behaviours. The study demonstrates that Chinese adolescents consider their parents' knowledge of their leisure-time activities as a sign of parental responsiveness rather than demandingness (Shek, 1999). This is consistent with other work indicating that Chinese adolescents consider control and restrictiveness as a sign of love and care from parents (Chao & Sue, 1996; McBride-Chang & Chang, 1998).

Studies also indicate that Hong Kong adolescents perceive their parents as less accepting than Western young people. They also consider their parents to make higher demands on their behaviour than Western young people do. In a retrospective study of adults' perceptions of their parents' behaviour during their adolescence, compared with respondents from Taiwan and Mainland China, adults from Hong Kong perceive their parents as demonstrating less affection, less empathy and being more controlling (Berndt *et al.*, 1993). Berndt and colleagues (1993) show that adults from Hong Kong rated their mothers as warmer than their fathers. Similarly, Shek's (1998a) study on Chinese adolescents' perceptions of parenting styles shows that fathers were perceived as relatively less responsive to and concerned about their adolescents' needs but as harsher in regard to disciplining. Women respondents perceived their mothers as being less harsh and demonstrating more demands in parenting. This echoes a popular Chinese saying, "strict father, kind mother" (Shek, 1998a).

Another issue that troubles many families in Hong Kong is conflict between parents and their adolescent children. Yau and Smetana's (1996) study shows that parent–adolescent conflict is more serious and frequent when adolescents perceive their parents as being more controlling and less responsive to their needs. In addition, mothers were usually perceived as warmer than fathers. Concerning conflict resolution, 45% of respondents indicated that they will obey their parents' final decisions. Most of the respondents, however, preferred to make their own decisions to resolve conflict, consistent with other studies in Euro–American culture showing that adolescence is a period of autonomy seeking (Yau & Smetana, 1996).

Chinese parents also considered adolescents' academic achievement as an important parenting issue. Gorman (1998) shows that Chinese mothers of adolescents will help their offspring to become productive members of society through different means. Chinese-American parents tend to be concerned about their adolescents' learning and academic performance, as well as their choice of college. Chinese-American mothers, in a qualitative study in which they were interviewed, considered themselves to have more involvement in their children's academic activities than American mothers and believed that they are able to contribute to their children's success at school through such involvement. This is generally consistent with Chao's (1994b) concept of training as a Chinese parenting style, with Chinese parents wishing to help adolescents to be successful in society.

Gorman (1998) identifies the subtle nature of the interaction between Chinese-American parents and their adolescent children. Although no overt rules are set, most children know what their parents' expectations are. Chinese parents tend to convey messages about their expectations through encouragement and argument to help their children to make appropriate decisions. Although the parents studied closely monitored their children, they were not restrictive and harsh. Rather, they showed love and concern, rather than imposing rules on adolescents. The mothers influenced their children in a subtle way; they were not overtly warm, as in Western culture, but were clearly motivated by love and concern. Gorman (1998) has given one example from this qualitative study to illustrate this point. Rather than saying that she was not satisfied with her child's academic achievement, the mother in question would say that the marks that the child had obtained were not good enough. This is different from Baumrind's description of the authoritarian parenting style and can be understood as a way for Chinese mothers to show their concern and care, which more closely resembles Baumrind's idea of authoritativeness (Baumrind, 1968).

McBride-Chang and Chang (1998) show that the classification of authoritative, authoritarian and permissive parenting styles may not be appropriate with regard to capturing the ways in which Hong Kong parents and their children interact. Adolescents' and parents' descriptions of parenting styles could not easily be classified into Baumrind's typology. It has been suggested that there may be cultural differences in the interpretation of the questionnaire. For example, a question on parental requirements for obedience may seem controlling to Westerners but very common in Chinese culture, in which obedience is emphasised to a greater extent (Chao & Sue, 1996). The same study uncovered a negative relationship between autonomy and authoritative parenting style (McBride-Chang & Chang, 1998) and between autonomy and school achievement. This may be because adolescents who were detached somewhat from their family were less influenced by their parents. They also received less support for their emotional well-being and with their academic work. This would affect their school achievements. The authors highlight the contrast of this with Western studies, in which the granting of autonomy is positively related to academic achievement. Moreover, this study indicates that no direct relationship exists between parenting style and academic achievement. As discussed here, this may be because parenting style is more strongly associated with student achievement in early years than in adolescence. Nevertheless, the study results indicate that parenting style has a subtle influence on adolescents in academically oriented but not in low-achievement schools (McBride-Chang & Chang, 1998).

Furthermore, supportive parenting behaviour is positively correlated with higher self-esteem in Chinese adolescents (Cheung & Lau, 1985; Lin & Fu, 1990). Communication and trust are among the elements described by Chinese-American adolescents as the most important aspects of their relationship with their mothers (Russell, Crockett & Chao, 2010). They articulated this kind of communication as a form of respect toward each other. Adolescents in this study stated that their mothers in general indirectly show that they care. These findings are generally consistent with the work of Gorman (1998), which show that Chinese parents express their concern and care in a subtle way. Another important expression of maternal care highlighted by adolescents was instrumental support, such as preparing meals for them, accompanying them to places and going shopping together (Russell, Crockett & Chao, 2010). From adolescents' point of view, they notice their parents care for them when they observe that their parents are making sacrifices for the family. Indeed, the study data indicate that respondents' mothers did not show love or support directly, and while the young people indicated that they valued verbal love and concern, this was not absolutely necessary, since love was being expressed in a non-verbal way. Although no study of this kind has yet been carried out in Hong Kong, anecdotally, this is consistent with what Hong Kong Chinese parents do to show their care and concern. Parental sacrifice is an indication of parental support and care but will not be spoken of explicitly.

In terms of their relationships with their fathers, the American-Chinese adolescents involved in this study described their fathers as teachers to their sons; they are strong, commanded respect and provided discipline. Respondents also perceived their fathers' role as providers and teachers as the basis of their good relationship (Russell, Crockett & Chao, 2010). This shows that Chinese-American adolescents still hold a traditional concept of the father figure as a strong man and a teacher of children to be true; they regarded fathers who upheld this kind of role as people they respect and with whom they were more willing to establish good relationships. Similar to their relationships with their mothers, they considered direct and open communication as an ideal. The majority of the time, they could only perceive paternal love and care through indirect actions regarding provisions for their needs.

A recent study indicates that Chinese-American adolescents and their European counterparts differ in the ways in which they understand autonomy (Russell, Crockett, & Chao, 2010). Chao (2005), quoted in Padmawidjaja & Chao, 2010) articulates the idea of 'contingency autonomy' to describe the parenting practice of Chinese parents. The seeking of autonomy is understood as a primary developmental task for adolescents (Collins & Steinberg, 2006). Nevertheless, this concept was developed from the Western perspective of the self, whereas Chinese adolescents have a different interpretation of autonomy. Chao (2005) uses the concept of 'contingent autonomy' to distinguish from the Western understanding of autonomy. This concept denotes the culturally specific parenting practices that exist in regard to the way parents must be satisfied that their adolescents can act responsibly before they are granted autonomy. Moreover, a study of the perception of autonomy among Chinese adolescents in America (Russell, Crockett & Chao, 2010) indicates that respondents perceived their parents as over-protective. In addition, they were more likely to make decisions based on parental advice and often told their parents about their decisions. Rather than considering this as controlling, they saw it as a form of filial obligation (Russell, Crockett & Chao, 2010). This demonstrates the culturally specific perceptions of Chinese adolescents' relationships with their parents.

Chinese adolescents in this study also described the nature of the independence they experienced in their culture. They defined independence with regard to their relationship with their parents. They understood that their parents knew what was best for them, and they had the autonomy to follow their parents' preferences. For Chinese-American boys in particular, autonomy was negotiated with parents and was sensitive to their concerns. This is the concept articulated by Chao (2005) as contingent autonomy, as discussed above. This is a culturally specific way of interpreting autonomy.

Changes in the attitudes of modern Chinese adolescents

Chinese parent–adolescents relationships differ from those the West, with an emphasis on filial piety, conforming to family traditions and practices, respecting parents' and seniors' views and obeying rules and regulations. Children living in a Confucian society perceive parental warmth, even with a certain amount of control and dominance, in relating to their parents (Lau & Yeung, 1996). In particular, however, parents with traditional beliefs with regard to expecting strict obedience from their adolescents, together with a growing awareness of pursuing personal values among Chinese adolescents, may cause difficulties to arise in the parent–adolescent relationship. Shek (1999), working in Hong Kong, shows that Chinese adolescents demonstrate signs of individuation. In addition, a strong discrepancy emerges between parents' expectations of how adolescents will behave and what the adolescents actually do. This indicates the beginning of a departure from traditional thinking about strict parental obedience, toward a desire for more individuation and autonomy. For example, Lau (1992) shows that there has been a growth in the emphasis placed on personal values (such as the pursuit of personal goals different to family expectations and freedom from family monitoring) in the Chinese societies of Mainland China, Singapore and Hong Kong. In contrast to this, Hong Kong Chinese parents may still hold the belief that their adolescents should be strictly obedient in regard to their parents' orders and expectations, creating potential conflict.

Studies indicate that traditional collectivistic beliefs about what has been described as traditional Confucian ideology may not be fully applicable to modern Chinese young people. Gradual changes have been observed among traditional Chinese family practices (Ho & Kang, 1984). Adolescents also increasingly endorse values that are more individually oriented, such as the pursuit of personal goals and autonomy from their parents and families (Lin & Fu, 1990). It can also be observed that Chinese family roles are no longer so strictly defined among Chinese families in the East (Lim & Lim, 2005). Chinese high school students show greater preferences than their US counterparts toward the idea that schools should teach them to be more creative in facing challenges. They have also been shown to perceive personal assets, such as intelligence and wealth, as essential (Lau *et al.*, 2000). Other research shows that Chinese college and high school students treasure personal goals, such as freedom and achievement (Lau & Wong, 1992). These findings indicate that Chinese young people are departing from the collectivist ideology and moving toward a more individualistic view.

The shift among young Chinese people from adherence to a Confucian collectivistic ideology to a more individualistic view speaks to the importance of carrying out contemporary studies so as to understand these adolescents better. Although there are some commonalities within societies influenced by Confucian ideology, such as Singapore, Hong Kong, Taiwan and Mainland China, it is also important to be aware of the different cultures within these societies. For example, the one-child policy of Mainland China has altered the traditional large family size of Chinese culture and has had a unique impact on the nation, which is not shared by other societies that have not employed such a policy.

In an open society such as Hong Kong, many aspects of traditional Chinese culture have not been fully accepted by young people and their parents. Nevertheless, traditional cultural beliefs continue to have an influence, despite ready acceptance of elements of Western and other cultures. Based on the author's clinical experience, it is not uncommon in Hong Kong for parent–adolescent relationships to become intense when there is conflict between the parents' requirement for conformity and the adolescents' need for more autonomy and to attain personal goals. Conflicts arise because Hong Kong Chinese parents are no longer able to maintain traditions. Parents expect their children to respect them but find they do so less and less; furthermore, they cannot address this simply by asserting their power in the family. Some parents adopt democratic child-rearing practices and exercise little control over their adolescents' behaviour. In more dysfunctional families, the child may hold the power over their parents. It is therefore important for parenting programmes to help parents to restore the hierarchy within their families.

Parenting and adolescents' anti-social behaviour

Having considered the culturally specific parenting practices of Chinese parents and parent–adolescent relationships in Chinese culture, the way in which parents and adolescents interact shapes the behaviour of the latter in Hong Kong. There is little research on delinquent behaviour in Hong Kong Chinese society (Leung & Fan, 1996; Shek & Ma, 1997). The lack of studies in this area cannot be interpreted as a lack of concern for the topic in society; there is in fact considerable concern and speculation about the cause of such behaviour in Hong Kong (Leung & Fan, 1996). The diverse conclusions drawn from different studies present some difficulties for forming a single conclusion about the factors associated with anti-social behaviour in Chinese adolescents. Nevertheless, some studies do shed light on its characteristics. Adolescence brings concerns, worries and uncertainties for parents as well. Part of their concern arises from the common stereotype of adolescents as difficult, oppositional and moody (Steinberg & Silk, 2002). Such negative stereotypes influence parents' negative perceptions of adolescents. Their children are entering a period of life in which there are a lot of difficult decisions to be made and challenges to be faced. One of these difficulties is the poorly defined role of parents. While there are clear suggestions available about what needs to be done for a child of 2 years of age, there is no such guidance for dealing with a 15-year-old. Such confusion leads to difficulties and uncertainty with regard to parenting adolescents (Coleman, 2001).

The biological changes caused by puberty, together with the search for personal identity, affects young people's relationships with their parents and increases the distance between them. This increases negative aspects of the relationship, such as conflict, complaining and anger, and decreases positive aspects, such as support, smiling and laughter (Steinberg & Silk, 2002). Parents of adolescents also begin, at this stage, to notice changes in the ways in which their offspring think. They are beginning to approach matters in more advanced and adult-like ways. Such changes may challenge the established parent–child relationship. Adolescents may also challenge their parents by bringing in new ideas for family discussions, decisions and arguments. The development of more adult thinking may lead to adolescents forming expectations that they should be treated like adults. These changes require parents to adapt.

In addition, an adolescent has much more power than a child. They have higher cognitive ability, more physical strength and the power to stimulate and influence family conflicts. They have more opportunities than children to leave the family situation and harm themselves and others. Furthermore, adolescents have more autonomous relationships with other adults and peers. This includes sexual relationships, which many parents find threatening. All these factors taken together make the parenting task more complex (Garbarino & Kelly, 1986). Thus, parenting an adolescent is completely different to parenting a child. They need more communication with their parents and the feeling of being loved and cared for.

Studies have shown that there are two distinct groups of adolescents that display delinquent behaviour. The first group, the majority, displays anti-social behaviour that is confined to adolescence. The second group, the minority, displays anti-social behaviour that begins in childhood and continues into adulthood (Moffit, 1993). This view is supported by other studies (see, for example, Loeber, 1982; Patterson, 1992).

A growing number of studies describe the impact of parenting on criminality, violence and anti-social behaviour (Loeber & Farrington, 1998). Such research describes the relationship between parent–adolescent conflict and delinquency (Patterson, 1982), as well as running away from home (Adams, Gullotta & Clancy, 1985). Familial conflict is related to lower levels of self-esteem and depression in adolescents (Rutter *et al.*, 1976) and to deterioration in the quality of family relationships (Demo, 1991). Such conflict is more common when adolescents perceive their parents as not supporting them, physically and emotionally (Hall, 1987). It has also been identified in a local study that parent–adolescent conflict is related to anti-social behaviour and poor psychological well-being in adolescents (Shek, 1998a). Furthermore, it has been identified from studies that adolescents' involvement in crime, drugs and alcohol is partly related to parent–adolescent conflicts (Montemayor, 1983).

Dekovic (1999) suggests that the lack of emotional bonding between adolescents and their parents in conflictual relationships is associated with the ways in which adolescents externalise behavioural problems. Similarly, the Ontario Child Health Studies show that family dysfunction is strongly related to conduct disorder. This is independent of the influences of other correlates and psychiatric disorders (Offord, Boyle & Racine, 1991). In addition, Snyder and Huntley (1990) report that there is a lack of intimacy and mutuality between anti-social adolescents and their parents. These parents demonstrate more anger, blaming and defensiveness toward their adolescents than in 'normal' families. Studies also show that parenting has a significant influence on children's development. For example, longitudinal studies indicate that criminal offending is transmitted from one generation to the next and confined to certain families (Rutter, Giller & Hagell, 1998). Farrington's study of inner-London boys (Farrington, 2003) shows that 63% of young men with fathers who had been convicted of an offence also had criminal records. Young people who are violent offenders tend to live in poor housing with large families and come from lower socio-economic classes; their fathers tend to have erratic job records, including periods of unemployment. The same study shows that the most important early precursors of aggression and violence in boys are harsh attitudes and discipline from a parent at age 8 and having older siblings who are delinquent or have behavioural problems. The violent offenders studied also tended to come from families with parents who displayed cruel attitudes, used harsh methods of discipline and tended to be in conflict with each other. A survey of the parents demonstrated they held authoritarian child-rearing attitudes (Farrington, 1991). Abusive and severe physical punishment in childhood, as well as during adolescence, has a negative impact on the emotional and mental well-being of adolescents (Henricson, 2000). Studies show that violent delinquents tend to have rejecting, punitive, aggressive or alcoholic parents. Some research suggests that criminal parents are less likely to provide adequate supervision to their adolescent children (Rutter, Giller & Hagell, 1998). In addition, the strength of the parent–child bond and the extent of the child's attachment to the parent is a principal factor explaining the presence of delinquent behaviour (Hirschi, 1969).

As in some studies carried out in the West, some of the work done in Hong Kong indicates that anti-social behaviour in adolescents is associated with parenting style. Shek and Ma (1997) studied 2,972 adolescents aged 11 to 19 years old in Hong Kong to identify whether or not paternal and maternal parenting styles were associated with anti-social and pro-social behaviour. They show that adolescents with a more negative perception of parental treatment, concern or leniency engaged more in deviancy and undesirable sexual activities and showed more anti-social behaviour and aggression. The data show that parental concern and kindness are negatively related to anti-social behaviour, whereas leniency is positively related to it (Shek & Ma, 1997). This is consistent with other evidence (see, for example, Maccoby & Martin, 1983) that suggests that parental style and negative perceptions of parental treatment are both associated with anti-social behaviour.

Chinese culture emphasises harmony and obedience, which may be one of the reasons why less anti-social behaviour is reported among Chinese adolescents than their Western counterparts. Anti-social behaviour has been defined as activities such as damaging school property, taking something without asking the owner and school misconduct and status offences (Feldman *et al.*, 1991). The arrest rate of Hong Kong juveniles was 0.16% for the age group 7 to 15 years between 1966 and 1970, which increased slightly to 0.27% from 1976 to 1980 (Cheung & Lau, 1985). In contrast to this, the corresponding figure was 0.53% for the same age group in Canada in 1966. This suggests that juvenile crime was much less serious in Hong Kong than in the West in the 1970s (Leung & Fan, 1996). Leung and Fan (1996) suggest that the fact that Chinese parents usually suppress aggressiveness and encourage impulse control may be a reason for the low arrest rates. Chinese people also show a high level of conformity toward high-status targets, and their behaviour is more closely governed by internalised rules (Leung & Fan, 1996).

Leung and Fan (1996) indicate that most studies of delinquent behaviour in Hong Kong are descriptive in nature and are not guided by theories. In their review of descriptive studies from the 1970s to the 1990s, they show that adolescents were more likely to display anti-social behaviour if their parents did so as well. In addition, members of single-parent families in which insufficient parental concern and care was evidenced tended to engage in delinquent behaviour (Leung & Fan, 1996). On the other hand, some studies have been carried out based on theories developed in the West. In discussing the work of Ng (1975) on juvenile delinquency in Hong Kong, Leung and Fan (1996) indicate that this study is based on the control theory developed by Hirschi (1969), and the results are consistent with Western findings. The control theory (Hirschi, 1969) proposes that delinquent behaviour arises because of the weakening of social control, which can also be conceptualised as social bonds. Hirschi further classifies social bonds into four types: attachment (the relationship with significant others), commitment (the pursuit of a widely valued life goal), involvement (submergence into socially accepted activities) and beliefs (the values and beliefs that an individual holds) (Leung & Fan, 1996).

Ng (1975) indicates that family, school, peers, living conditions, employment conditions, leisure activities and social attitudes are all related to juvenile delinquency in Hong Kong. Ng studied 479 randomly selected juvenile offenders aged 12 to 20 years old with a control group of 491 adolescents with no criminal records. The comparison indicates that non-delinquent adolescents had better relationships both in their family and in school than the delinquents.

Non-delinquents also showed better academic performance and had higher aspirations educationally. On the other hand, the delinquent group was more involved in socially stigmatised activities, such as gambling and smoking, and was more negative about the police and less accepting of conventional moral standards (Leung & Fan, 1996).

There is also a relationship between affiliations with deviant friends and anti-social behaviour (Elliott & Menard, 1996; Farrington, Ohlin & Wilson, 1986). Berndt (1979), and Steinberg and Silverberg (1986) show that adolescents experience lower levels of peer pressure during the pre-adolescent period. Such pressure increases through the middle years of adolescence. Eventually, peer pressure decreases in late adolescence. A lack of pro-social friends can be responsible for anti-social behaviour (Elliott *et al.*, 1985). The social learning model suggests that a strong association with anti-social friends will enhance the way in which adolescents learn more about deviant attitudes and make it more likely that they will subsequently engage in anti-social behaviour themselves.

In addition, unsupervised wandering and associations with delinquent peers are predictors of having a court record at ages 10 to 14 years old (Stoolmiller, 1994). A delinquent boy and his friend at age 14 are more likely to affect each other in regard to talking about rule breaking than non-deviant dyads. In addition, these exchanges are positively associated with future anti-social behaviour. Furthermore, Stoolmiller (1994) confirms earlier findings that unsupervised wandering, association with delinquent peers and anti-social behaviour are closely linked in boys from childhood to early adolescence (Stoolmiller, 1994).

A follow-up study by Ng (1980) shows that the delinquent group reported more negative relationships with parents, stronger associations with delinquent peers, more involvement in socially unacceptable leisure activities and stronger endorsements of unconventional moral beliefs and values. The results indicate that the influence of peers was stronger than other variables influencing juvenile delinquency (Leung & Fan, 1996). This is further confirmed by Mok (1985), whose work is also based on control theory but involved respondents from secondary schools. These results indicate that the delinquent group reported poorer relationships with their families and adhered to fewer socially approved beliefs and values.

Parental monitoring has recently been shown to be negatively associated with adolescents running away in Hong Kong (Cheung, Liu & Lee, 2005). This study gathered data from 951 grade 7 students in Hong Kong and measured how parents monitor their children (Stattin & Kerr, 2000). Other dimensions measured included social support at school and friendships. The results show that respondents who had run away at least once had significantly less parental monitoring before the age of 10. They also had less teacher support than those who had never run away. However, those who had some experience of running away scored higher with regard to friendships (Cheung, Liu & Lee, 2005), which is to say they were subject to stronger influence from their peers than their families. These research findings are generally consistent with previous work in Euro–American cultures that highlights the affiliation between anti-social behaviour and deviant friends (Elliott & Menard, 1996; Farrington, Ohlin & Wilson, 1986) and lack of parental monitoring (Stoolmiller, 1994).

Furthermore, one study on the emotional autonomy of Hong Kong adolescents shows that high levels of such autonomy is correlated with participation in problematic behaviour (Chou, 2003). This study involved 512 adolescents who responded to a questionnaire on emotional autonomy. This concept, derived by Steinberg and Silverberg (1986), has three dimensions: the de-idealisation of parents, in which adolescents realise that their parents are not absolutely powerful; non-dependency on parents, whereby adolescents are less likely to rely on their parents when they have problems in interpersonal relationships or at school; and individuation, wherein adolescents no longer believe that their parents know or understand them. The results indicate that individuation was strongly correlated with problematic behaviour among the adolescents (Chou, 2003). This suggests that, when adolescents in Hong Kong develop poor relationships with their parents and feel their parents do not understand them, there will be a strong correlation with problematic behaviour.

Parenting and parent–adolescent conflicts

As described by Scaramella and Conger (2004), some studies operationalise conflict in terms of the frequency of interpersonal disputes or disagreements. In addition, some studies define parent–adolescent conflict as an intensity of negative emotion (Scaramella & Conger, 2004). However, the first of these approaches is inappropriate, since it is the intensity of the conflicts between parents and adolescents, and not the frequency of the disputes in itself, that best captures the idea of the emotional volatility between them. Emotion may or may not be expressed during disagreements, since parents and adolescents may resolve their conflicts without this.

Prinz (1976), quoted in Fitzpatrick and Norbeck (1997), defines parent–adolescent conflict in a board sense including some behavioural expression like interruption, disagreement, tension, defensive and supportive communications or even aggression. It also includes negative communications between parents and adolescents including both verbal and non-verbal interactions. The definition also includes some emotional aspects when parents and adolescents face difficulties. These are anxiety, emotion, hostility and antagonism. This definition posits parent–adolescent conflict as something that includes *both* disagreement and the expression of negative emotions.

In this book, parent–adolescent conflict will be defined as the disagreement and opposition behaviour between parents and their teenage children, together with the expression of negative emotional response between parents and their teenage children.

There has been an increase in the number as well as the quality of research in the area of parent–adolescent conflict in the past 25 years, compared with the situation before then (Holmbeck, 1996). Several scholars have carried out integrative reviews in this area (see, for example, Holmbeck & Hill, 1986; Collins &

Laursen, 1992; Collins, 1995; Steinberg, 2001). These reviews present a clear picture of how parents' and young people's relationships change from childhood to adolescence and also begin to clarify how family processes impact adolescents' development and mental health.

The first step is to consider the issues that may give rise to conflict between parents and adolescents. One study, based on a retrospective analysis of adolescent perceptions (Fitzpatrick & Norbeck, 1997), proposes nine categories of problematic interactions, as described by adolescents. These are: family relations, extracurricular activities, sex, romantic relationships, career/education, living circumstances, money/material items and behavioural problems (Fitzpatrick & Norbeck, 1997). This study also indicates that fewer conflicts were reported from those adolescents who had lived away from their parents for a while than those who had moved away more recently. In addition, males recalled more conflicts involving unlawful activities than females did.

The work of Tesser and colleagues (1989), using the Issues Checklist (IC) developed by Prinz and colleagues (1979), indicates that the most frequent issues identified were concerned with daily household chores and relationships with siblings. This is consistent with previous findings that suggest that conflict typically involves mundane issues, rather than serious problems. In addition, Smetana (1989) reports conflict over everyday issues, such as rule breaking, failing to comply with parental requests about matters such as schoolwork and home chores, general disobedience, the adolescent's choice of activities, social life and friends, fighting with and teasing siblings, failing to finish tasks and personal hygiene. This indicates that parent–adolescent conflict usually involves normal, everyday events of family life, such as household chores, family rules and obligations, personal habits, choices and relationships (Montemayor, 1983; Smetana, 1989). Arguments about major issues, such as sex, drugs and politics, are less frequent by comparison.

Perspectives in understanding parent–adolescent conflicts

Canary, Cupach and Messman (1995) contend that there are three possibilities for the causal relationships of parent–child conflict. One is the unidirectional approach, which focuses on how parental behaviour affects children. In this view, conflict is understood as the child's non-compliance with parental control. Parents can therefore modify their behaviour to increase their effectiveness. The second possibility is that the parent–adolescent relationship is bi-directional, which emphasises the way in which both parties influence each other. The third option is termed the "spiral of recursive feedback loops", according to the system properties of the parent–child interaction. At the very least, parent–adolescent relationships are a bi-directional process, with one party affecting the other (Steinberg, 1988).

This process is affected by many factors, such as the temperament of adolescents. Adolescents who reach puberty early (that is, who mature early) have more conflicts with their parents. Temperamental characteristics, including high impulsivity, are a feature in increasing levels of conflict (Dekovic, 1999). Adolescents who easily become angry at minor issues with their parents may have more difficulty controlling their emotional expressions than those who display more tempered emotions. Although the characteristics of individual adolescents may contribute to parental conflict, Dekovic (1999) suggests that this also depends on how parents respond to young people with these characteristics. Therefore, the characteristics of adolescents are affected by how the environment responds to them (that is, the goodness or poorness of fit). If the adolescent's characteristics are consonant with the environment, he or she can adjust well to it and vice versa.

From a developmental perspective, the transition to adolescence and the onset of puberty are the main reasons for parent–adolescent conflict. As discussed above, parenting adolescents can be a stressful experience for adults (Silverberg & Steinberg, 1990). The onset of puberty, together with adolescents striving for independence, leads to different levels of conflict among parents and their adolescent sons and daughters. Such conflict within families used to be considered as a normal process in which parents and adolescents negotiated a new relationship with each other as the latter went through a period of formulating their own identities and adult selves. These ideas are well described by psychoanalytic theorists (Erikson, 1968; Blos, 1967), who suggest that adolescence is a period of identity crisis and individuation, which implies conflict with parents, and, further, that this is a process that is in fact developmentally desirable.

Evidence confirms the relationship between puberty and an increase in disagreements between parents and adolescents. This is the case for both boys and girls (Holmbeck & Hill, 1991). More mothers than fathers are involved in conflict, particularly with daughters (Montemayor, 1986). Conflicts between mothers and daughters are more frequent than in other combinations of parent and child (Montemayor, 1983). The higher frequency of interactions between daughters and mothers, compared with fathers and daughters, may explain this, as may the possibility that girls share more of their personal and relationship problems with their mothers (Youniss & Smollar, 1985). In contrast, recent studies (Dekovic, Groenendaal & Gerrits, 1996) report a lack of gender differences in parent–adolescent conflict, which is explained by the fact that gender based expectations are beginning to disappear. Such inconsistent results may also be due to methodological weaknesses in different studies.

Scholars working from a developmental perspective have argued that during early adolescence, normative physical, cognitive and social-maturational changes initiate a process through which the parent–child relationship is transformed from one in which the parents make most of the decisions affecting the young person to one in which the adolescent gains independence and legitimacy in regard to personal decision-making. Such a proposition is confirmed by studies showing that parent–adolescent conflict increases from early to middle adolescence and declines in late adolescence because maturational changes lead to a restructuring of the parental relationship (Smetana, 1989).

Parent–adolescent conflicts, therefore, according to the developmental perspective, should be considered as a necessary process with regard to facilitating the renegotiation of boundaries and roles in order to transform parental relationships (Allison, 2000). In addition, conflict serves an important function in enhancing negotiation skills and learning how to consider alternative views (Steinberg, 1990). It is part of a normal developmental process originating from the idea that adolescents need to separate themselves from the family (Steinberg, 2001). Conflict also provides the context for psychosocial development and, in particular, the development of psychological autonomy and identity (Phinney, Kim-Jo & Vilhjalmsdottir, 2005). This is a very important developmental crisis, as described by Erikson (1968), necessary in order to achieve individuation (Blos, 1967). The literature also suggests that conflicts between adolescents and parents in most families are relatively infrequent, short lived and mild (Montemayor, 1986), further strengthening the view of this as a normal phenomenon. Drawing on the theoretical basis of the developmental perspective, parents often need to accept the changes in their adolescent children over this period and facilitate their progress through this stage of changing identity (Steinberg, 2001).

In contrast to this notion of parent–adolescent conflict displaying a curvilinear change in negative affect, the social relations perspective argues that relationships naturally strive to maintain homeostasis, and so exhibiting negative affect will not follow the developmental process. From this perspective, the relationship between parents and adolescents will not change at all or will do so slowly and gradually, rather than consisting of developmentally linked fluctuations (Laursen & Collins, 1994). The extent and intensity of conflict are also different in different relationships. For example, the mother–adolescent relationship should give rise to more intense displays of emotional affect, both positive and negative, than less emotionally close interactions (Laursen & Collins, 1994). Studies of variations in the frequency of interpersonal disputes during adolescence generally report findings consistent with the social relations perspective. A reduction in the rate of parent–adolescent disputes over mundane issues has been observed (Collins, 1990; Laursen, Coy & Collins, 1998). Nevertheless, the social relations perspective is unclear in regard to what actually constitutes gradual change, so a general decline in the frequency of disputes can be used to both support and disconfirm this approach (Scaramella & Conger, 2004).

The mediated-effect model has been suggested by writers such as Peterson and Taylor (1980) and Brooks-Gunn and colleagues (1994). Based on the direct-effect model (that is, biological changes in puberty are posited as the direct cause of parent–adolescent conflict), it augments this by suggesting there are some mediating factors alongside puberty that lead to conflict. These include the character and temperament of the adolescent and parents, adolescent and parental responses to the social and physical changes of adolescents during puberty, ethnicity, peer and school factors and other major life events (Holmbeck, 1996).

The behavioural family system model is proposed by Robin and Foster (1989). It hypothesises that adolescent developmental factors, together with deficits in family skills and inappropriate functional interaction patterns, create the potential for discord (Robin & Foster, 1989). The model has been evaluated and found to be effective in improving the problem-solving skills of mother–adolescent dyads in clinical settings (Robin *et al.*, 1977).

In this model, parent–adolescent conflict is conceptualised as resulting from the adolescent experiencing drastic physiological, cognitive, emotional and behavioural changes. The major psychosocial change is the attempt to become independent from the parents, which interrupts the previously established homeostasis of the family. The system then reacts in an attempt to recover its homeostatic balance. A conflict therefore arises. Nevertheless, conflict is normal during this period of adjustment. How the family reacts to it determines whether the normal perturbation of early adolescence is resolved or whether it escalates into a problem (Robin & Foster, 1989). For example, different family members may have different views on conflict between parents and adolescents (Steinberg, 2001). Parents will be more bothered by conflict with their adolescents than with their siblings. In addition, Silverberg and Steinberg (1987) identify a relationship between parental mental health and parent–adolescent conflict. Parents experience more stress when interacting with an adolescent who is more inclined to make differentiations from his or her family of origin during puberty or is the same sex as the parent; stronger feelings are also experienced by unemployed and divorced parents. More parent–adolescent conflict is reported in divorced, single-parent and step-parent families than in those in which the parents are still together (Montemayor, 1983; Wallerstein, 1985; Garbarino, Sebes & Schellenbach, 1984). High frequency of conflict is also associated with changes in family context, such as unemployment (Elder, 1974), insularity (Wahler, 1980) or the adolescent being abused (Garbarino & Gilliam, 1980).

The family system perspective adds to the communication model by suggesting that the relationship between parents and adolescents is not an equal one and so genuine negotiation is impossible (Robin & Foster, 1989). It further addresses the issue regarding the way in which the nature of family disruption is rooted in a breakdown of hierarchy; the parents fail to act as parents and the adolescent is in charge of the family. Parent–adolescent conflict can be viewed as a result of the triangulation and 'detouring' (Minuchin, 1974) that occurs within the family. It may be considered as covering up or hiding covert or submerged conflict between parents, detouring them through the adolescent in a process called triangulation. The behavioural family system model thus considers problem-solving, communication skills, belief systems, cognitive distortion and family structure as the key dimensions influencing parent–adolescent conflict.

There are other approaches to conceptualising parent–adolescent conflict. Caffery and Erdman (2000) propose the use of a systems approach and attachment theory. In this theoretical proposition, the attachment relationship between parent and adolescent is interactive and is both affected by and affects the family process. Thus, secure attachments for all members are important to family functioning. This model further postulates that there are three patterns of parent–adolescent relationship associated with insecure attachment when the adolescent was a child: recklessness and accident-prone behaviours, inhibition of exploration and precocious competence in self-protection. These are defensive patterns of behaviours that the child perceives as a lack of protection from their caregivers in their childhood. When the child matures into adolescence, he or she may exhibit anger directed at the parents for what he or she perceives as a lack of interest or concern about their well-being, leading to conflict.

It has also been suggested that it is more important to consider how parents and adolescents solve these conflicts than to focus on avoiding them, as set out in the social problem-solving model (Chang, D'Zurilla & Sanna, 2004). This model suggests that adolescents and parents are more adaptive to parent–adolescent conflict if they have stronger problem-solving skills. Three styles of problem-solving have been identified: constructive or rational, impulsive-carelessness and avoidance (Doorn, Branje & Meeus, 2008).

A longitudinal study carried out by Shek and Ma (2001) shows that parent–adolescent conflict is predictive of anti-social behaviour. In addition, adolescent anti-social behaviour at time point 1 of the study predicted parent–adolescent conflict at time point 2. Father–adolescent conflict was more pervasive than mother–adolescent conflict in Hong Kong Chinese culture. The study also suggests that father–adolescent conflict is particularly predictive of anti-social behaviour (Shek & Ma, 2001).

In addition, the home life of chronic delinquents is characterised by disorganisation and hostility, with their parents unable to instil in them proper standards of behaviour and self-control (Moffit, 1993). Parent–adolescent conflict predicts future contact with delinquent peers (Mags & Galambos, 1993). More male juvenile delinquents than non-delinquents have poor relationships with their parents. Finally, depression is significantly related to parent–adolescent conflict (Cole & McPherson, 1993; Dekovic, 1999).

It is suggested that poor quality parent–adolescent relationships are related to a higher tendency to externalise problem behaviours (Dekovic, 1999). A poor relationship reduces opportunities for adolescents to internalise their parents' values. On the other hand, adolescents who have a positive relationship with their parents communicate more with them about their daily activities and disclose their thoughts and feelings more. As discussed earlier, such disclosure increases parents' knowledge of their child's whereabouts, which in turn has been correlated to low levels of anti-social behaviour (Dekovic, Wissink & Meijer, 2004).

Parent–adolescent conflict in Hong Kong

The work of Shek and Ma (1997), together with that of Yau and Smetana (1996), provides an understanding of parent–adolescent conflict in Hong Kong. Compared with the international literature, the findings of studies in Hong Kong are consistent with each other and different from those obtained from Western cultures. Yau and Smetana (1996) studied 120 lower-class adolescents in Hong Kong, sampled from three different secondary schools, collecting mainly qualitative data about the nature and frequency of parental conflict. They show that adolescents and parents in Hong Kong tend to have conflict over everyday issues at a similar frequency as found in Western studies. Nevertheless, conflict over academic achievement ranked as the third most frequent issue in the former context, suggesting that families in Hong Kong focus more on their children's academic outcomes than their Western counterparts. In addition, the adolescents reported conflict over their parents' own behaviour, such as smoking, leisure activities and their relationship with the other parent. This indicates that Hong Kong Chinese adolescents expect their parents to behave decently and that their parents' misbehaviour affects their relationship. This is an interesting finding that is different from that obtained in studies of other cultures.

There is also a gender difference in regard to conflict in Hong Kong, with girls generating more conflicts than boys (Yau & Smetana, 1996) and more difficulties arising with mothers than with fathers (similar to Western findings). This may indicate that the trend in Hong Kong is similar to the West insofar as mothers spend more time taking care of adolescents on a day-to-day basis, resulting in more opportunities for conflict.

As in the Western research findings, adolescents in Hong Kong justify conflict as the pursuit of personal jurisdiction, which may indicate a need for individual autonomy. In terms of conflict resolution, 45% of adolescents in Yau and Smetana's (1996) study reported that they would conform to their parent's decision in order to resolve conflict. However, when asked about their choice of resolution, they stated that they would have preferred to make their own decisions. This is consistent with Western findings, in that adolescents strive for independence independent from their parents (Yau & Smetana, 1996). It also suggests that adolescents in a collectivist culture may tend to resolve conflicts with their parents by conforming to their wishes. A study by Fuligni (1998), comparing beliefs and expectations from parents of Chinese and European adolescents, indicated that Chinese adolescents held greater respect for parental authority than their European counterparts. This seems to be consistent with findings from the international literature, which indicate a preference for negotiation in Western cultures, suggesting a difference between collectivist and Western cultures in regard to conflict-resolution styles.

In terms of parenting style, this study showed that conflicts occur more frequently when parents are more controlling and less responsive to their adolescents' needs (Yau & Smetana, 1996). This is consistent with other findings that suggest that more conflict is associated with less responsive, less empathic and more controlling parents. Young people in Hong Kong value parent–child relationships, which predicts the level of life satisfaction among young people in Hong Kong (Shek, 1998a, 1999). The role of the family is therefore crucial for Hong Kong adolescents, since traditional concepts of the importance of conformity to family values are still an important element that concerns Chinese adolescents, who tend to be particularly relationship oriented (Leung, McBride-Chang & Lai, 2004). These findings are consistent with the idea that parents who demonstrate high levels of affection, nurturance and empathy toward their child (that is, the elements of authoritative parenting) serve as a secure base for children to face challenges arising outside the family (Bowlby, 1988).

The above review of studies carried out in Hong Kong suggests that the way in which adolescents negotiate and resolve conflict is culturally patterned (Markus & Lin, 1999). According to this view, there will be a difference in the nature and manifestation of parent–adolescent conflicts in collectivist (such as Chinese) and individualistic (for example the US) cultures. In a culture that values individual autonomy, the direct expression of one's own view and feelings, together with open disagreement in conflict, seems to be the most appropriate way to respond to a disagreement. Direct confrontation may not be seen as appropriate in cultures that value harmonious relationships (Phinney, Kim-Jo & Vilhjalmsdottir, 2005).

Kapadia and Miller (2005) review studies on conflict resolution and show that, in collectivist cultural groups, individuals demonstrate more conformity and are other-oriented. In individualistic cultural groups, individuals are more assertive and self-oriented. In collectivist cultural groups, such as those to which Chinese-American adolescents belong, young people concede to parental expectations in conflict resolution, rather than insisting on their own will (Yau & Smetana, 1996).

Furthermore, parenting beliefs are different across cultures. The traditional Chinese family structure places emphasis on filial piety and hierarchical relationships (Chan & Leong, 1994). This ideology requires children to respect their parents and care for them when they are elderly. Traditional Chinese families do not want their children to openly display negative emotions, such as anger or aggression. Children are not permitted to bring shame and dishonour to the family through any kind of misbehaviour. Behaviour that brings honour to the family includes achievement, obedience and obligation to one's parents. Chinese families are child-centred, and more emphasis is placed on the parent–child bond than the marital bond (Lim & Lim, 2005). These traditional beliefs affect adolescents and their responses to parental conflict in Chinese culture.

From the above review, it may be concluded that, in Hong Kong, most of the conflicts identified are about homework and academic achievements, with a culturally specific concern with Hong Kong Chinese parents' behaviour (such as smoking or certain leisure activities) which may not appear in Western studies. Hong Kong Chinese adolescents tend to conform to the wishes of their parents in order to achieve conflict resolution. As shown in Western studies, the underlying reason for conflict is the need to strive for autonomy. In addition, the gender difference in Hong Kong is similar to that found in Western studies. It can also be seen that there is less conflict between parents and adolescents if the latter perceive the former to be warmer and less controlling. This may imply that an authoritative parenting style may be appropriate in Hong Kong. Nevertheless, the evidence also indicates that parenting styles among Chinese parents are different from those identified in Western typologies. Culturally specific approaches to parenting, such as training (Chao, 1994a), may be more desirable approaches to describing Chinese parenting than the authoritative style derived from Western work.

Parenting and adolescents' emotional problems

Chou (1999) indicates that there is a strong correlation between adolescents' psychological well-being (that is, they had fewer depressive symptoms) and their subjective perception of good relationships within their families. In addition, Ma and colleagues (2000) show that Hong Kong Chinese adolescents with good parental influences and parent–adolescent relationships demonstrate less delinquent and more pro-social behaviour (Ma *et al.*, 2000).

On the basis of the above review, it can be seen that a poor parent–adolescent relationship, low levels of parental monitoring, a high level of involvement with delinquent activities and peers and a parental record of delinquent behaviour are all factors associated with juvenile delinquency in Hong Kong. Such a conclusion is generally consistent with Western findings. As Leung and Fan (1996) comment, it may be tempting to conclude that Western theories are enough to explain Chinese culture. However, one must be aware that these studies were based on theories and evidence developed in the West, and there is a lack of cross-cultural comparison studies. Furthermore, no attempt has been made to develop culturally sensitive concepts to explain delinquent and anti-social behaviour in Chinese culture (Leung & Fan, 1996).

Chinese parents place particular emphasis on their children's academic performance and achievements, so this also affects Hong Kong adolescents. There is evidence that some of the undesirable behaviours demonstrated by adolescents are partially related to these kinds of parenting beliefs. Yip, Ngan and Lam (2003) show that self-harm among adolescents is related to having had an unhappy childhood and poor quality family life, such as that characterised by divorce and harsh parental discipline. In addition, the Chinese belief in obedience may prompt parents to use strict discipline to prohibit their adolescent children from self-harming further, which would also prevent them from expressing their feelings. Further control of adolescents' behaviour, together with measures intended to inhibit their feelings, may actually provoke further self-harm (Yip, Ngan & Lam, 2003). In contrast, adolescents with supportive and empathic parents showed more positive outcomes. This study shows that Chinese beliefs about obedience and the Chinese culture's emphasis on harmony may inhibit adolescents' feelings about unpleasant family situations and provoke further undesirable behaviour on their part.

Another important characteristic of Hong Kong Chinese adolescents is the extent to which they are burdened heavily by examinations and coursework. Chan (1998) looks at stressful life events and adaptation outcomes among Hong Kong adolescents. Major and minor life events concerning school, families and peer relationships were reviewed in terms of their relationship with the adolescent's emotional well-being. The life event checklist used here consisted of 42 items, based on Johnson and McCutcheon's (1980) Life Events Checklist. Six teachers were invited to review the applicability of these items, and six questions were deleted because they were not applicable to Hong Kong Chinese culture. Two questions concerning the emigration of good friends and families were added, as these are relatively common life events in Hong Kong. A total of 800 students responded to the questionnaire, in which they were asked to indicate whether these events had happened last year, rate their perception of them as 'good' or 'bad' and evaluate them based on a scale of 0 to 3. The results indicate that the adolescents experienced seven or eight stressful life events a year, more than half of which they perceived as bad. They perceived bad events as having twice the impact of good events. The most frequently reported stressful life events were academic issues (Chan, 1998). This suggests that Hong Kong Chinese adolescents tend to perceive life events negatively and that academic issues are the primary focus of their stress.

Parenting and adolescents' suicidal behaviour

Another issue that has a significant impact on Hong Kong Chinese society is adolescent suicide. Currently, suicide is one of the leading causes of death among adolescents in Hong Kong, China and in many other places around the world. It is also an issue that is considered important around the world. Previous studies have shown that, in the United States, suicide is the third leading cause of death in adolescents (ages 10 to 14 years old) and the second cause of death in those aged 15 to 34 years old (CDC, 2015). It is the leading cause of death in adolescents between the ages of 15 and 24 years in Hong Kong (Yip *et al.*, 2004). Studies conducted in Hong Kong showed that 26.8% of a sample of adolescents had experienced suicidal ideations in the past 12 months (Chan, Miranda & Surrence, 2009). Furthermore, 13.7% of adolescents have thought about attempting suicide, and 4.7% had actually attempted suicide in a separate study conducted with adolescents in Hong Kong (Shek & Yu, 2012). The suicide rate of adolescents in Hong Kong is lower than in Europe (Sun, Hui & Watkins, 2006). In fact, at 19.5 suicides per 100,000 inhabitants, it is among the lowest in the developed world. Nevertheless, it is an important topic in Hong Kong, since tragedies like this, when they do occur, arouse a lot of concern. Suicide brings shame to the family and has a great impact on friends and schoolmates. Evidence indicates that adolescents who have low self-esteem and mental health issues, especially depression, correlate with adolescent suicide in Hong Kong. In particular, how adolescents perceive family relationships and the level of support they receive from teachers are significantly associated with levels of adolescents' self-esteem and their levels of depression (Cheung & Lau, 1985; Lau & Kwok, 2000). Shek (1997) also indicates that Chinese adolescents who experience relatively more conflict with their parents tend to report lower levels of self-esteem, less hope and lower levels of life satisfaction. Poor family relationships also have a significantly stronger association with depressive symptoms among Chinese adolescents than their Western counterparts (Greenberger *et al.*, 2000).

A recent study of the relationship between family, teachers and peer support and depression shows that more than 50% of adolescents participating reported different degrees of depressive symptoms. A total of 26% of the sample had had suicidal thoughts and 6% of them had formed the intention to commit suicide. These findings support the assumption that family, teachers and peer support are important predictors of suicidal thoughts (Sun *et al.*, 2006). Family cohesion has an effect on suicidal thoughts, which are in turn mediated by self-esteem. The findings of this study suggest that low levels of family cohesion and high levels of family conflict lead to adolescents using depression as a way to cope with the situation in question, which in turn may lead to suicidal ideation (Chan, Miranda & Surrence, 2009). Unlike in Western countries, where evidence shows that low levels of family expressiveness are directly related to suicidal ideation, this relationship was not strong in this study. The author suggests that Chinese culture does not emphasise open communication and that it may not be a necessary condition for the prevention of suicide (Sun *et al.*, 2006).

Studies have indicated that depression and lower levels of self-esteem among adolescents correlate significantly with adolescent suicide in Hong Kong (Lee *et al.*, 2006). In addition, adolescents who have stressful relationships with their peers and families, as well as feelings of loneliness and increased impulsivity, are associated with suicidal ideation in Hong Kong (Chan, Miranda & Surrence, 2009). International studies indicate that having a family history of suicide (Runeson & Åsberg, 2014) and a personal history of attempted suicide are strong predictors of completed suicide (Gould *et al.*, 2003). In addition, poor family relationships, such as lower levels of familial adaptability and family cohesion, are predictors of adolescent suicidal attempts (Sheftall *et al.*, 2013). Parent–adolescent conflicts have also been identified as a common factor of completed and non-fatal suicidal episodes (Wagner, Silverman & Martin, 2003), as well as being related to suicidal thoughts among college students (Lamis & Jahn, 2013). Furthermore, a high number of conflicts between parents and adolescents, low levels of cohesion within the family and ineffective parenting are strong risk factors for youth suicide and depression. In particular, a conflict-ridden and unsatisfying father–child relationship is related to adolescent suicide (Wagner, Silverman & Martin, 2003). Family discord and negative relationships with parents are also associated with adolescent suicide (Consoli *et al.*, 2013). These international studies are consistent with local studies. Studies conducted in Hong Kong have indicated that high levels of parent–adolescent conflict and low levels of warmth in families correlated with adolescents' suicidal ideation in Hong Kong (Lai & McBride-Chang, 2001). Poor communication between adolescents and their parents also correlated with suicidal ideation and hopelessness (Kwok Lai & Shek, 2010).

Parenting and adolescents' positive outcomes

As noted above, research on parenting styles in Western culture is usually based on Baumrind's typology (permissive, authoritative and authoritarian styles) (Baumrind, 1968). Maccoby and Martin (1983) build on the permissive parenting style and distinguish two separate patterns: indulgent and neglecting (Darling & Steinberg, 1993). Indulgent parents are defined as being high in responsiveness but low in demandingness, while neglectful parents are low in both aspects. Extensive research in this area consistently shows that an authoritative parenting style is beneficial to the adolescent's development, with better psychological and behavioural adjustment than non-authoritatively raised peers (Collins & Steinberg, 2006). Authoritative parenting produces adolescents with self-esteem who cope better and show more maturity than those brought up in a non-authoritative style (Coleman & Hendry, 1999).

Gray and Steinberg show that each component of authoritativeness (that is, warmth, firmness and psychological autonomy-granting) contributes independently to healthy adolescent development (Steinberg, 2000). Behaviour such as kissing, hugging and giving compliments and praise exemplifies parental warmth and acceptance (Russell, Crockett & Chao, 2010). Adolescents in authoritative homes, compared with those whose parents are less supportive, achieve more success in school, report less depression and anxiety, score higher on measures of self-reliance and self-esteem and are less likely to engage in anti-social behaviour (Steinberg, 2001). In addition, parents who adopt a warm and supportive parenting style report less conflict with adolescents than those whose style is more coercive (Ambert, 1997).

A high level of parental monitoring is one of the protective factors against anti-social behaviour for adolescents (Patterson & Stouthamer-Loeber, 1984; Snyder, Dishon & Patterson, 1986). Parental monitoring also has strong associations with all indicators of adjustment for both boys and girls, with the exception of depression in boys (Jocobson & Crockett, 2000). Parental monitoring can be defined as "knowledge of their child's whereabouts, activities, and friends" (Jocobson & Crockett, 2000: 66). Poor monitoring of adolescents is strongly associated with anti-social behaviour (Patterson & Stouthamer-Loeber, 1984; Aseltine, 1995; Barber, 1996). Levels of parental monitoring are different in moderate and chronic offenders (Patterson & Stouthamer-Loeber, 1984). Evidence suggests that high levels of parental monitoring and positive family relationships are associated with low levels of anti-social behaviour.

Nevertheless, not all families experience difficulties with parent–adolescent relationships. Those with close and non-conflicted relationships will have adolescents with better mental health than those for whom there are problems with parents. Most such families have already developed conflicts before the children reach adolescence (Steinberg, 1990).

Patterson and Stouthamer-Loeber (1984) demonstrate that parental family management skills are related to adolescent anti-social behaviour. Such skills are seen as having four components: monitoring, discipline, problem-solving and reinforcement (Patterson & Stouthamer-Loeber, 1984). Consistent parental discipline, such as the use of time out and loss of privileges, has a significant long-term effect on reducing anti-social behaviour (Patterson, 1982). However, the other two components (problem-solving and reinforcement of good behaviour) are not directly related to anti-social behaviour, but rather to positive child behaviour, academic skills and pro-social peer relationships (Patterson & Stouthamer-Loeber, 1984).

The affective quality of the parent–child relationship is crucial in the development of anti-social behaviour. This refers to the emotional climate or 'atmosphere' of the relationship (Dekovic, Wissink & Meijer, 2004). When children have positive relationships with their parents, this may function as protection against anti-social behaviour and delinquency (Dekovic, Wissink & Meijer, 2004).

In reviewing the above scientific literature on adolescent anti-social behaviour, we come to three important conclusions. First, those who show anti-social behaviour early in childhood are more likely to develop into chronic offenders (Leober, 1982). Second, parental monitoring and discipline are important predictors of adolescents' anti-social behaviour (Leober & Dishion, 1983). Third, another such predictor is the association with delinquent peers (Stoolmiller, 1994). Protective factors include satisfactory parental monitoring, discipline and positive family relationships.

Furthermore, young people involved in crime have a history of being subjected to one or more forms of harsh or erratic discipline, emotional or physical neglect or inadequate supervision (Farrington & West, 1990). Parents' deviant behaviour predicts the development of delinquency in their children. There are four negative parenting approaches related to the development of delinquency in young people in Euro–American culture: neglect and failure to supervise effectively, conflict between parents and children, parental criminality and family disruption, such as inter-parental conflict (Henricson, 2000).

Conclusion

It has been documented that parental conflict leads to undesirable outcomes for adolescents. How parents adapt to the changing needs of adolescents and how young people adjust to their own developmental changes will determine their ongoing relationships. The ways in which parents and adolescents adjust to their new relationships will in turn determine whether or not there will be conflict and, if so, what the outcome of that conflict will be. As far as parents are concerned, research evidence suggests that parent–adolescent conflict is more intense if parents adopt a more coercive style of parenting. Conversely, a warm and supportive parenting style is beneficial in reducing conflict. How well parents and adolescents adjust will be moderated by other relationships within the family and its overall cohesiveness. Nevertheless, the ways in which parents and their adolescent children resolve conflict and perceive their respective roles is culturally specific. It is necessary to be aware of the context within which parents and adolescents relate within a specific culture and how this culture affects conflict resolution.

The review presented here indicates that Chinese parents still hold culturally specific parenting beliefs. These include highly valuing family harmony, obedience and good behaviour, and the belief that children should not bring shame to the family. These beliefs may be one of the reasons why Hong Kong Chinese adolescents show little anti-social behaviour and have a relatively low arrest rate. In addition, Chinese parents' belief that education is a key means of social mobility and an indication of achievement that will honour the whole family coexists with their use of an authoritarian parenting style and their high level of involvement in their children's learning. A culturally specific concept of training can be used to describe this parenting practice, which concentrates on helping adolescents to become successful and responsible citizens. Chinese families focus on their children's academic achievements, such that their parenting focuses more on learning in school than the relationship as such. Moreover, the subtle nature of Chinese parent–adolescent relationships shapes the lack of overt communication between parents and adolescents, despite the fact that the latter accept this kind of relationship. The love and care of Chinese parents tends to be expressed through doing things for their adolescents, rather than directly expressing their feelings to each other. Furthermore, Chinese adolescents who have more emotional autonomy demonstrate more negative behavioural problems than those with less. This differs from a Western understanding in which more emotional autonomy is usually found to be associated with higher levels of academic achievement. Nevertheless, Chinese parents also face a changing situation whereby adolescents may begin to seek more autonomy and individuation, become more open about expressing their feelings and look for a trusting relationship with their parents. Such changes in the thinking of Chinese adolescents create a discrepancy between their parents' beliefs in strict obedience and conforming to their parents' will. This suggests a possible theme in parenting programmes whereby more information needs to be provided to help parents understand this discrepancy and hence reduce conflict. In addition, Chinese adolescents have begun to develop a need for more open communication and to enjoy a trusting relationship with their parents. This is in contrast to the subtle expression of love and care performed through parents doing things for their adolescent children. Chinese parents may therefore benefit from learning more about how to verbally and overtly express their love and concern.

Finally, this review shows that Chinese parenting beliefs are different from Western constructions. When adapting Western programmes for use with the Chinese population, we need more local examples, as well as more awareness that parents may still hold many traditional Chinese parenting beliefs. This suggests that adjustment and adaptation are needed when using Western programmes in Hong Kong. This discussion does have some limitations, in that many of the studies referred to are based on Chinese-American populations. Although there are many similarities between Chinese-American and Hong Kong Chinese people, they do live in different cultures and, therefore, some differences in the ways in which they perceive adolescents and parents are to be expected. In addition, there are not enough studies on the relationship between Hong Kong Chinese parents and adolescents. For example, the expected patterns of interaction between

Hong Kong Chinese adolescents and their parents have not been properly studied. Caution should be taken not to over-generalise about Hong Kong Chinese adolescence based solely on the discussion set out in this chapter.

Note

1 In Hong Kong, students are classified into three different groups in secondary school: those with good academic results are in Band I and those with poor outcomes in Band III.

3 Parenting programmes

Introduction

Group parenting programmes are one of many approaches to supporting parents of adolescents. Despite their proliferation, however, there is still a lack of consensus on their goals. Some researchers suggest that the overall objective of such programmes should be to strengthen parents' informal support systems, while others think they should try to prevent child maltreatment through developing skills. Still others regard parenting programmes as a form of 'parent involvement' (Cheng-Gorman & Balter, 1997). Furthermore, parenting programmes encompass a wide variety of formats, like group meetings, newsletters, videos and so on. Such a diversity of formats and approaches gives rise to different styles of programme delivery, serving different target groups and achieving different aims.

This chapter considers the outcomes of parenting programmes and presents an overview of the evidence for the effective elements of a parenting programme and the benefits they can realise for parents and children. Since most of the models used in parenting programmes have been developed in a Euro–American cultural context, it is also necessary to consider the benefits which Chinese Hong Kong parents might realise from joining a culturally sensitive programme. The final section provides an overview of the results of different evaluations of parenting programmes in Hong Kong.

Defining parenting programmes

Barlow, Johnston, Kendrick, Polnay and Stewart-Brown described a parenting programme as a

> focused, short-term intervention aimed at improving the quality of the parent–child relationship by improving parenting practices; aspects of parental functioning such as mental health, attributions and cognitions; the child's emotional and behavioural adjustment, and family functioning more generally.
> (2005: 1)

The terms 'parent training', 'parental education', 'parenting programme' and 'parenting support' are used interchangeably (Cheng-Gorman & Balter, 1997). Croake and Glover (1977: 151) defined parent training programmes as the "purposive training activity of parents who are attempting to change their method of interaction with their children for the purpose of encouraging positive behaviour in their children". Fine (1980: 5–6) defined parent education as "a systematic and conceptually based program, intended to impart information, awareness, or skills to the participation aspects of parenting". Hoard and Shepard (2005) differentiated 'parent training' from 'parent education'. From their perspective, parent training focuses on intervening in existing parenting practice, while the goal of parent education is to prevent problems that arise from parenting practice. Parent training also focuses on the special needs of a particular group of parents, while parent education caters for the needs of the general population. This distinguishes a parent education programme, which could be delivered by professionals or non-professionals, from parent training, which refers to tackling a targeted problem, setting clearly defined objectives and employing evidence-based practice. Furthermore, discussion of these terms draws attention to the current issue of viewing 'parent education' as a term which implies an expert delivering parenting information to lay persons. It also highlights that this involves a power differential between experts and parents rather than a partnership. In this sense, the term 'parenting support' is preferred to 'parenting programme'.

According to Barth and colleagues (2005), a parenting programme should comprise four elements. Firstly, it should include an assessment of parenting problems, perhaps drawn from previous studies on parenting style or theoretical concepts of parenting practices that will bring about positive outcomes for families. Secondly, parents should then be taught new skills. Thirdly, they should be able to use those new skills with their children through such means as homework assignments or role play during sessions. Finally, parents should receive feedback.

Parenting programmes have also been referred to as 'interventions' that help people to adopt better parenting skills (Patterson, 1982). In this study, the term 'parenting programme' will be used to refer to any programme that focuses on bringing about an improvement in parenting skills or which addresses other factors that may be interfering with effective parenting (Forehand & Long, 1988). It will also encompass any programme that promotes parents' efficacy (Barlow, Coren & Stewart-Brown, 2002) or enhances parents' parenting attitudes, their parenting knowledge and parenting skills. These skills are essential for the promotion of children's healthy development in all aspects and in all stages (Mahoney, Kaiser & Girolametto, 1999). The term also refers to all parenting support and educational programmes delivered mainly to parents. These usually take place in groups and involve meetings of around two hours per week (Barlow, Shaw & Stewart-Brown, 2004).

Historical development of parenting programmes

Parenting programmes have been in existence since the nineteenth century (Medway, 1989). It is recorded that as early as the 1930s, adults were already participating in educational groups for parents (Fine & Henry, 1989). It has been estimated that over 50,000 parenting classes are currently being delivered in the US; most are small classes offered within the community by churches, schools and other community-based organisations (Long & Adams, 2001). Such a demand for parenting education indicates a need for parents to know more about the skills involved. Greer (1986) showed that 75% of survey respondents reported that parents face more challenges today than before.

In terms of the history of US parenting programmes, before the 1920s these tended to be more informal and less organised. As more and more parents asked for help, parenting programmes continued to expand, with social workers and other helping professionals becoming involved. In the late 1930s, however, there was a decline in interest following the debate about whether parental or institutional child-rearing brought about better outcomes for child development. From the 1940s onwards, parental training began to grow again and involve more people from different professions and the private sector to provide services (Croake & Glover, 1977).

The content of parenting programmes has also changed over time, covering a variety of topics in different eras and contexts. For example, some have aimed to help parents understand their children better by educating them on child development norms, child-rearing techniques, methods of discipline and emotions and their expression (Croake & Glover, 1977). Early attempts focused more on the teaching of moral virtues (Medway, 1989). These values also change over time. The moral virtues drawn from teaching philosophies employed in early attempts at parental education stressed the need for parental control, but over time focus shifted to more egalitarian parent–child relations. Interest in parenting programmes declined in the 1930s as more responsibility was given to institutions like schools in teaching children (Hoard & Shepard, 2005). A renewed focus emerged in the 1960s as studies indicated better outcomes were observed among children whose parents were more involved in their learning and development. In addition, evaluations of some parenting programmes over this period indicated that they were successful, despite methodological limitations such as a lack of control groups (Croake & Glover, 1977). The 1960s also witnessed advances in the evaluation of parenting programmes, with the use of random subject assignment and the use of control groups. This period, leading into the 1970s, also saw advances in the technology of parenting programmes, with the advent of the Head Start programme in the US and the popularity of Parent Effectiveness Training (PET; Gordon, 1975 and Systematic Training for Effective Parenting (STEP; Dinkmeyer & McKay, 1976).

The need for knowledge and skills led to a proliferation of parenting programmes. There was a growing recognition that parents have an essential influence on their children's development (Loeber & Farrington, 1998). Governments therefore began to provide support for parent education. Professionals in different disciplines also started to create different forms of parenting programmes. Such diversity gave the general public greater opportunity to select the type of parenting programme that suited them, but also led to diversity in the aims and objectives of programmes and therefore to different methods of evaluation being used.

For a long time, parenting programmes have been considered as lacking evidence for their effectiveness. This has been because of the diversity of their objectives and outcomes, and also because programmes have tended to be delivered by professionals from different backgrounds and even non-professionals. Very little in the way of consensus on the expected outcome of different parenting programmes has been reached. Some writers argue for the importance of measuring indicators of children's behavioural change, while others focus on changes in the parents. The extent of the diversity has made it difficult to arrive at an agreed set of objectives and outcomes that could be compared across different parenting programmes. In addition, it has also led to variability in programme outcomes, whereby positive results have been achieved for some of the outcome measurements but not others within the same study (Medway, 1989).

Types of parenting programme

Despite the variety of formats, parenting programmes have traditionally been categorised by their philosophical orientation. Medway (1989) identified three different categories: behavioural, reflection and Adlerian. Smith and Pugh (1996), discussed by (Barrett, 2003), categorised programmes as either behaviour- or relationship-focused (Barrett, 2003). This section considers the content and theoretical basis of behavioural parenting programmes and reflects on the humanistic (based on the Rogerian approach) and Adlerian models.

Behavioural parenting programmes focus on actual and observable parenting activities and their consequences for the behaviour of children and adolescents, as well as the environmental variables that maintain particular behavioural patterns. This approach is based on behavioural psychology as proposed by psychologists such as Skinner. Behaviourists attempt to train parents to apply empirically validated procedures and techniques in their parenting practices. The principle is that behaviour can be learned by the use of reward and punishment. Some of the ways in which behavioural programmes seek to achieve this are teaching parenting skills like setting and maintaining boundaries and praising children when they display the desired behaviours. There are some well-established behavioural programmes teaching parenting skills, such as Webster-Stratton's video-modelling programme, the Positive Parenting Programme (Sanders, 1999) and parent–child interaction therapy (Eyberg & Robinson, 1982). There is robust evaluation evidence for the success of behavioural parenting programmes in many of the positive behavioural outcomes observed (Moran *et al.*, 2004).

Most behavioural parenting programmes take the form of a structured course lasting 6 to 12 weeks, delivered in community or school settings. The focus of the group work is to teach parents skills how to supervise and monitor their children. It also teaches parents how to set boundaries and discipline children through communication and negotiation (Moran *et al.*, 2004). There is an extensive body of evidence that using these specific parenting skills will lead to good outcomes for young people.

Webster-Stratton's programme is based on the coercion theory developed in Patterson's work on the aetiology of conduct disorder and misbehaviour (Patterson, 1982, quoted in Webster-Stratton, 1997). Patterson shows that parents of children with conduct problems use more violent disciplinary techniques and are more critical of their children's behaviour, they are unable to monitor their children's misbehaviour and they are more likely to ignore pro-social behaviour and to reinforce misbehaviour (Webster-Stratton, 1997). The Webster-Stratton programme consists of a 10- to 12-week video training course accompanied by group work. Its development was heavily guided by the modelling literature;

it attempts to enhance the modelling effects by including parents and children of different cultures. In terms of evaluation, five randomised controlled trials were carried out by Webster-Stratton (1997) with more than 500 children aged 3 to 7 with early onset conduct problems. The programme was demonstrated to be effective in helping parents to adopt positive parental attitudes and engage in positive parent–child interactions as well as in significantly reducing parents' reliance on violent and critical disciplinary approaches. When compared with control groups, child conduct problems were found to be significantly reduced (Webster-Stratton, 1997).

Reviews indicate that parenting programmes which aim to reduce the anti-social behaviour of school-age children and adolescents have had positive outcomes. Multisystemic Therapy (MST; Henggeler *et al.*, 1998) and Fast Track have been shown to be effective in treating juvenile offenders and young people with conduct problems in the US (Moran *et al.*, 2004). These programmes address risk factors in several areas and are multi-component, including parent groups for parents, social skills training for children, time for parents and their children to share and home visits. In addition, the Adolescent Transition Programme (Dishion, Patterson & Kavanagh, 1992), a parenting programme which aims to reduce problem behaviours in children and adolescents, is effective in reducing parent–child conflict and anti-social behaviour (Moran *et al.*, 2004).

Reflective parenting programmes place particular emphasis on enhancing parents' awareness of the positive and negative aspects of their parenting skills. They also enhance parents' ability to understand and accept their child's feelings (Medway, 1989). Such an approach leads indirectly to better outcomes for children. It can be assumed that changes in parental attitudes will lead to subsequent shifts in how they interact with their children, in turn leading to behavioural change in the latter. Some advocates of this approach consider changes in parental attitudes to be the appropriate measurement of effectiveness, rather than children's behavioural outcomes themselves.

The humanistic approach is based on Carl Rogers' concept of person-centred psychotherapy, which suggests that a patient is best placed to identify a unique solution to a particular situation in an empathic environment. In the parenting context, this approach requires the prioritisation of the need to respect and empathise with the world view of parents, who can then be helped to develop a realistic approach appropriate to their circumstances. The humanistic approach focuses more on the circumstances of parents themselves, making it difficult to measure their children's behavioural outcomes (Barrett, 2003).

Parents trained using this approach are taught to employ communication techniques drawn from person-centred therapy, such as empathy, active listening and so on. From this theoretical approach emerged PET, which consists of eight three-hour training sessions that focus on building close, warm relationships between parents and children through acceptance and the creation of a democratic framework for decision-making. In addition, parents are encouraged to use environmental modification rather than punishment to tackle their children's negative behaviours (Gordon, 1975). This approach advocates a 'no lose' approach to resolving conflict and encourages parents to agree a mutually acceptable solution with their children (Henricson & Roker, 2000).

Moran *et al.* (2004) showed that these types of parent training programme are effective in terms of success reported by parents (such as reducing stress and changing attitudes) but less so when the outcomes for children are considered. Reflective training is also more effective with older children and the effects are usually short-term (Moran *et al.*, 2004).

The Adlerian parent training programme was developed by Rudolph Dreikurs based on Alfred Adler's personality theory of child-rearing. This theoretical work led to the launch of the STEP programme. In STEP, parents are reminded that children's behaviour is purposive. The influence of the family atmosphere, birth order and the child's private logic provide the framework upon which the Adlerian parenting programme is based (Dreikurs & Soltz, 1964). There are three widely used programmes deploying the Adlerian approach: STEP (Dinkmeyer & McKay, 1976), Active Parenting Today (Popkin, 1993) and Positive Discipline (Nelsen, 1996). The principles of this approach focus on democratic parenting through the use of "logical and natural consequences", family meetings and a focus on the child's purposive behaviour (Chang & Ritter, 2004) to control children's behaviour.

Besides the categories of parenting programmes described above, advances in technology have facilitated further developments, and considerable amounts of information on parenting adolescents are available via the Internet. In addition, parents can access support via traditional media, such as books, videos, newsletters, magazines and leaflets (Henricson & Roker, 2000). Henricson and Roker (2000) highlighted a study in the US by Bogenschneider and Stone (1997) which found that circulating bi-monthly advice newsletters to parents of adolescents resulted in higher levels of parental monitoring than were found in the control group. Bogenschneider and Stone (1997) sent newsletters to over 700 parents of early adolescents. The parents were asked to fill in a questionnaire concerning their parenting beliefs and practice. The results indicated that there was an improvement in parenting behaviour, parent–child relationships and family functioning where parents had read the newsletter. In addition, the parents who received the intervention engaged in more discussion with their adolescents about risky behaviour (Bogenschneider & Stone, 1997).

Another source of support for parents of adolescents is telephone helplines. Henricson (1997) indicated that more than 80% of parents using such services indicated that they had changed their parenting mindset, methods and practices as a result. Although telephone helplines have many limitations, they can provide a starting point for delivering initial consultations to people seeking advice on their parenting practices (Henricson & Roker, 2000).

Evaluation of parenting programmes

Hoard and Shepard (2005) showed that previous reviews of parenting programmes have indicated that a limited number of treatment outcomes could be identified conclusively from research in this area. In addition, many parenting interventions have primarily been created to meet service delivery needs; they therefore lack empirical and theoretical support and do not use standardised measurements and indicators to evaluate outcomes (APA, 1993, quoted in Hoard & Shepard, 2005).

Reviews of the effectiveness of parenting programmes offer some idea of what they can achieve, such as the work of Dembo and colleagues (1985) and Medway's (1989) meta-analysis of parent education programmes, Moran *et al.*'s (2004) review of what works in parenting support programmes and the work of Cheng-Gorman and Balter (1997). Barlow, Shaw and Stewart-Brown (2004) also reviewed culturally sensitive parent education programmes and provided essential information on how they have been developed.

Medway's meta-analysis of 27 studies on parenting programmes carried out between 1973 and 1984 included PET, Adlerian approaches and behavioural programmes. The evidence indicates that the benefits to participants were approximately 62% greater than those experienced by the controls. Methodological weaknesses included the lack of follow-up measurement of the outcome of the intervention. These studies also did not use measurements with high validity and reliability (Medway, 1989).

Dembo and colleagues (1985) came to a similar conclusion regarding behavioural programmes, finding that both parents and children participating in the courses demonstrated more positive changes in behaviour. Most of the studies reviewed used random assignment of subjects. Some report mixed results in which the outcome varied according to the type of assessment used, with parent-recorded and independent observer evaluations yielding less favourable results.

One of the programmes being evaluated is called the Adolescent Transition Programme, developed by the Oregon Social Learning Center. The method involved in the training programme uses video scenarios to help parents to learn approaches such as positive reinforcement, monitoring, limit-setting and relationship skills. It is normally run in the community. Components for parents and teenagers are different. This programme has been found to be effective in reducing parent–child conflict and reducing aggressive and delinquent behaviour among children and adolescents ((Moran *et al.*, 2004).

Cognitive-based parenting programmes include PET (Gordon, 1975), which is based on the work of Carl Rogers. This approach emphasises democratic relationships within families. It also emphasises the adoption of a 'no lose' approach to conflict resolution among family members, which seeks to improve parent–child communication. Other cognitive programmes, like those based on the theories of Adler (1927), emphasise parents' understanding and comprehension of their children's behaviours, thoughts and emotions. There does not seem to be a definitive consensus on the effectiveness of such cognitive programmes (Moran *et al.*, 2004). The results very much depend on the methodology involved: more rigorous and better-designed studies have better effect sizes. Despite these methodological issues, the evidence suggests that these programmes do have considerable benefits for parents. Cognitive programmes do not provide the same level of success in children's as in parents' outcomes (Moran *et al.*, 2004).

Furthermore, the evaluation of parenting programmes shows that interventions focused on parenting attitudes and beliefs tend to work better when they involve parents from higher socio-economic classes or who are better educated and whose children are older and engage in less serious delinquent behaviour. Programmes that work less well typically involve parents who are poorer, whose children are younger and where the family has serious background difficulties (Moran *et al.*, 2004).

In the school context, parenting programmes usually take the form of group-based courses or one-off talks (Roker & Richardson, 2001). Sometimes these programmes or other support are provided because there has been a crisis or specific difficulties during a certain period. Provision is thus piecemeal and unsystematic. Roker and Richardson's (2001) study on the needs of parents in group parenting programmes delivered in a school context showed that parents of adolescents face many challenges. The majority have disputes over household issues like pocket money and bedtime. Less common problems are the involvement of young people in crime or drug use. Roker and Richardson's (2001) participants also struggled to resolve conflicts within the family. These findings are consistent with similar work suggesting that conflict usually arises out of the daily family routine (Yau & Smetana, 1996). In addition, the results also indicate that parents need more information about adolescents' development, opportunities to meet other parents to discuss issues and someone to help and support them (Roker & Richardson, 2001). The same study also reported the evaluation of a course for parents, which indicated that the majority of parents were positive about it and also felt they had gained support in their parenting. Participants also felt they now communicated better with their adolescent children, understood them better and were more satisfied with their relationship after the programme (Roker & Richardson, 2001). These results are promising for the provision of parenting support and running group-based programmes in a school setting.

Another school-based parenting project, the Adolescent Transitions Program, has been documented by Dishion and Kavanagh (2000). This programme was a multilevel family-based intervention delivered in secondary schools. It included universal, selective and indicative strategies for serving families with young adolescents. The universal level involved the setting up of a resource centre for parents in the school and offering self-help materials like videos and leaflets for them to use on-site. The other component involved providing parenting programmes using a family management curriculum in addition to some personal consultations offered by professionals. The curriculum focused on helping parents to use incentives to promote positive behavioural change in adolescents. It also helped parents to set limits for their adolescents and to learn skills essential to monitoring their adolescents. Family communication and problem-solving skills were also taught. The results of the evaluation indicated that significant reductions in parent–child conflict were observed when participants were videotaped engaging in joint problem-solving tasks. There was also a reduction in anti-social attitudes at school as observed by teachers on those children who were identified as "high-risk children" whose parents had received the service. There was also an indication of reductions in substance use and early onset use of tobacco (Dishion & Kavanagh, 2000).

There is also evidence that both parents and their adolescent children can benefit from joining a parenting programme that focuses on reducing conflict between them. For example, Guerney, Coufal and Vogelsong (1981) documented an early attempt at a group-based parenting programme in their study of the Parent Adolescent Relationship Development Programme. Components of this programme include teaching communication skills, conflict-resolution skills and problem-solving skills. The evaluation compared programme participants with a group receiving group therapy and a no-treatment group. The results showed that the experimental group achieved significant improvement in empathic skills and constructive self-expression. There was also improvement in general communication patterns and in the general quality of relationships in the experimental groups (Guerney, Coufal & Vogelsong, 1981). This early study highlighted a promising design in which both parents and adolescents received training in communication and problem-solving techniques. Similar results are also identified in an evaluation of another parenting programme focused on training problem-solving and communication skills (Robin & Foster, 1989). This training programme aimed to improve deficits in communication skills and to address cognitive distortions and inappropriate patterns of functional interaction in the family over 8 to 12 sessions. The therapist helped each family to learn skills that are important for problem-solving to aid families in changing their negative communication patterns (Long & Adams, 2001). Long and Adams (2001) also reviewed other work, indicating that this approach has achieved improvement in mother–adolescent dyads (Foster, Prinz & O'Leary, 1983), and indicated success among studies that involved adolescents diagnosed with attention deficit hyperactive disorder (ADHD) (Barkley *et al.*, 1992). However, these studies have some limitations in that they were mostly carried out by the developer of the programme and report only short-term effects (Long & Adams, 2001).

Bavolet (1987) reported on an evaluation of a US parenting intervention called the Family Nurturing Program that involved both parents and adolescents. This also showed evidence of benefits to participants. The study involved parents and adolescents from families that had been reported to the local Department of Social Services on suspicion of abuse and/or neglect. It also included adolescents who had been identified by the courts as delinquent and families seeking to reduce perceived parent–adolescent conflict. The programme content involved teaching parenting and communication concepts to parents and adolescents separately, brief relaxation exercises and time for parents and adolescents to communicate after each of the presentations. Participants were also assigned home exercises. The results show that belief in corporal punishment significantly decreased among the parents, who also significantly improved their empathic awareness of their adolescents' needs and development, their understanding of appropriate expectations and their knowledge of behaviour management (Bavolet, 1987).

Again, these results indicate that such an intervention showed promise. Bavolet (1987) also reported a significant reduction in family conflict, an increase in family cohesion and improvement in the quality of family relationships. In other words, a parenting programme addressing conflict management, communication with adolescents and understanding of their development showed promising results in terms of outcomes for parents and their relationship with their adolescent children. Although these findings are very positive, there is no indication that a control group was used for comparison purposes in this study.

An evaluation by Clarke and Churchill (2010) indicated the effectiveness of a parenting programme for parents of adolescents based on the Webster Stratton and Positive Parenting Programme (Triple-P) programmes, which were developed for parents of younger children, together with principles from cognitive behavioural therapy to facilitate parents' learning. The programme consisted of eight weekly two-hour sessions. It was delivered by two trainers who had been trained specifically to deliver it. The evaluation of short-term indicators of parenting styles, level of conflict and behavioural difficulties among the adolescents showed significant improvement in the adolescents after the eight-week course. The qualitative data also showed that the adult participants benefited from reminders of parenting tips, a feeling of being supported, a sense of greater confidence in their parenting and learning a number of useful skills.

An evaluation of a course named Living with Teenagers in southern England was conducted by Coleman and Roker (2001). This was a school-based course which ran over ten weeks in early 1997. The qualitative data from interviews with participants showed that parents found this course very useful. Nevertheless, the quantitative data indicated that some parents felt less confident afterwards; they felt that they were less influential over certain areas of their teenagers' lives.

Another review by Woolfenden, Williams and Peat (2003) described outcomes of parenting skills training programmes in both the UK and the US. A US programme called Parents who Care (Catalano & Hawkins, 1996: 77), created for families with adolescents aged 12–16, demonstrated significant short-term improvements in family discipline, reduced tolerance of anti-social behaviour of the parent and increased family bonding. This programme consisted of five to six two-hour workshops that aimed to reduce risks and strengthen protective factors within family settings associated with substance abuse, delinquency and other behavioural problems. The programme content included discussions aided by a trained facilitator with parents of the risk and protective factors associated with the teenage years, effective communication and family management.

Some US preventive services target key behaviours during pre-teen years to protect adolescents from adverse outcomes. A number of effective sex education programmes have been offered in the US through schools to improve parent–teenager communication regarding sexual activities. These programmes were based on developmental theories which help to reduce risk and strengthen protective factors. The outcome evaluation found some short-term improvement.

Woolfenden, Williams and Peat's (2003) review also indicated that parents who scored highly enmeshed or highly disengaged on the family communication scale and those parents who had mental health issues did not benefit from parenting programmes (p. 69). In addition, parents did not benefit when they had less motivation to seek out such programmes.

On the other hand, adolescents with behavioural problems improved after joining Multisystemic Therapy (MST), which is a US programme based on cognitive behavioural principles and parenting support. Evaluation of MST found it to be effective in reducing adolescents' aggressive behaviour but showed less positive results in the improvement of parenting skills and family functioning (Woolfenden, Williams & Peat, 2003).

Ghate and Ramella (2002) studied the effectiveness of parenting programmes provided by Youth Offending Teams in the UK. Their target parents were not in receipt of an Order but could benefit from preventive intervention. Although the courses provided varied across different teams, their impact was largely positive and demonstrated improvements in parent–child communication, supervision and monitoring in the short term. However, there was no way of determining whether these changes could be attributed to the programmes or to some other intervention.

Another British study compared the outcomes for young people referred to specialist family support and social work teams (Biehal, 2006). Family support teams provide services that consist of training parents to understand how to change their communication patterns with their adolescent children. They also help parents to learn how to establish agreed boundaries for adolescent behaviour. Nevertheless, Biehal's study did not demonstrate any improvement in promoting changes in child and family functioning over mainstream social work teams.

Summing up the above evaluations of parenting support for parents of adolescents, we cannot attribute positive changes to the programmes themselves. Nevertheless, the review does indicate that parents perceive improvements in themselves as well as in their adolescent children after joining the programmes.

Parenting programmes and educational work are particularly important for families with teenagers, especially those catering for their developmental needs (Molina, Pastor & Violant, 2011). As indicated in Table 3.1, the literature shows that various forms of parenting support have been used to support parents of adolescents (aged 10–14). An early example, Patterson and Stouthamer-Loeber (1984), demonstrated that parental family management skills (four components: monitoring, discipline, problem-solving and reinforcement) were favourable to non-conflictual parent–adolescent relationships. Parenting programmes developed with components including focus on the affective quality of parent–child relationship (Dekovic, Wissink & Meijer, 2004), consistent parenting (Patterson, 1982) and reinforcement of good behaviour (Patterson & Stouthamer-Loeber, 1984) seem to benefit both parents and their adolescents, reducing conflict (Guerney, Coufal & Vogelsong, 1981; Robin & Foster, 1989; Dishion & Kavanagh, 2000; Long & Adams, 2001; Cojocaru & Cojocaru, 2011). Behavioural parenting programmes based on the principles and curriculum of the Webster Stratton and Triple-P programmes for parents of adolescents benefited parents by giving parenting tips; making them feel supported and more confident

Table 3.1 Evaluation of different parenting programmes for parents of adolescents

Programme	*Content*	*Method*	*Outcomes*
Triple-P Adolescent (UK) (Clark & Churchill, 2010)	Eight weekly two-hour sessions by trained facilitator Learning parenting skills	Cognitive behavioural approach	Reduction in conflict with adolescents Changing parenting styles
Parenting Early Intervention Pathfinder Evaluation (UK) (Lindsay *et al.*, 2008)	Incredible years, Triple-P and Strengthening Families Strengthening Communities	Cognitive behavioural and social learning approach	Improvements in parents' mental well-being, parenting skills and their sense of being a parent Improvement in behaviour of adolescents (ages 8–13)
Adolescent Transition Programme (US) (Dishion & Kavanagh, 2000)	Incentives promoting positive behavioural change Limit-setting and monitoring skills Relationship skills	Multilevel approach family intervention	Reduction in parent–child conflict Reduction in teachers' reports of externalising problems Improved parenting practice
Living with Teenagers (UK) (Roker & Coleman, 1998)	Understanding adolescent development Communication skills Conflict-management skills	Ecological approach	Qualitative data indicate that the programme is very useful Quantitative data show that parents are less confident post-programme
Problem-Solving Communication Training (Robin & Foster, 1989)	Improving communication Addressing cognitive distortion Problem-solving skills	Social learning approach	Improved mother–adolescent dyad Improved behaviour of adolescents with ADHD
Parents who Care (Catalano & Hawkins, 1996)	Protective factors Effective communication Family management	Behavioural and systemic approach	Improvement in family discipline, less tolerance of anti-social behaviour
Family Nurturing Programme (Bavolet, 1987)	Teaching concepts to parents and adolescents Brief relaxation exercises	Discussion with facilitator	Improved understanding of adolescents' needs Appropriate expectations of adolescents
Parent Adolescent Relationship Development Programme (US) (Guerney, Coufal & Vogelsong, 1981)	Teaching communication Problem-solving and conflict-resolution skills	Social learning approach	Improvement in empathic and expressive skills Improved communication patterns Improved quality of relationships

in their parenting ability; and teaching them a number of useful skills (Clarke & Churchill, 2010). Another parenting programme based on social learning principles was found to be very useful and was rated very highly by parents in qualitative data, but quantitative data indicated that some parents felt less confident about certain aspects of their parenting and also less influential over certain areas of their teenagers' lives (Roker & Coleman, 1998). The use of social learning theory has provided active skills training for parents to help them to improve their relationship and daily positive interaction with their children. It also involves learning effective disciplinary strategies to reduce parenting stress, coercive discipline and conflict (Sanders & Woolley, 2005). The effectiveness of various parenting programmes that applied the social learning approach has been indicated (Prinz & Jones, 2003; Sanders *et al.*, 2004; Prinz & Dumans, 2000). Furthermore, a recent evaluation of parenting programmes in the UK taking the social learning and behavioural approach, which involved more than 3,000 parents in different local authorities, indicated improvements in parents' mental well-being and in their adolescents' (ages 8–13) behaviour (Lindsay *et al.*, 2008).

In contrast, a study in the UK has indicated a different result. Macdonald and Turner (2005) indicated that foster parents were satisfied with the programme they studied and reported an increase in their confidence about handling difficult behaviour in their children. No statistically significant differences were found between the experimental and control groups, but Macdonald and Turner's (2005) results indicate that participants expressed satisfaction with the intervention and perceived their confidence to have increased.

From these evaluations of parenting programmes, it is possible to conclude that there are certain essential elements which need to be included when designing a programme to reduce parent–adolescent conflict, such as parents' knowledge of adolescents' development; communication and conflict-resolution skills; and opportunities to share experiences with other parents. All of these elements have led to positive results. In addition, when studying programme effectiveness, it is important to carry out both quantitative and qualitative evaluation, unlike some previous studies which have used one or the other. A better understanding of the effectiveness of programme design can be gained by using a control group where possible. This has not always been done in previous studies, making it impossible to confirm whether successful outcomes can be attributed to the programme itself or to other factors.

Evaluation of culturally sensitive parenting programmes

The review presented above focuses mostly on interventions undertaken in Euro–American cultures. This section now turns to look at research on the outcomes of parenting programmes aimed at ethnic minority families. The purpose is to enhance understanding of the effects of parenting interventions on non-Western populations and how such families might benefit. Barlow, Shaw and Stewart-Brown (2004) and Cheng-Gorman and Balter (1997) provided essential reviews of the outcomes of culturally sensitive parenting programmes. Three main types of programme have been identified: translated, culturally adapted and culturally specific (Cheng-Gorman & Balter, 1997). A translated programme is simply a traditional parenting programme that has been translated into the native language of the target population. Despite the linguistic modification, it remains essentially unchanged. In a culturally adapted programme, the intervention is designed to incorporate the indigenous values and cultural traditions of the target population. A culturally specific programme is designed to facilitate successful parenting within a specific group's culture. These programmes are not derived from previous programmes but are designed specifically for a particular target culture (Cheng-Gorman & Balter, 1997).

Cheng-Gorman and Balter (1997) also presented a review of quantitative studies on the efficacy of programmes for African-American, Hispanic, Native American and Asian-American parents. Only two published studies on African-American parenting programmes could be identified. These dealt with culturally adapted versions of STEP and PET (Alvy, 1988). The two programmes involved 48 parents, of whom 19 were classed as having low and 29 as high attendance. The results show that high-attendance parents had higher parental acceptance scores than members of the low-attendance group. The mean change in the quality of their relationship with their children reported by the high-attendance group was also higher than in the low-attendance group (Cheng-Gorman & Balter, 1997). Although positive results were reported in this study, we need to exercise caution in interpreting the findings since the study suffered from methodological flaws: failure to use standardised measures, report the demographic background of participants and use control groups. Myers and colleagues (1992) conducted a two-year quasi-experimental study using two groups and a pre-test–post-test design. Four variables were investigated using self-reported measures to test the efficacy of the programme: parental acceptance of their children, positive parenting practices, quality of parent–child relationship and child behaviour. The results indicated no significant overall effect on parenting practices, behaviour or the children's problems (Cheng-Gorman & Balter, 1997). Looking at programmes aimed at Hispanic parents, Johnson and Breckenridge (1982) demonstrated a significant effect when control and experimental groups were compared on extroversion and destructive scales (Cheng-Gorman & Balter, 1997). In addition, Johnson and Walker's (1987) follow-up study of experimental and control groups in a Houston, Texas intervention five to eight years after completion of the programme indicated that control group children displayed significantly more behavioural problems than the children of programme participants (Cheng-Gorman & Balter, 1997). Although some positive changes were indicated, these evaluations also suffered from methodological problems, such as over-reliance on mothers' self-reported data and use of only one type of indicator to measure change.

Barlow, Shaw and Steward-Brown (2004) showed that the results of culturally specific programmes are mixed. In their review of outcomes from several effective black parenting programmes, they indicated that some of these resulted in improvements in parents' perception of children's emotional problems, while others did not. In addition, the results of four studies evaluating the effectiveness of the culturally adapted versions of STEP and PET also show mixed outcomes. Some studies have shown that parents who attended a programme improved, while others did not state clearly what content had been adapted. Nevertheless, the results of qualitative studies do indicate that parents themselves perceived a benefit from interventions. They felt their relationship with their children had improved and they enjoyed being a parent more (Barlow, Shaw & Steward-Brown, 2004). Such mixed results indicate a need for more rigorous methodology. It is also necessary to consider carefully in what circumstances an adapted programme will bring promising outcomes for parents and their children in other cultures.

Other research indicates that joining a culturally adapted parenting programme will benefit Chinese parents and their children. For example, one qualitative study shows that parents and children improved their communication as a result of one such intervention. In addition, the parents were also able to understand their children's lives better. They were better equipped with listening skills, which helped improve their relationship with their children (Yuen, 1997, quoted in Barlow, Shaw & Steward-Brown, 2004). Parents learn the importance of allowing their children greater autonomy, which helps improve their self-confidence. Chinese parents also gain a sense of support from other parents on the programme (Chau, 1996). A supportive environment is helpful in reducing parental stress. The results are encouraging even when Chinese parents participate in an adapted programme.

Mixed results have been identified in culturally sensitive parenting programmes. There are no consistently positive results across all the different measurements adopted by researchers. Nevertheless, some promising initial findings suggest that Chinese parents can benefit from improving communication with their children and adopting some Western ideas, like allowing children more autonomy and thus becoming more independent. This suggests that Chinese parents can accept some aspects of Western parenting ideology. Nevertheless, Barlow, Shaw and Steward-Brown (2004) also showed that when value conflicts arise in an adapted programme, some Chinese parents may drop out, while others adapt their parenting style to match the values being advocated. When adapting a Western programme for use with Chinese parents, it is thus important to strike a balance between accommodating participants' own culture on the one hand and introducing new parenting concepts on the other. Such new ideas may benefit those who can accept them. Nevertheless, more rigorous studies of culturally sensitive parenting programmes are needed to provide further evidence of which elements within them help parents from a particular culture, and how far facilitators should adapt a programme to make it more acceptable to parents.

Evaluation of parenting programmes in Hong Kong

Parenting practices in Hong Kong society have deep roots in Confucianism. Parenting has long been regarded as a natural practice that does not need to be learned. Following one's parents' traditional child-rearing methods is usual in Chinese societies. The concept of filial piety and the maxim "spare the rod, spoil the child" are examples of traditional Chinese parenting beliefs (Chapter 4 presents a detailed consideration of culturally sensitive Chinese parenting practices). In addition, in Hong Kong Chinese society, parents are concerned about their practice and keen on attending courses. It has been suggested that advances in society and the continuous drop in the birth rate mean that Hong Kong parents are now more concerned about raising children of high intellectual ability (Tsang, 2004). Despite a lack of rigorous evaluation of parenting programmes in Hong Kong, it is possible to consider how such programmes have been developed and to what extent they been found to be effective.

The development of parenting programmes in Hong Kong started in the 1970s in response to growing concern about the social causes of violent crime. In 1975, the Chinese University of Hong Kong completed a study, *Social Causes of Violent Crime among Young Offenders in Hong Kong* (Ng, 1975). This recommended the launch of a new service named "Family Life Education" (FLE) to promote better parent–child relationships and reduce juvenile delinquency (Tsang, 2004). Since then, parenting programmes have become part of the service provided by social welfare agencies. The government funds most of these programmes. Excluding those organised by private practitioners, it has been estimated that more than 500 parenting programmes are delivered each year in Hong Kong (Cheung, 2001).

Despite the proliferation of such interventions, few studies have evaluated their effectiveness (Cheung, 2001). Most Hong Kong practitioners use opinion questionnaires to collect parents' satisfaction. The focus is limited to the timing, venue, format and content of the programme, and very few practitioners consider using scientific methods to evaluate effectiveness (Education and Manpower Bureau, 2003). Parenting programmes were originally intended to be preventive and developmental in nature. In its early days, FLE was generally focused on promoting concepts of positive parenting (Yue, 1989). Later, as public concern about the programme's effectiveness grew, FLE workers began to operate at three different levels: mass programmes (such as promotional game stalls, exhibitions and public lectures) intended to reach the wider public; courses aimed at larger audiences of a few hundred people; and small-group teaching.

In 1979, the White Paper *Social Welfare into the 1980s* outlined the Hong Kong government's policy of subsidising non-governmental organisations (NGOs) to provide FLE services at the district level while the Social Welfare Department was responsible for the overall planning, coordination and administration of services. Another publication, *The Consultancy Report on Family Service Review* (2001), proposed the integration of FLE with related services to improve overall effectiveness (Social Welfare Department, 2006). The philosophy of providing FLE services assumes that the family is the primary socialising agent of an individual. The integrity of the family has a significant effect on the healthy development of a person's physical and mental health. In addition, rising levels of marital breakdowns, single parenthood and youth problems have resulted in significant changes to family structure within Hong Kong society (Social Welfare Department, 2006). Such changes put extra pressure on families. The FLE service was thus used as a means to promote healthy family development while also reducing the juvenile delinquency rate in Hong Kong.

The mode of delivery of parenting programmes in Hong Kong includes lectures, groups and promotional activities (Tsang, 2004). It also includes formats like public education through the mass media, talks, small-group programmes, family life camps and so on. Most programmes are delivered by NGOs, private practitioners and governmental education or health departments (Education and Manpower Bureau, 2003). Lectures and parenting groups aim to promote awareness or to train parents to adopt new strategies. Promotional activities aim to arouse public awareness of the importance of parenting programmes (Tsang, 2004).

Officially, parenting programmes have been targeted at the general population since their inception in the 1970s. With changes in the needs of society, the focus of FLE in Hong Kong shifted from parents-to-be to young adults approaching marriage. Nonetheless, according to a 2001 study of the four FLE teams, parents and adolescents were still the major target groups served, while pre-marital couples and parents-to-be formed the smallest proportion of users (Tsang, 2004).

A review of parenting programmes in Hong Kong shows that the most common topics covered include communication skills with children, positive parenting skills, knowledge of child development, the parental relationship, moral education for children, sex education and strategies to improve children's performance at school. Additional efforts have also been made to address the needs of different forms of family structure. This includes single parents, step-parents, new immigrant families, at-risk families and families with children who have behavioural or emotional problems or disabilities. These approaches meet the needs expressed by parents. There has also been change in the popularity of topics from the 1970s to the 1990s. In the early 1970s to 1980s, there was great demand for programmes focusing on "how to bring up filial and compliant children" and "how to make children achieve". The early 1990s saw an increasing interest in learning about the different "roles of fathers and mothers in parenting and family affairs" (Tsang, 2004).

In the late 1990s, a trend emerged to find out more about how to promote children's self-esteem and the development of emotional and moral intelligence. Parents wanted to know how to adjust their parenting style in order to raise children with these characteristics. There was also a growing interest in information technology with the approach of the millennium (Tsang, 2004). Such a change in the content of parent education indicates a growing concern among Hong Kong parents to raise children with high intellectual ability. It also shows that practitioners have tended to focus more on the needs expressed by parents than on evidence or theory when developing their programmes.

This last point is confirmed by Tsang (2004), who indicated that only some of the parenting programmes in Hong Kong are theory-driven or evidence-based. Those which are tend to be based on three theoretical approaches: the behavioural method (Ho *et al.*, 1999; Leung *et al.*, 2003), PET (Cheung & Yau, 1996) and STEP (Kwok, 1994). Besides these, some other approaches used by practitioners are Harris' (1969) transactional analysis model (Tsang, 2004), the Satir Model and the eclectic approach (Education and Manpower Bureau, 2003). It appears that practitioners are particularly keen on using cognitive behavioural approaches and social learning theory. It has been assumed that cognitive changes in parents subsequently lead to behavioural changes in their parenting practices. In addition, practitioners assume that Chinese parents lack an empathic understanding of their children (Cheung & Yau, 1996). This is based on the belief that Chinese culture requires strict obedience and compliance from children and therefore children's psychological needs are denied. Practitioners tend to assume that improvements in parents' empathic and communication skills will improve their relationships with their children and therefore have an impact on juvenile delinquency.

Studies on parent–child relationships tend to support such an assumption. Shek and Ma (1997) showed that adolescents who have a more negative perception of parental treatment, parental concern or leniency engage in more deviancy, undesirable sexual activity, anti-social behaviour and aggression. Nevertheless, there is no strong evidence for the kind of parenting education programme that can best help Hong Kong parents to establish better relationships with their adolescent children. In addition, the simple assumption that parents lack communication skills and empathic understanding takes no account of the special nature of parenting in Chinese culture where *guan* (governing and training) is emphasised. Nor are the special ways in which Chinese parents characteristically express concern and love properly addressed within this model.

Ho and colleagues (1999) showed that a parent training programme based on a behavioural approach and using parent management training (Forehand & McMahon, 1981) was effective in reducing conduct problems in children. Subjects were recruited from the "child and adolescent psychiatry team" at the Queen Mary Hospital in Hong Kong. The training consisted of 8 to 12 sessions of behavioural treatment. Twenty-five subjects were treated, and the results demonstrated significant reduction in behavioural problems and an improvement in parent–child interaction (Ho *et al.*, 1999). Nevertheless, the study involved only 25 subjects and no control group, so the results cannot support a definitive conclusion.

Meanwhile, a more rigorous study of the Triple-P programme has recently been conducted, launched by the Department of Health in Hong Kong. The sample comprised Hong Kong Chinese parents whose children had been diagnosed with early onset of conduct-related problems. The results indicated some effectiveness in reducing reported behavioural problems (Leung *et al.*, 2003). Although this programme seems to demonstrate some success in helping parents whose children have behavioural problems, its target group is limited to parents of children aged 5 to 7. Furthermore, the programme is more oriented towards social learning and behaviourism rather than communication and relational skills. However, this evaluation is of the most scientifically rigorous studies available in this area. Another parent training programme based on the Triple-P behavioural approach (Sanders, 1999) has been studied (Leung *et al.*, 2003). This is a comprehensive, multilevel preventive programme involving non-intrusive parent management techniques to change unrealistic and dysfunctional parenting beliefs (Sanders, 1999). Ninety-one parents with children aged 3 to 7 participated in the project. Measurement included questionnaires which the parent participants were required to complete before and after the programme. The measures used included the Eyberg Child Behaviour Inventory (Eyberg & Ross, 1978) and the Strengths and Difficulties Scale (SDQ; Goodman, 1997). A waiting list control group was used to compare differences post-intervention. The results showed that the programme was effective in reducing children's behavioural problems (Leung *et al.*, 2003). Although these two studies both indicate that a behavioural approach to parenting training can be effective against behavioural problems, the subjects' children were all of primary school age rather than adolescents. In addition, the latter study relied heavily on parents' self-reporting of their children's behavioural changes.

One study of a parallel group programme delivered for parents with adolescent children found post-test improvements in conflict management compared with the control group (Yeung, 1998). However, Yeung's study has a number of drawbacks: the participants were overwhelmingly from middle-class families and were not randomly assigned to experimental or control groups, introducing the possibility of bias. Nevertheless, it is one of the most scientifically rigorous recent studies of programmes for Hong Kong parents of adolescent children.

Parenting groups which emphasise communication with children have been found to be effective with middle-class Hong Kong Chinese mothers. A study of the effectiveness of STEP (Kwok, 1994), which aims to improve the parenting skills and attitudes of Chinese parents of children aged 6 to 11 in Hong Kong, showed that STEP is effective in achieving its objective as well as improving children's behaviour. Kwok's sample was drawn from a middle-class area of Hong Kong. Nevertheless, this study identified gender difference among mothers and fathers and the programme was less effective in changing fathers' parenting attitudes. Kwok (1994) found that fathers were not keen on adopting the 'I-message' skills taught in the programme. I-message is a non-blaming message that shows the receiver how their behaviour is affecting the sender. Chinese fathers are less emotionally involved with their children and are traditionally taught not to express their emotions (Kwok, 1994), and therefore may not accept the need to learn this skill.

Similarly, Cheung and Yau's (1996) study on the effectiveness of PET for Chinese parents showed that after participating in the programme, working-class mothers with at least a secondary school education demonstrated improvements in their ability to empathise with their children and to listen to them actively. All the participants were mothers with at least one school-age child, although the authors did not make clear what level the children had reached. The training programme emphasised the learning of active listening, sending 'I-messages' and a 'no-lose' method of conflict resolution. Parents were particularly taught to be sensitive to their children's feelings and to understand the messages conveyed (Cheung & Yau, 1996). The results showed that participants benefited from this programme with an emphasis on developing empathic skills. However, the study did not measure changes in the children's behaviour.

A more recent and rigorous study on parent training in Hong Kong was carried out by a research team at the governmental Education and Manpower Bureau. The researchers set out to evaluate different formats of parent training used in Hong Kong through a review of the use of PET, the Satir Model (Satir, 1983) and the eclectic approach (Education and Manpower Bureau, 2003). This involved 201 parents who participated in ten parenting programmes organised by three Hong Kong NGOs. Parent participants were randomly assigned to experimental or control groups and all were asked to complete the Eyberg Child Behaviour Inventory (Eyberg & Ross, 1978) and Parenting Stress Index (PSI) pre- and post-intervention to enable measurement of changes. The post-intervention questionnaires had to be completed within two weeks of completion of the programme. The results showed that the participants' children demonstrated fewer behavioural problems and participants themselves felt less stress.

The above review also shows that participants' satisfaction with the service-provided outcomes were influenced by facilitators, and significant differences in pre- and post-intervention scores were demonstrated where the group leader had a Bachelor or Master of Social Work, but not a diploma. In addition, significant changes were obtained in groups led by facilitators with five years or more social work experience, showing that facilitators with more experience can produce better results. In addition, the review has also looked at the effect of the theoretical framework of programmes on child behaviour and parental stress. Theoretical basis had a significant primary effect on the latter. The relationship between the number and length of sessions and programme effectiveness was also measured, indicating that the greater the number of sessions provided, the greater the difference between pre- and post-intervention scores. The results also show that the more time a mother spends with the target child, the greater the change observed in the child's behaviour (Education and Manpower Bureau, 2003). Furthermore, this review indicates that certain elements are important when implementing a parenting programme. First of all, it should cover communication skills, which are of great importance in parenting teenagers. The evidence indicates that Chinese parents benefit from better communication with their children after taking part in a parenting programme, and also feel more competent. Therefore, facilitating participants' sharing and self-help is another important element of a successful programme.

Studies of parenting programmes in Hong Kong indicate that behavioural training is effective in reducing problematic behaviour in children. Cognitive programmes like PET and STEP are effective in reducing parental stress and improving parents' confidence. Furthermore, facilitators who have higher educational attainment and more social work experience produce better results. Nevertheless, there are limitations to this research given that very few attempts have been made to consider culturally sensitive parenting practices among Chinese families. Most studies have borrowed directly from Western theories and used them in the Hong Kong context. In addition, there is a general lack of methodological rigour in evaluations, such as the absence of control groups or randomised controlled trials. Furthermore, there have been few attempts to address parents' experiences by such means as asking them how they had perceived the programme and how they had found it helpful.

There have also been very few attempts in Hong Kong to evaluate parenting programmes for parents of adolescents rather than young children. Less attention has been paid to measuring the efficacy of parent training in reducing adolescent anti-social behaviour, nor has there been much focus on the topics which need to be included for a particular type of parent or the appropriate duration of interventions. It is therefore important when designing programmes for parents of adolescents to use a control group and to set out a theoretical basis that caters to the behavioural and cognitive elements of parenting with an emphasis on Chinese parenting style.

Conclusion

In Hong Kong, the initial policy aim of parent training was to reduce juvenile delinquency and improve family relationships. Despite the proliferation of programmes in Hong Kong, few rigorous studies have been conducted to investigate their efficacy. Practitioners have mainly been interested in parents' satisfaction levels, with very few attempts being made to examine the behavioural changes in their children. Less attention has been given to parents of adolescents, with no studies so far having explored their experiences after joining such a programme. Furthermore, because the outcomes of research are mixed, no firm conclusions can be drawn about whether parenting programmes have been effective in bringing about positive outcomes for parents and adolescents. There is therefore a need to focus on using more rigorously designed studies to investigate the outcomes of parenting programmes, and to develop a better understanding of whether they are benefiting parents and adolescents, in order to be accountable to funders and service users. Finally, particular attention also needs to be paid to the specific Chinese culture in Hong Kong since parents and adolescents in this context hold different assumptions about parenting from their Western counterparts. Drawing directly on Western theories to underpin parenting programmes may not be appropriate for Hong Kong Chinese parents. There may therefore be a need to develop more culturally sensitive parenting programmes to meet the needs of these parents.

4 Methodology of evaluating parenting programmes

Introduction

This chapter focuses on the methodology adopted in evaluating parenting programmes. Evaluation research has a long history of providing evidence for effective and appropriate use of public funding of initiatives to tackle social problems. It can also serve as a means to review the implementation of interventions regarding, for example, appropriateness of content, time of implementation and number of sessions. Summative evaluation is the term usually referred to when we ask the question of whether the programme/ intervention achieves its purpose, while formative evaluation focuses more on the planning and implementation of the programme. Summative and formative evaluations are both very important to our understanding of the effectiveness of a programme's outcome(s) and of the implementation process. A design employing a mixed method of quantitative and qualitative approaches can help us to have a clearer picture of how promising a programme is for helping participants improve along the desired track. Mixed methods can also answer the question of how suitable the implementation process and content of a programme are for the participants. This commonly used method of quantitative and qualitative approaches in programme evaluation is also discussed in this chapter. In addition, the methodology commonly used to analyse data is discussed.

Evaluation research

Evaluation has been defined as "a form of applied research which aims to produce information about the implementation, operation and ultimate effectiveness of policies and programmes designed to bring about change" (Clarke & Dawson, 2005: 35). The systematic evaluation of social programmes has a long history, dating from as early as World War I, when efforts were directed at assessing the effectiveness of national educational and public health programmes in the US. Since these programmes involved large public expenditure, there was a need to know whether they worked (Rossi, Lipsey & Freeman, 2004). Programme evaluation became more popular in the 1950s, when there was more effort put into reducing social problems like juvenile delinquency and testing out innovations in psychotherapy (Babbie & Rubin, 1989). Methods for evaluation research then started to emerge, such as Hayes' (1959) monograph on evaluation, Suchman's (1967) review of evaluation research and Campbell's (1969) call for social experimentation. These writers set the scene for using experimental and quasi-experimental studies as the basis of evaluation. Today, evaluation research is an important means of judging whether public funding for human services is effective in achieving its designed aims. It also provides evidence of whether the service provided is effective in reducing the social problem. Thus,

> programme evaluation is the use of social research methods to systematically investigate the effectiveness of social intervention programmes in ways that are adapted to their political and organisational environments and are designed to inform social action to improve social conditions.
>
> (Rossi, Lipsey & Freeman, 2004: 16)

Programme evaluation is "undertaken to inform decisions, clarify options, reduce uncertainties and provide information about programmes and policies" (Patton, 1986: 14, quoted in Clarke & Dawson, 2005: 35).

One of the traditions regarding the methodological quality of evaluation is defined by Farrington (2003) with reference to Cook and Campbell's (1979) use of experimental and quasi-experimental designs. This calls for various forms of validity: statistical conclusion, internal, external and construct (Farrington, 2003). These criteria, together with the idea of establishing causal relationships (that is, where cause precedes effect), have come to be regarded as the major criterion of methodological rigour. Thus, randomised controlled trials (RCT), experimental and quasi-experimental designs and statistical analysis have all been used to indicate methodological rigour in evaluation.

Nevertheless, such an approach has been criticised by Pawson and Tilley (1997), who argue that the use of experimental designs can only answer the question of 'what works' while ignoring the issue of "what works for whom in what circumstances" (Pawson & Tilley, 1997). The Campbell tradition can lead to mixed findings, since it lacks the power to examine how and why a programme is successful in a particular context or situation. This is because the experimental paradigm considers all the programmes delivered to be generally the same. The service recipients will experience nearly the same process, but other variables that have a possibility of affecting this are considered outside the control of the evaluator (Blamey & Mackenzie, 2007). This results in programme outcomes being combined across different groups of individuals in different settings to whom a programme was delivered. In addition, the political, social, organisational and individual dimensions should also be taken into consideration in evaluation processes. The 'realistic evaluation' approach, proposed by Pawson and Tilley (1997), stresses the importance of understanding the context within which the programme takes place. This is also important when a researcher attempts to replicate the intervention in a future setting or in generalising the possible causal pathways in the intervention process. The realistic evaluation approach further suggests that evaluation research should focus on the mechanism, that is, the complex process of human understanding and interaction (Pawson & Tilley, 1997) within the programme that brings about success or failure. On this basis, it is more desirable to design a programme evaluation using both quantitative and qualitative methods in order to have the best understanding of the programme results.

Paradigm and mixed methodology

The combination of quantitative and qualitative approaches denotes methodological pluralism (Fuller, 1996). This has been defined as

> the belief that no single approach to research is best overall, rather, what is important is that the methods be appropriate for the questions under investigation. No single research method is inherently superior to any other: all methods have their relative advantages and disadvantages.
>
> (Barker, Pistrang & Elliott, 2002: 245)

Thus, the essence of methodological pluralism is to use the method that best fits the measurement of what we want to measure. Both quantitative and qualitative approaches are useful (Hanson *et al.*, 2005), and the choice depends on the research questions (Tashakkori & Teddlie, 2003). In this paradigm, no single approach is superior to other methods. It is more productive, for the methodological pluralist, to fit the method to the research question. In other words, the study is driven by the research question, not by the research method (Barker & Pistrang, 2005). Mixed methods is regarded as another major approach or paradigm alongside quantitative and qualitative research (Johnson, Onwuegbuzie & Turner, 2007).

Mixed-methods research has been defined as "the class of research where the researcher mixes or combines quantitative and qualitative research techniques, methods, approaches, concepts or language into a single study" (Johnson & Onwuegbuzie, 2004). According to Brannen, this means "adopting a research strategy employing more than one type of research method. The methods may be a mix of qualitative and quantitative methods, a mix of quantitative methods or a mix of qualitative methods" (2005: 4).

Furthermore, the application of 'mixed methods' in evaluation research has been regarded as essential by writers such as Riggin (1997), quoted in Rallis & Rossman (2003). Evaluation entails three primary activities: description, comparison and prediction (Rallis & Rossman, 2003). Underlying these is the demand for value judgements about the merit and worth of the intervention being evaluated. Evaluation theorists have long suggested that the methodology to be applied is grounded in the theoretical paradigm of the researcher, stakeholder or both (Rallis & Rossman, 2003). It therefore emerged that using a quasi-experimental study with a waiting-list comparison group would best identify the impact of the parenting programme.

In addition, the evidence suggests that combining quantitative and qualitative research has further advantages; it can enable triangulation. Triangulation provides an analysis that helps to provide richer data and initiate new modes of thinking by explaining the differences in the findings that emerge within two datasets (Johnson, Onwuegbuzie & Turner, 2007). Furthermore, the 'triangulation design model' of the data-mixing methodology (Creswell & Plano Clark, 2007) helps to triangulate, or to gather at the same time and integrate, both quantitative and qualitative data in order to best understand a research problem. The two datasets will be presented separately in this thesis and will be synthesised in the discussion section to explore whether there is supporting or conflicting evidence for the results. A researcher may also transform one type of data into another (for example, quantitatively counting the codes of qualitative data). Therefore, the adoption of a mixed methodology in evaluation research can serve two important objectives. Firstly, seeking participants' views of the programme means their ideas, thoughts and feelings (which may not be available through quantitative data alone) can be identified. In addition, further interviews with participants may allow unexpected data to emerge. Thus, the qualitative data could serve the purpose of enriching the quantitative data. Secondly, the quantitative data could also be cross-checked using the qualitative data to explain or further justify the results. Furthermore, quantitative data can help to explain anything that is not clear from the qualitative data by indicating the proportion of parents who experienced changes. As a result, methodological triangulation can serve the purpose of confirming and/or combining the two datasets to enrich the findings.

Finally, previous studies of programme evaluation have also suggested a similar design. Nastasi and colleagues (2007) used an experimental pre–post control group design (summative programme evaluation) and final-session participant evaluation strategies to seek students' and teachers' views on a programme. Afterwards, they reanalysed the formative evaluation data. They also used the qualitative data to inform their practices when they were using culturally sensitive measures and to develop the scale used in their quantitative studies. In other words, they used the qualitative data to inform the quantitative analysis. The use of mixed methods thus enhanced the validity of the programme evaluation as well as its reliability (Leahey, 2007). Such an approach can also help to uncover unexpected dimensions. Further, it can enrich our explanations of theory, integrate theory and/or enrich the explanations of findings. It has also been argued that using both quantitative and qualitative approaches enables us to form a better understanding of the world generally.

Evaluation design

The above discussion focused on methodological pluralism, adopted here, where rather than conforming to a particular form of research design, one should select the most suitable evaluation design for achieving the evaluation objective. The most important objective of evaluation research is to indicate whether the intervention is effective in achieving its aims. It is also important to know if the intervention really causes the changes in service recipients. One design used to address this is the single-group, pre-test–post-test design method. This method measures one group twice, before and after the treatment. We can therefore identify any changes occurring in the subject between premeasures and post-measures. There is a difficulty in this method, however, in controlling for other factors that influence the participants. For example, we cannot measure the natural maturity of a participant in a one group pre- and post-test design (Dooley, 2000).

To avoid such time-related rival explanations in the design, a lot of studies in the evaluation of parenting programmes have adopted a control or comparison group. This method allows us to compare those who did not receive any programme intervention with those who did at the same time. In such a design, instead of comparing the pre- and post-scores of only one group of participants who receive the intervention, we compare the pre- and post-test scores of the intervention group and the comparison group. This method can help us to identify between-subject differences between those who joined the programme and those who did not (Dooley, 2000). In comparing the pre-test scores of the two groups, we try to identify any pre-intervention differences between the intervention group and the comparison group. When comparing the post-test scores of the intervention and comparison groups, we can protect against the assumption that both groups experience the same time-related influences. This kind of design is called a quasi-experimental design. Such a design can help us to control for some extraneous variables.

Another form of design is the true experimental design, which controls for both time-related and group-related threats. A true experimental design involves two or more differently treated groups and randomly assigns people to these groups. True experimental designs control for group differences by randomly assigning every subject to any group to prevent group differences between subjects and uses a comparison group to control for time and maturation factors (Babbie & Rubin, 1989). Nevertheless, such a design has the disadvantage that we do not know how long our intervention will last. The timing of when we measure the outcome could affect our results. For example, if we measure the outcome immediately after the intervention, we are not able to capture how much change might occur after the participants practice the learned skills at home. In such a case, some designs measure the outcome after three months or more to test how long the changes last. In addition, in real-life situations, we also need to consider ethical issues in randomly assigning participants to different intervention situations. It would be unethical to ignore the needs of the participants or the problems that they have when they decide to join the intervention. A review by Shulruf (2004) has indicated that the majority of studies (26 out of 34 evaluations) on the effectiveness of parenting programmes adopted a methodology that involved comparing the outcome indicators before and after the intervention. Only a minority of post-intervention measures were identified. There were also eight programmes that had follow-up measures after the programme finished. This review has indicated that the most common design for evaluating the effectiveness of parenting programmes is to use pre- and post-intervention measurements with follow-up measures after the programme has finished.

As well as the importance of study design, there is also the significant issue of properly engaging with parents who attend a programme (Whittaker & Cowley, 2010). One of the indicators for the success of a programme is the participation/dropout rate of participants. As indicated in our review of effectiveness in this article, poor attendance in the parenting programme and participant dropout is an area lacking attention in research papers. There are barriers like personal life factors, structural barriers and cultural barriers that affect the participation of parents in parenting programmes. To develop a clear understanding about all those who drop out from the programme, a proper evaluation should incorporate measurements that survey dropouts and/or low-attendance parents to understand the reasons why they drop out of the programme. This information is essential for improving how we plan and deliver parenting programmes in the future. It also helps to provide a better evaluation of the effectiveness of a programme and to understand how a programme could be delivered in a more successful way.

Outcome measurements

As well as making careful decisions on how the evaluation is designed, there is another issue of importance in deciding what to measure as indicators of success.

The following are the common impact/outcome issues that interested us (Parent Education & Support Forum, 2002).

Impact on Parents

- Better knowledge of child and adolescent development
- Improved understanding of their children's and adolescents' problems
- Improved communication skills with children and adolescents
- Improved communication skills with spouse and other family members
- Adopting a more positive attitude towards their children's and adolescents' behaviour
- Improved skills in solving conflict with their children and adolescents
- Improved coping strategies in dealing with anger
- Better insights into one's parenting style, parenting beliefs and parenting skills
- Changes in behaviour, such as acquiring more skills in positive parenting (for example: giving praise, letting go etc.)
- Having more support from parent participants
- Improved mental health of parent participants (for example: reduced parenting stress; more parenting confidence; less depression; less anxiety towards parenting etc.)
- Improved help-seeking behaviour, such as joining suitable parenting programmes in the community, knowledge of where to seek help whenever there is a problem related to child-rearing and being able to access benefits, health and employment services when needed

Impact on children and adolescents

- Improved interaction with parents and family members
- Reduced conflict with parents and other family members
- Less depression, anxiety and anti-social behaviour
- Improved performance at school and in school attendance
- Improved relationship with peers and schoolmates

Process issues

- Delivery of service to parents (how acceptable, enjoyable and culturally appropriate is it?)
- Practical issues like accessibility and convenience of facilities
- Availability of support services like child-care facilities during the programme
- Meeting special needs among parent participants
- Recruitment processes like publicity and referral systems
- Attendance and retention

Quantitative measurement

The previous section lists some of the common indicators in which the evaluation study is interested. One way to understand how successfully the indicators were achieved in the programme is to employ some standardised measurements. These measurements should be administered before and after the programme. In addition, if a comparison or control group is designed into the evaluation, we must also administer the questionnaire to the comparison or control group so that we can compare the results of the intervention. The advantage of administering standardised tests is that they have usually been rigorously tested for validity and reliability by specialist researchers. It is recommended that the questionnaire is not changed or shortened, since this will affect the validity and reliability of the test. Furthermore, when the test was not originally developed in our own culture, we may also need to consider the validity of the measurement. We may need to administer tests that have been translated and validated in our own culture so that cultural differences in understanding the questionnaire have already been accounted for in the validation process.

When considering what measurements should be included in our evaluation, we must first answer the question of what the objectives of the programme are and then design the intervention strategies accordingly. Parenting programmes have been designed to achieve different objectives. An overview of common programmes internationally shows that a few important themes can be drawn from the objectives of parenting programmes. There are programmes that aim at enhancing participants' understanding of child or adolescent development. These programmes help participants to understand the psychological and social development of children and adolescents to help parents establish realistic expectations of their children. These programmes employ scales like the Knowledge of Child Development Inventory (Larsen & Juhasz, 1986). This inventory can be used to measure participants' "knowledge of child development" from 0–3 years. It covers children's social, emotional and cognitive development. On the other hand, some programmes are designed to reduce children's behavioural problems (Sanders *et al.*, 2000). These parenting programmes employ a behavioural approach to enhance parents' knowledge regarding parenting their children in order to reduce their children's behavioural problems. One of the measurements that is commonly used in these kinds of parenting programmes is the Strength and Difficulties Questionnaire (Goodman, 1997). This scale has a rather balanced view of a child in that both strengths and difficulties are measured. The third commonly addressed area in parenting programmes is the mental health of participants, which is measured before and after the programme. Two common measurements scales are the Beck Depression Inventory (Beck & Steer, 1987) and the Rosenberg Self-Esteem Scale (Rosenberg, 1965). Examples of these programmes include those studied by Patterson and colleagues (2002) and Baydar, Reid and Webster-Stratton (2003), and they aim at improving parents' mental health. The fourth objective of parenting programmes is to encourage parent participants to adopt more positive parenting attitudes. These programmes mostly use cognitive behavioural or social learning approaches to enhance parents' understanding of positive parenting attitudes (Conners *et al.*, 2006). The fifth aspect concerns the parenting behaviour of the parents. Programmes focusing on this are concerned with not only the attitude of parents after the programme but also the parenting behaviour of parent participants. Other parenting programmes are concerned with the interactive behaviour of parents and children (Goemans *et al.*, 2016). These parenting programmes adopt videotaping parent–child interactions. The trained observer then codes the interaction between children and parents to determine the effectiveness of the programme (Sanders *et al.*, 2000).

In the present study, which will be illustrated in more detail in Chapter 5, several indicators were adopted:

- Chinese version of the Parent–Adolescent Conflict Scale (PAC: Robin & Foster, 1989) (to measure any change in parent–adolescent conflict levels)
- Chinese version of the PSI (Abidin, 1995) (to measure any change in levels of parenting stress before and after the programme)
- Chinese version of the SDQ (Goodman, 1997) (to measure any change in adolescents' emotional and behavioural problems before and after the programme)
- Chinese version of the Modified Chinese Parenting Belief questionnaire (CPBQ: Lieber, Fung & Leung, 2006) (to measure any change in attitudes towards parenting before and after the programme)

The literature on the evaluation of parent training programmes in Hong Kong indicates the use of the above measurement to identify the success of programmes. Cheung (2001) has measured parental efficacy, parental empathy, availability of social support and parent satisfaction level. A more rigorous study by the Education and Manpower Bureau (2003) has measured behavioural changes in children, parenting stress, facilitators' background and programme information. Leung and colleagues (2003) have evaluated parent training programmes through looking at children's behaviour, parental efficacy and client satisfaction. In conclusion, the variables included in this study are parent–adolescent conflict, parenting stress, children's behavioural change, change in parents' attitudes to parenting and satisfaction of participants with the programme. Each variable will be further explained in the sections which follow.

PAC

The PAC scale developed by Robin and Foster (1989) has been translated into Chinese by Shek *et al.* (1995) and used in other relevant studies, such as Shek (1998b), who reports high internal consistency and temporal stability. This is a 20-itemed scale indicating parent–adolescent conflict from a parents' perspective.

Chinese version of PSI

Parental efficacy was measured using the PSI Short Form (PSI–SF) (Abidin, 1995). This questionnaire was first developed as part of Abidin's (1995) work on parenting education. Its primary function is to perform early identification screening using pre- and post-test measures of intervention and individual diagnosis (Abidin, 1995). The PSI–SF is a 36-item self-report measure used to reflect the extent of stress experienced by an individual when caring for a child or adolescent (Tam, Chan & Wong, 1994). It was originally developed through factor analysis of the full-length PSI. The PSI–SF scale consists of three factors: Parental Distress (PD), Parent–Child Dysfunctional Interaction (PCDI) and Difficult Child (DC). The validity and reliability of the PSI–SF scale is close to that of the original long form (Abidin, 1995). The stress score of the PSI–SF ranges from 36–180, with the majority of the items on a five-point scale (Lam, 1999). In this study, the PSI–SF was used to measure parenting stress before and after the intervention. This scale has been translated into Chinese and found to have high validity (Lam, 1999).

SDQ

The Chinese version of the SDQ (Goodman, 1997) was used to consider adolescents' behavioural problems. It is "a one-page questionnaire for assessing the psychological adjustment of children and youths" (Goodman, 2001: 1337). It was originally developed for the purpose of screening for children and adolescents' problems and is also intended to measure treatment outcomes and as a research tool (Goodman, 2001). The scale consists of 25 items divided across five areas and is available in different languages, including Chinese. It measures emotional symptoms, conduct problems, hyperactivity, peer relationships and pro-social behaviour. The questionnaire has the advantage of including both positive and negative descriptions. Respondents use a 3-point Likert scale to indicate how far these items apply to the individual child or adolescent. The questionnaire can be completed by parents, teachers or the adolescents themselves. It is also easy to administer and has been validated in various studies (for example, Leung *et al.*, 2003), and is available free of charge for use by non–profit-making research and the public sector (Goodman, 2001).

Chinese version of the modified CPBQ

This scale was used to measure changes in attitudes before and after the parent training programme. Previous studies suggest participation in this type of programme can lead to such shifts. This scale was developed by Lieber, Fung and Leung (2006), the first of whom approved its use in the present study. It consists of four dimensions of Chinese child-rearing beliefs; authoritativeness, autonomy, shaming and training. These four aspects have been identified by the authors as culturally specific parenting practices among Chinese families. A modified (that is, shortened) version of the scale was used in this study.

The following are the items included in the four subscales of training, shaming, autonomy and authoritative parenting (Lieber, Fung & Leung, 2006). Respondents are asked to indicate whether they agree or disagree with each statement.

Training scale items

- Close monitoring to show children that you care
- Mothers should make sacrifices for the benefit of children's education
- Parents should continuously monitor and correct behaviour
- Children should be reminded often of the conduct rules
- Parents must train children for hard work and discipline
- Parents should correct a child's misbehaviour
- Children should confess and repent after transgressing
- Harsh discipline is sometimes for the child's own good

Shaming scale items

- A good child is a child who is obedient
- Later in life children will be grateful for harsh discipline
- Children should be shamed when disobeying rules
- Shaming children helps them learn to behave
- Parents should be ashamed of a child's public misbehaviour
- Sometimes making children afraid gets them to listen
- A child's disobedience should be disciplined consistently
- Three-year-olds should restrain themselves and respect others

Autonomy scale items

- A child should know they have unconditional parental love
- Parents should stimulate exploration and learning
- Self-esteem is the basis for happiness and actualisation
- Children have their own ways of understanding things
- A child is uncomfortable with unexpected parental moods
- Parents should keep children's lives fun and pressure free
- Children are by nature born innocent
- A child's own sense of self is most important
- Parents and children must sometimes adjust to each other
- Children should be allowed to choose their own playmates

Authoritative scale items

- Parents should seek opportunities to praise children
- Even a child's conflicting feelings/ideas deserve respect
- Children's ideas deserve attention and respect

- Whenever reasonable, children should be treated as equals
- The expression of emotion should be encouraged and assisted
- Children's comprehension of feelings should be assisted
- Children listen better to parents who spend time with them
- Expressing opinions and feelings should be encouraged
- Parents should try to justify their requests to children

The questionnaire was distributed to parents before and after the programme to enable the capture of any changes in their beliefs. It was also used to indicate whether contemporary Hong Kong Chinese parents agree or disagree with traditional beliefs, enabling the proportion of those who endorse such cultural positions to be evaluated.

Parental comments on the programme

A questionnaire was developed and used to evaluate the satisfaction levels of the participants in the parenting programme. It was designed to identify which elements within the parent training programme participants had found useful and not useful in reducing conflict with their adolescents. The questionnaire was also used to explore any culturally sensitive elements that participants had found useful and any aspects which they considered to have not been culturally sensitive enough. The survey also sought opinions on the way the facilitator had led the programme and to explore what kind of activities within the parent training programme the participants had found most useful.

Qualitative design

Qualitative interviewing was undertaken to meet the objective of exploring any unidentified aspects of the intervention. For example, we wanted to know how parents feel when they participate in the programme. It is hard to ask participants to put their feelings down on paper. Even though we used some purposefully constructed questionnaires to capture these answers, qualitative interviews can enrich our understanding by providing more in-depth information on feelings and thoughts from the participants than that expressed when they fill in a questionnaire. In addition, there may be some aspects that were not covered in the validated or culturally translated questionnaires. We need to use qualitative interviews to understand these aspects. For example, we may want to know more about how the participants view the parenting strategies that have been introduced in the parenting programme. One of the particular skills that we introduced to participants was teaching them to give more autonomy to their adolescent children. However, due to Chinese culture, for example, participants may not totally agree with this approach to parenting. When we conducted interviews with participants on this, we were able to find out more about participants' thoughts. Because of keen competition to get accepted to university in the local context, parents preferred a higher monitoring of their adolescents' academic work rather than giving them more autonomy (Low, 2016). This example indicates the importance of interviewing participants to understand more than the questionnaire can tell us about the reasons behind their behaviour.

Depending on the purpose of the interview and what data one would like to collect, there are two commonly used interview methods. This first is semi-structured group or individual interviews. The advantage of this kind of interview is that interviewers have a clear guide and instructions on how to conduct the interview. It can also provide reliable and comparable qualitative data when you are interviewing more than one group of participants. To achieve methodological rigour, it is always more desirable to have clear objectives for the interview and to write down clearly the interview guidelines before launching the interviews. Interview guidelines can maintain the consistency of the interview content across different groups. It also helps to maximise comparability between different interview groups and individual participants. In addition, it can reduce interviewer bias between different interviewers. It can also help the reader of the research report to judge the quality of the interview methods. Nevertheless, more structure in the interview may reduce the natural, conversational nature of it. It also reduces the interviewers' flexibility in probing further with questions to understand more about the thoughts behind the answers of the participants. To solve this problem, one way is to use a semi-structured interview, in which an interview guide has been prepared for the interview but the interviewer can still probe further into any answers. This is useful in cases where it is not exactly clear what was meant or where further explanation is needed to understand the full picture. We may also use standardised open-ended interviews to guide interviewers in asking standardised questions. Meanwhile, we can also train them to ask probing questions to clarify meaning and to further understand the thoughts behind the answers (Babbie & Rubbin, 1989).

The second commonly used qualitative data collection method is unstructured interviewing. This is in contrast to semi-structured interviewing, where there are some pre-determined questions for the subject. Nevertheless, for the purposes of evaluation, the interviewer may need to be purposeful and sometimes directive. Interviewers must have a clear idea about the objectives of the interview. The objective of the unstructured interview is to fully understand the interviewees' experiences, attitudes or beliefs (Parent Education & Support Forum, 2002). It has the advantage of helping the evaluators understand more about undiscovered experiences among participants. This includes, for example, their experiences in new parenting methods or in newly developed or culturally adapted programmes. However, this kind of interview is more time consuming and expensive. It generates large amounts of data, but it may be difficult to compare and analyse this data between different groups of participants.

Data analysis

Quantitative data

Having collected quantitative data before and after the intervention, we needed to analyse the data by comparing the differences between groups. As per the above the discussion, we were interested in within-group differences, that is, any change within individual participants. We were also interested in between-group differences, that is, the differences between experimental groups and control groups. The first step in the process was to put those data into a computer and perform a normality test. The purpose of this test was to determine if the data that we had in hand were normally distributed, which would determine the kind of statistical test that we would use in our data analysis. If the normality test indicated that the data were normally distributed, then we would use a parametric test, since parametric tests hold the assumption that the data are normally distributed. Conversely, if the test results indicated that the data were not normally distributed, we would adopt a non-parametric test instead.

After testing the normality of the data, we needed first to compare any differences among the demographic data of the experimental groups. If we identified any group differences before the intervention, we would need to control that variable when comparing the results of the two groups. We usually use a chi-square test to test any differences in the demographic data between two groups. After comparing any differences in demographic data, we would apply either a parametric or a non-parametric test to compare the group differences. The following illustrate the example of the quantitative data analysis methodology adopted in the study, which will be further explained in the next chapter.

Differences between experimental and control groups

A series of chi-square and t-tests were performed to analyse any differences between the experimental and control groups. A series of analysis of variance (ANOVA) tests were also carried out to determine whether there were any statistically significant differences between various demographic variables and conflict levels. Results of PAC before and after the intervention were compared and the scores analysed against demographic variables such as gender, age of participant, age of partner, marital status, number of children living at home, adolescent's age, adolescent's gender, number of years residing in Hong Kong and country of origin. The scores from the control and experimental groups were also compared. Multivariate ANOVA tests were also performed to compare differences in the parent–adolescent conflict scores, parenting attitudes, parenting stress and adolescents' behaviour between the experimental and control groups.

Dropouts

As far as possible, all the parents who dropped out were contacted and asked to fill in the same set of questionnaires as those who had stayed in the group. They were also asked why they had dropped out. All the data were compared with those from the experimental and control groups to see if the dropouts had any significant characteristics.

Qualitative data analysis

In the present study, which will be further illustrated in the next chapter, a particular objective of the qualitative aspect of the study was to identify any culturally specific elements of the parent training programme through the semi-structured interviews. In addition, it was anticipated that any unexpected comments on the programme would also be recorded. A deductive as well as inductive approach to data analysis was adopted. Since the aim was to identify any culturally sensitive elements in the programme mentioned by the participants, all references to Chinese parenting were coded. In addition, any remarks about their likes and dislikes with respect to the programme were recorded and coded in order to enable their perceptions of it to be explored. Finally, any unexpected themes that emerged during the semi-structured interviews were also coded and analysed.

All the semi-structured group interviews were tape recorded. Afterwards, they were transcribed by the researcher and analysed using the procedures described below.

Coding of data

Coffey and Atkinson (1996) suggest a procedure for coding qualitative data: (1) notice relevant phenomena; (2) collect examples of those phenomena; and (3) analyse these phenomena in order to reveal potential meanings. This coding method was followed. All the transcripts were read line by line to identify any relevant phenomena falling within the objectives of the qualitative data collection. That is, note was taken of any culturally sensitive elements mentioned by the participants, such as parenting beliefs, parent–child relationships and so on.

Open coding

In open coding, there are no preconceived categories about what to code. The aim is to develop sense out of the data rather than having preconceived ideas to identify. This method corresponds to grounded theory as developed by Glaser and Strauss (1967). Under this methodology, the theory is generated from the data rather than the researcher forming preconceptions about the data, having a set of codes in mind and then identifying the themes from the data. Open coding serves as a step for identifying any special themes emerging relevant to culturally sensitive elements, likes and dislikes regarding the parenting programme and other unexpected themes.

Development of themes

There were some recurring themes within the transcripts, such as involved parenting beliefs, conflict-resolution strategies and effective elements of the programme. Particular attention was paid to these themes.

Focused coding

Once the themes had been developed through open coding, the stage of focused coding, in which the transcripts were read line by line to focus on those themes, was launched.

Looking for patterns

The first step in analysing the transcript after coding was to look for any patterns in the coded data. For example, there may be a pattern whereby those parents who make more positive comments about the parenting programme have daughters rather than sons. This could be analysed in terms of gender differences in the pattern of conflict between parents and their teens or in terms of mothers' and/ or daughters' responses to changes in parenting approach after the programme.

Relating the qualitative and quantitative data

When mixed methodology is adopted in a study, issues of relating quantitative and qualitative data become important. Greene, Caracelli and Graham (1989) identify five purposes of mixed method evaluation: triangulation, complementarity, development, initiation and expansion (Caracelli & Greene, 1993). In this study, the data were combined for the purposes of expansion. The quantitative methods were used to assess the outcomes of the programme, while the qualitative methods played the supporting role of examining the programme's processes (Caracelli & Greene, 1993).

In addition, Greene, Caracelli and Graham (1989) also group mixed-method data analysis and interpretations into four categories: no integration; analyses separate but some integration during interpretation; integration during both analysis and interpretation; and analysis procedure not reported (Caracelli & Greene, 1993). In the study illustrated in the next chapter, the two sets of data were analysed separately. Afterwards, the datasets were also compared to consider any inconsistencies or contradictions between them, in order to ensure that any supporting or conflicting evidence for the results could be considered. In addition, the qualitative analyses were considered as an expansion of the quantitative data. The combined results are presented in the chapters which follow.

Precautions in combining quantitative and qualitative data

It is possible for the quantitative and qualitative data to point in different and contradictory directions after analysis. For example, the quantitative data may show deterioration or no change before and after the programme while parents may regard it as a success. Precautions were taken in collecting the qualitative data, with probing questions used to ensure parents gave examples when commenting on the programme and to encourage them to illustrate their points further.

Another problem is that there is still no one single method of analysis for both quantitative and qualitative data; some researchers use different strategies to analyse the quantitative and qualitative data together, and there is still no consistent methodology for such analysis (Johnson, Onwuegbuzie & Turner, 2004). It would not be possible to use hermeneutics (that is, the study of interpretation theory) to interpret the quantitative data or to have enough statistically significant results for the qualitative data. Finding a consistent method of the same analysis is problematic. A further, consistent rule is needed in this process to maintain the quality of the mixed methodology and compare the two datasets.

In addition, there remains controversy around the best time to combine the data and at what stage of the study this should be done (Johnson, Onwuegbuzie & Turner, 2004). In addition, the question of how to ensure the validity and reliability of the mixed approach is still not settled. Researchers have used a variety of means to do so, but there is still no agreement on how best to do this.

Furthermore, researchers' preconceptions, personal and professional experiences in undertaking the research and prior beliefs about the outcome of the study all need to be avoided when undertaking research (Malterud, 2001). Having been a social worker for over 16 years, the author has developed acknowledged preconceptions about the value of parenting training programmes in relation to adolescents' well-being. Precautions were taken in the data analysis, particularly where positive feedback from the participants was concerned, as the author recognised a tendency to be over-sensitive to positive feedback and results while overlooking negative feedback. As Malterud (2001: 484) puts it:

> [the] investigator should take care not to confuse knowledge intuitively present in advance, embedded in preconceptions, with knowledge emerging from inquiry of systematically obtained material.

Ethical issues

This study considered ethical issues in the context of the framework introduced by the UK Economic and Social Research Council (ESRC) in 2005. The ethical issues arising in this study were reviewed and approval was granted by the ethics committee of the School for Policy Studies, University of Bristol. Before filling in the questionnaires, participants were informed verbally and in writing of the potential risks and benefits of participating in this study. For example, participants were required to fill in forms relating to the conflicts between themselves and their adolescent children, introducing the potential risk that recalling memories of such conflicts may arouse psychological discomfort. Nevertheless, participants also had opportunities to learn new parenting skills, gain support from other parents and reduce their stress. These points were set out in the written consent form as well as explained verbally by the researcher.

In addition, all the participants were reminded that they were joining the programme voluntarily. They were notified verbally and in writing that they could stop whenever they wanted to. They were also informed of similar programmes that they could join in the event they did not want to participate in the study but did want to benefit from intervention. In other words, no participants were obliged to participate in the study. Informed consent was obtained immediately after recruitment. All participants were required to fill in written consent forms for participating in the research study and the programme. They were also required to attend the group interview after the programme sessions and had to consent in order to be contacted if they dropped out.

To preserve confidentiality and anonymity, the questionnaires did not require the names of the participants to be entered. In addition, the researcher was the only person to read the completed questionnaires, and the electronic data were stored on a password-secured memory stick which was locked away whenever it was not in use by the researcher. Finally, in the interests of independence, three facilitators were invited to run the programmes rather than the researcher leading the sessions.

In the qualitative study, participants in the parenting programme were invited to attend a semi-structured group interview. During the discussion, it was possible that details of conflicts between parents and adolescents would be disclosed, with the chance that someone might disclose a coercive parenting practice such as physical child abuse. In such an event, it was not possible to maintain confidentiality. An agreement had been made before the study commenced that if any form of child abuse were disclosed during the interviews, the researcher would notify the social worker attached to the school and would also report it to the research supervisor. These points were included on the written consent form and participants were also told about them verbally.

Another potential ethical consideration is whether the researcher might use a different method from the one stated at the outset as a means to achieve the 'expected' results. This creates an ethical issue insofar as the researcher would then be using different methods to achieve a desired outcome, rather than systematically drawing conclusions from what emerges from the data. Particular attention was paid to this issue, especially in the data analysis phase, where grounded theory was employed, to avoid contamination of the findings by the researcher's preconceptions.

There is also an issue of confidentiality when both quantitative and qualitative data are collected from the same sample. If the participants in both are the same, there is a possibility that respondents to the quantitative study will be capable of being identified through the semi-structured interviews. Precautions were taken to keep the identity of parent participants confidential so that the researcher could not identify those informants through the semi-structured interviews.

Conclusion

This chapter illustrates some common approaches to evaluating parenting programmes. The most important point to note is that it is vital to set up clear objectives for evaluating parenting programmes. This can help us to have a clear idea of what to evaluate and to employ suitable strategies in the evaluation. Both quantitative and qualitative methods could be employed to achieve our evaluation objectives. An important means to achieving methodological rigour involves the choice of suitable validated scales to measure our expected outcomes. These outcomes include both parents' outcomes, children's and adolescents' outcomes and parent–child relationship outcomes, all of which are common indicators of the effects of the programme. This chapter also argues for the importance of employing a mixed approach in evaluating parenting programmes. Employing systematic evaluations could enhance evidence-based practice in parenting programmes in Hong Kong.

5 Culturally sensitive parenting programme

Example from Hong Kong

Introduction

The present study investigates the effectiveness of a school-based group parenting programme for parents of adolescents in Hong Kong. This study attempts to consider the effectiveness of a school-based group parenting programme in reducing parent–adolescent conflict in Hong Kong. It also looks at parents' perceptions of, and responses to, the programme to identify what elements they perceived as being most helpful, and examines the extent to which the approaches used were culturally sensitive.

This study is constructed around three research questions. Firstly, how effective is a parenting programme in reducing conflict between parents and their adolescent children? Previous studies have investigated the nature and extent of parent–adolescent conflict (Yau & Smetana, 1996). This study adds to that literature by addressing whether a group parenting programme could help reduce such conflict. The available evidence suggests that parenting practices can act as a protective function against adolescent anti-social behaviour. For example, parental supervision may dissuade adolescents from engaging in problematic activities (Dishion & McMahon, 1998). Parenting programmes have also been found to be effective in improving parent–adolescent relationships, reducing anti-social behaviour and reducing adolescent substance use (Dishion & Andrews, 1995). However, this is based on studies conducted in Western, Euro–American cultures. The literature does not provide any evidence about parenting programmes aimed at reducing parent–adolescent conflict in Hong Kong Chinese culture, despite the sizeable differences between this and Euro–American culture. The present study therefore sought to explore whether or not parenting programmes are effective in reducing parent–adolescent conflict within a collectivist culture like Hong Kong.

The second research question focuses on participants' views about which of the approaches to parenting or managing conflict suggested in the programme they find most effective. Previous work on the effectiveness of parenting programmes has provided some information on which types of training are most effective in changing behaviour and outcomes for children under 12 in Hong Kong (Ho *et al.*, 1999; Cheung & Yau, 1996; Kwok, 1994; Leung *et al.*, 2003). However, these studies did not try to delineate which specific elements of the programme were effective in bringing about the observed changes in children's behaviour and parental attitudes, beliefs and practices.

The third research question focuses on which of the culturally sensitive elements of the programme are regarded as effective by participants in helping them to reduce conflict. As explained above, parenting programmes in Hong Kong have a long tradition of being premised on Western theories like the humanistic (Kwok, 1994), and behavioural (Leung *et al.*, 2003) approaches. Nevertheless, studies have indicated that Western typologies of parenting style are insufficient to describe Chinese parenting practices (McBride-Chang & Chang, 1998). Chinese approaches are based on somewhat different assumptions and expectations to those described by Baumrind. This study aims to fill this gap by exploring which strategies, as informed by the parenting programme, have the most impact on parent–adolescent conflict. Qualitative data on participants' experiences of the programme will be collected. Transcripts of group interviews will be analysed in relation to traditional Chinese parenting styles.

Chinese parenting styles have been characterised as containing a unique concept of 'training' (Chao, 1994b). This term has a positive connotation in Chinese, meaning that parents will be both warm and firm. Chinese parenting also involves specific concepts such as filial piety, hierarchy, strict obedience and the maintenance of interpersonal harmony, all of which are unique to Confucian Chinese beliefs (Lieber, Fung & Leung, 2006). It may therefore be suggested that if most participants describe the culturally sensitive elements of the programme as effective in terms of their traditional Chinese parenting beliefs, then these aspects can be considered helpful.

Adaptation of parenting programmes in Chinese culture

The reason there is a pressing need to adapt parenting programmes in Chinese culture was because majority of the parenting programmes in Hong Kong have borrowed material developed in the Euro–American culture, with little attention paid to developing a culturally sensitive approach. However, direct use of Western-developed training materials may not be appropriate for programmes that aim to improve adolescent outcomes in Hong Kong Chinese culture. The relationship between parenting style and adolescent outcomes has been found to differ across different cultures (Sorkhabi, 2005). We also have little knowledge of any culturally specific parenting elements that may be essential to facilitating positive adolescent development in the Hong Kong context. This suggests that there is a need to develop culturally sensitive approaches to parenting programmes in Hong Kong.

Cultural issues in designing and implementing parenting programmes

In the present example, all the facilitators were instructed to adapt the programme so that it was more suitable to the needs of local participants. It has been suggested that a culturally sensitive parenting programme should be sensitive to the influences of specific risk and protective factors, or of different parenting approaches or practices. For example, there may be culturally specific aspects of the parent–child interaction that serve as protective factors against anti-social behaviour, such as understanding the adolescent's development and communicating effectively. The programme should also take into consideration the acculturation, identity and lifestyle preferences of the group. Furthermore, it also needs to consider the family's migration and relocation history; levels of trauma, loss and possible post-traumatic stress disorder (PTSD) related to war experiences or relocation; work and financial stressors; and language preferences and impediments due to English being a second language (Kumpfer *et al.*, 2002). These criteria are useful in adapting programmes in Euro–American societies where most of the ethnic minority participants were immigrants from Asia. Nevertheless, some of them could be used to adapt the parenting programme in this study. In this study, the use of local examples to reflect the lifestyle of parents and adolescents in contemporary Hong Kong was encouraged. In addition, the ways in which parents resolve their conflicts with adolescents in Hong Kong are different from those used in Western cultures. Facilitators were instructed by the researcher to be aware of these culturally sensitive elements. Finally, facilitators were encouraged to use their own social work experiences to illustrate the points within the programme package. A suggested approach to adapting the programme was given to all three facilitators for their reference.

An example of a culturally sensitive parenting programme

The parenting programme that has been adapted in this study was The Challenging Years, which was originally published by Surrey County Council under the title of Living with Teenagers. The authors of this programme were Sonya Hinton and Angela Taylor. After noticing the promise of its effectiveness, Young People in Focus then worked with the authors to publish the programme and rename it The Challenging Years. This is a programme, based on social learning theory, to help parents learn communication and conflict-resolution skills. It also allowed parents to reflect on their parenting practice and used interactive workshops to facilitate reflecting and learning by parent participants. A brief summary of the four weekly two-hour programme content is as follow:

- Week 1: "Understanding the teenage years". Parent participants were facilitated in an interactive way to reflect on their perceptions of teenagers nowadays
- Week 2: "Talking to teenagers". This week's programme focused on helping participants to identify and practice good listening skills, learn about different styles of communication and practice helpful ways of communication
- Week 3: "Parenting style". Participants were able to talk about different styles of parenting and consider how their upbringing affects their parenting practice
- Week 4: "Dealing with conflicts". Participants were able to consider conflicts between themselves and their teenagers. Participants were also able to practice approaches in problem-solving with their teenagers

This is a social learning programme in which parent participants were able to learn different communication skills and problem-solving skills through understanding and retaining of all the skills with the help of the facilitators. They were also able to learn and acquire all those skills through the time they practice these skills during the sessions. The programme also used an interactive and experiential approach in facilitating participants' learning throughout the programme.

This programme was selected because this programme content was consistent with the theory of change which generalised from the literature review. In addition, the programme is targeted towards parents in general, which is more acceptable to parents. Furthermore, the programme was designed in the UK and based on theory that developed in the West. The adaptation of this programme also aimed at understanding how far Chinese Hong Kong parents accept Western parenting ideas. Finally, the four-week design is also consistent with time that Chinese Hong Kong parents can commit to a parenting programme.

Evaluation methodology

This study adopted a quasi-experimental design with a comparison group. Questionnaires measuring children's behaviour, parenting stress and parenting beliefs were administered to determine any changes before and after the parenting programme. This chapter first presents an overview of the demographic data, with a statistical comparison of the experimental and comparison group and of those who dropped out. It then goes on to describe the pre- and post-test changes in scores on the SDQ, PSI–SF, PAC and CPBQ, and the results of the statistical tests performed to explore any significant reduction in these scores. The null hypothesis to be tested in this study is that there was no significant difference in scores before and after the programme. A significance level of 0.05 was used as the critical value for all statistical evaluations. Most of the statistical tests used were non-parametric because the data collected were unable to fulfil the assumptions of parametric testing; the data were not normally distributed, according to the test of normality, plus the sample sizes were small and the sample had not been drawn randomly from a normally distributed population (Corder & Foreman, 2009).

More specifically, in this study, a quasi-experimental design with a waiting-list control group was used to evaluate the effectiveness of a parent training programme in reducing parent–adolescent conflict, and adolescents' problem behaviour and parenting stress. After the evaluation, a semi-structured group interview was undertaken to obtain further details about which elements of the programme had best helped parents and which had been less acceptable, and to evaluate the effectiveness of the programme overall. Thus, the results of the qualitative analysis were intended to enhance understanding of the quantitative elements of the study. The results should also enable any unexpected perceptions of the participants about the programme to be explored.

Sampling

The sample was drawn from the secondary schools in the Northern District of Hong Kong. Letters were sent to each Parent–Teacher Association (PTA) inviting them to participate in this study by agreeing to launch a parent training group and inviting their members to join. Five schools agreed to participate; the timing and venue of the parenting programme were fixed between the school authorities and each PTA, who then informed the researcher of their decision. Leaflets about the programme were then sent to parent members. All parents gave written consent to participating in the study, including an agreement that if they did not complete all the sessions of the group they would be contacted for an interview. They were then invited to join the parent training programme provided that they fulfilled the following criteria. Firstly, they were a parent of at least one child in early adolescence (11–14). Secondly, they considered themselves to have frequent parent–adolescent conflict. Thirdly, they had not attended any counselling, family therapy or psychotherapy or received psychiatric treatment in the three months prior to recruitment to the study, nor did they have chronic mental health problems. Finally, all participants needed to have basic literacy skills and to be able to read and write Chinese.

All these requirements were designed to reduce the extraneous variables that could affect the results. If such factors are not controlled, there can be several implications for the study. Firstly, there is the threat of selection bias if the participants of the programme are very different from each other (Dooley, 2000). All participants were recruited from the same area (the Northern District) of Hong Kong. This was intentional in order to ensure, as far as possible, that they had the same socio-economic status.

Secondly, if participants are undergoing psychological treatments, for example counselling or family therapy, it would be impossible to determine whether any observed changes were as a result of the parent training programme or these other treatments. To keep this factor constant, only parents who had not received any such interventions over the previous three months were invited to participate in the study.

Thirdly, participants had to complete questionnaires as part of the study, which required them to be literate and have a basic understanding of Chinese so that they could participate in the group processes and fill in survey forms as required.

Finally, a quasi-experimental design must also deal with the problem of maturity, or the possibility that changes experienced by the client may arise from the natural process of maturity rather than the intervention. The use of a waiting-list control group helps to control for this factor.

Of the hundred-plus participants, most were mothers, with only seven fathers (less than 10% of the total) joining the programme. Previous studies (Shek, 1996) suggest a difference in parenting style between mothers and fathers in Hong Kong. For example, mothers show more warmth, and father–adolescent conflict has a more direct relationship with anti-social behaviour than conflict with the mother. Father–adolescent relationships have also been shown to be different from those with mothers. In addition, mothers exert more behavioural but less psychological control over children than fathers, and the mother–child relationship is generally more positive than the father–child relationship. Moreover, girls perceive that their free time and leisure activities are more closely monitored than boys' (Shek, 2005). These issues are reviewed in Chapter 4 and indicate a difference in relationships in terms of the parent's gender. The overwhelming representation of mothers joining the programme may indicate a greater need on their part to participate than fathers, since they tend to be the main caregivers and so may experience more difficulties. The traditional Chinese saying that "women are responsible for the home and men are responsible for outside home" is still widely believed. Where possible, the quantitative results will be compared in terms of the gender of the participant.

The experimental groups

Seven experimental groups were recruited from five different secondary schools in the Northern District of Hong Kong. A total of 101 parents participated in four weeks of two-hour sessions. The groups were conducted by three qualified and experienced social workers, all of whom had a close professional relationship with the researcher. In order to make sure that the contents of the programme were consistent across the different groups, the study adopted the Challenging Years parent training programme materials. The researcher attended at least one session of each group to observe the content and method of facilitation.

The control groups

Two waiting-list control groups of 26 parents each were recruited in schools A and B using the same criteria as for the experimental group. They received no service during the time they filled out the questionnaires, and were invited to join the programme after the experimental period had been completed. They were recruited on a voluntary basis from two other secondary schools (that is, schools where no experimental groups had yet been launched).

Data collection

Quantitative measures

Before the start of the programme, participants were asked to complete a newly developed questionnaire to collect demographic data. In addition, before and after the programme, participants were asked to fill in the following questionnaires:

- Chinese version of the Parent–Adolescent Conflict Scale (PAC: Robin & Foster, 1989) (to measure any change in parent–adolescent conflict levels)
- Chinese version of the PSI (Abidin, 1995) (to measure any change in levels of parenting stress before and after the programme)
- Chinese version of the SDQ (Goodman, 1997) (to measure any change in adolescents' emotional and behavioural problems before and after the programme)
- Chinese version of the Modified Chinese Parenting Belief questionnaire (CPBQ: Lieber, Fung & Leung, 2006) (to measure any change in attitudes towards parenting before and after the programme).
- Newly designed questionnaire designed to identify elements within the programme participants found useful and not useful and decide any culturally sensitive elements within the programme

Qualitative data collection

SEMI-STRUCTURED INTERVIEWS

Qualitative data were collected through a semi-structured group interview, facilitated by the researcher and carried out one week after the final session of the programme. A total of seven such interviews were conducted. The duration of each varied from 30 minutes to more than an hour depending on participants' responses. All the set questions were covered in each group as far as possible. The main purpose of these interviews was to expand the breadth of the quantitative study by exploring participants' views on the programme and the exploration of culturally sensitive elements within it.

The objectives of the interview were firstly to identify which elements within the programme participants had found useful and not useful in reducing parent–adolescent conflicts, and secondly to explore any culturally sensitive elements that participants had found useful in the programme or, alternatively, any parts of the programme which were not culturally sensitive enough. Participants were also asked to comment on the culturally adapted elements of the programme, and about their views of culturally specific methods of conflict resolution between parents and adolescent children, and culturally sensitive parenting practices. The interview also sought participants' opinions on the way the facilitator had led the programme and, finally, their views about which activities they had found most useful.

Study results

DEMOGRAPHIC PROFILES

The subjects in the experimental groups were recruited from schools in the Northern District of Hong Kong. All Parent–Teacher Associations (PTAs) in the district's secondary schools received a letter inviting them to participate in this study. Five schools agreed to do so and teachers were contacted via meetings or telephone calls to agree the preferred time and venue for the parenting programmes in each one. Leaflets and invitation letters about the programme were then sent out via the participating schools' PTAs to all parents of pupils in Forms 1 to 3 (that is, aged 11–14). Those parents who returned the reply slip and indicated that they agreed to join the programme as well as participate in the study were then enrolled. Participants also stated that they considered themselves to have some conflict with their adolescent children, that they had not received any counselling or social work services within the previous three months and that they had at least one child in the target age group 11–14. All participation was voluntary and the programme was delivered free of charge.

A total of 101 parents agreed to join the seven parenting programmes, although only 65 (64.4%) attended all the sessions and completed questionnaires before and after. Twenty-six parents from one of the schools also agreed to join the programme later and formed the waiting-list comparison group.

The parents in the experimental groups participated in four two-hour sessions delivered weekly and attended a semi-structured group interview after the last session. The programme content delivered to them was the Challenging Years (Hinton & Taylor, 2006), a parenting programme published by the Trust for the Study of Adolescence (now Young People in Focus). This programme was originally run by Surrey County Council in the UK under the name Living with Teenagers. It was developed for use with all parents of younger teenagers and does not focus on particular problems. The author attended at least one session of each group to observe the content and method of facilitation. In addition, it has a standardised manual which can help maintain consistency across different facilitators and groups. All three facilitators were experienced registered social workers in Hong Kong who had a close professional relationship with the researcher. They all attended a one-hour briefing session on the programme content and objectives. As shown in Table 5.1, the total number of parents who enrolled in the study was 101. The average enrolment per group was 14.42, with the largest having 19 parents and the lowest 10. A total of 65 of the 101 parents (64.4%) completed the before and after questionnaires. Thirty-six (35.6%) of the total participants dropped out before completing the programme.

The mean age of the participants in the experimental groups was 45.6, while in the comparison group it was 43.1 (Table 5.3). The mean age of the partners of experimental group participants was 47.1 and in the comparison group 50.6. A Mann-Whitney U-test, a non-parametric t-test of independent samples, was performed to explore whether there were any significant differences between groups in terms of age. The results indicated that there were statistically significant

Table 5.1 Recruitment and participation rate of experimental group

	No. of parents enrolled	*No. of parents completing the group and questionnaire (%)*	*No. of dropouts (%)*
Group 1	17	9 (52.5%)	8 (47.5%)
Group 2	16	7 (43.8%)	9 (56.2%)
Group 3	19	13 (53.8%)	6 (46.2%)
Group 4	10	7 (70%)	3 (30%)
Group 5	10	7 (70%)	3 (30%)
Group 6	13	8 (46.2%)	5 (53.8%)
Group 7	16	14 (77.5%)	2 (12.5%)
Total	101	65 (64.4%)	36 (35.6%)

Table 5.2 Gender of participants

Experimental groups		*Comparison group*	
Male	*Female*	*Male*	*Female*
13 (20%)	52 (80%)	1 (3.8%)	25 (96.2%)
X^2 (1) = 3.72, p = .05*			

differences between the experimental and comparison group (see Table 5.3). Participants in the former were older, as were their partners; the latter result may be explained by the fact that more mothers participated in the comparison group and it is common for husbands in Hong Kong to be older than their wives. When comparing mothers only between groups, a similar picture was obtained in that the mean age was slightly higher in the experimental (47.8) than the comparison group (43.1). Statistical test indicated that the difference was non-significant (see Table 5.3). Comparing gender of experimental groups and comparison group (Table 5.2), there were more father participate in the experimental groups (13, 20%) than the control group (1, 3.8%). Statistical test indicated a statistically significant different between the gender of experimental groups and comparison group (P >.05).

The mean number of children in the family for the experimental groups was 1.5 and for the comparison group 1.7. This indicated that the majority of participants in this study had no more than two children. The Mann-Whitney U-test found no statistically significant difference in the number of children between groups ($U = 708$; $z = -1.34$, with an associated probability of 0.18; that is, $p > .05$).

Concerning participants' marital status (Table 5.4), the majority (58, 89.2%) of parents in the experimental groups, and 24 (92.3%) of the comparison group, were married. Three (4.6%) of the parents in the experimental groups were divorced, and two (3.1 %) had remarried. In the comparison group, only two (7.7%) were divorced; all the others were still married to their original partners. This indicated that the participants who had enrolled in the programme tended to be married and live with their partners in a traditionally nuclear family structure. Chi-square test results indicated no statistically significant difference

Table 5.3 Age difference between groups

	Experimental groups	*Comparison group*	*Mann-Whitney U-test / Significance*
	Mean (SD)	*Mean (SD)*	
Age of participants	45.6 (4.9)	43.1 (4.3)	$U = 589.5$, $z = -2.17$ / .03*
Age of partners	47.1 (5.0)	50.6 (5.7)	$U = 531.5$, $z = -2.43$ / .01*
Age of mothers	47.8 (3.9)	43.1 (4.4)	$U = 518.5$, $z = -1.2$ / .23
Number of children	1.5 (0.7)	1.7 (0.6)	$U = 708.0$, $z = -1.34$ / .18

Table 5.4 Marital status of participants

	Experimental groups		*Comparison group*	
Married	58	89.2%	24	92.3%
Divorced	3	4.6%	2	7.7%
Remarried	2	3.1%	0	0
Others	2	3.1%	0	0
Total	65	100%	26	100%
X^2 (3) = 1.65, p = .65				

between the experimental and comparison groups in terms of marital status: X^2 (3) = 1.65, p = .65.

Concerning place of birth (Table 5.5), 43 (66.2%) of those in the experimental groups had been born in Hong Kong, compared with the comparison group, where this was the case for only seven (26.9%). Accordingly, a much higher proportion of the comparison group had been born in China than in the experimental groups. The chi-square test indicated this difference to be significant (X^2 (1) = 11.5, p = .001). One of the reasons for this is likely to be the 'Open Door' policy brought in 30 years ago, whereby women born in China who had married a man in Hong Kong could immigrate to the territory.

Mean number of years of residence in Hong Kong (for those who were not born there) was 17.9 for the experimental and 14.1 for the comparison groups (Table 5.5). In addition, parents in the experimental groups who had not been born in Hong Kong had lived there longer than those in the comparison group, although this difference was not significant (Mann-Whitney U = 224.5, z = –.31, with an associated probability of 0.76).

There were more mothers born in Mainland China in the comparison group than in the experimental groups. Mothers from Mainland China came from more traditional family backgrounds. They may be more conservative in parenting practice. This may affect their acceptance of new parenting ideas, and showed in their later joining of the programme. However, those born in Hong Kong were more open to Western ideas and more receptive to new parenting ideas. They were more motivated and likely to join the programme first. In addition, parents from Mainland China may still be adjusting to the living environment in Hong Kong and have less of an idea of joining a parenting programme. This affects their motivation to join the programme earlier.

Comparing the educational level of experimental groups and comparison group (Table 5.6), the parents in the experimental groups had a higher proportion of participants who were university graduates (4, 6.2%) compared with the comparison group (1, 3.8%), but the number with higher education in both groups was very small. The majority of the experimental group members were educated to secondary 4–5 standard (29, 44.6%). In the comparison group, the majority of the participants were educated to secondary 4–5 (16, 61.5%) as well. Statistical

Table 5.5 Place of birth and year of residence in Hong Kong of experimental and comparison groups

	Experimental groups (N = 65)	*Comparison group* (N = 26)	*Statistics*
Hong Kong	43 (66.2%)	7 (26.9%)	X^2 (1) = 11.55,
Mainland China	22 (33.8%)	19 (73.1%)	p = .001*
Mean years of residence (for those who were not born in Hong Kong)	17.9 years	14.1 years	U = 224.5, z = –.031, p = 0.76

***p* < .05**

tests indicated there was no statistically significant difference in education level between the experimental and comparison group (X^2 (6) = 4.27, p = .64).

In relation to the occupation of participants, we can conclude from Table 5.7 that the majority of both the parents in the experimental groups (32, 49.2%) and comparison group (16, 61.5%) were housewives. The second highest proportion of parents in experimental groups performed clerical work (11, 16.9%). Since the experimental groups had more highly educated parents, there was a higher proportion of experimental group participants (11, 16.9%) working as managers and professionals than in the comparison group (2, 7%). In addition, two parents who were unemployed joined the experimental groups, indicating the variety of parents was greater in the experimental groups than in the comparison group. Chi-Square tests indicated that there was no significant difference in occupation between the experimental and comparison groups (X^2 (8) = 8.02, p = .43).

Concerning the household monthly income of the experimental groups and the comparison group, the majority of the participants in these groups had an average household monthly income less than HKD 30,000 for the experimental groups (44, 67.6%) and comparison group (21, 80.8%) (Table 5.8).

Table 5.6 Education level of experimental and comparison groups

	Age of leaving school	*Experimental groups*		*Comparison group*	
Primary or below	11	2	3.1%	2	7.7%
Secondary 1–3	12–14	15	23.1%	4	15.4%
Secondary 4–5	15–16	29	44.6%	16	61.5%
Secondary 6–7	17–18	7	10.8%	2	7.7%
Post-secondary	Above 18	7	10.8%	1	3.8%
University or above	Above 18	4	6.2%	1	3.8%
Others	---	1	1.5%	0	0
Total	---	65	100%	26	100%
X^2 (6) = 4.27, p = .64					

Table 5.7 Employment of participants in experimental and comparison groups

	Experimental groups			*Comparison group*		
	Male (n = *13*)	*Female* (n = *52*)	*Total* (n = *65*)	*Male* (n = *1*)	*Female* (n = *25*)	*Total* (n = *26*)
Manager	5	3	8	0	1	1
Professional	1	2	3	0	1	1
Paraprofessional	1	1	2	0	0	0
Clerical	2	9	11	0	2	2
Service	1	3	4	1	3	4
Salesmen	1	1	2	0	3	3
Housewife	0	32	32	0	16	16
Unemployed	2	0	2	0	0	0
Total	13	52	65	1	25	26
X^2 (8) = 8.02, p = .43						

Table 5.8 Participants' monthly household income

HK$	*Experimental groups*		*Comparison group*	
0–10000	11	16.9%	8	30.8%
10001–20000	19	29.2%	4	15.4%
20001–30000	14	21.5%	9	34.6%
30001–40000	7	10.8%	1	3.8%
40001–50000	5	7.7%	1	3.8%
50001–60000	3	4.6%	2	7.8%
60001–70000	2	3.1%	0	0
70001–above	2	3.1%	0	0
No indication	2	3.1%	1	3.8
Total	65	100%	26	100%
X^2 (7) = 8.73, p = .27				

Again, statistical tests of significance between the experimental and comparison groups indicated that there was no significant difference between the two groups regarding monthly household income (X^2 (7) = 8.73, p = .27). Compared with the median monthly income of a household of four in Hong Kong (HKD 22,900) (Hong Kong Council of Social Service, 2010) in 2008, we can see the majority were lower than this income range, with only 32.4% of the experimental groups and 19.2% of comparison group falling within this range. This showed that a majority of parents were housewives and belonged to low income groups. Their average education level is secondary 5, which means they left school at age 16; most of them were born in China and migrated to Hong Kong later in their life, with an average of not more than 15 years of residence.

Children of participants

The mean age of the first-born child was 13.9 for the experimental groups and 14.8 for the comparison group, indicating a higher mean age of the comparison group when compared with the experimental groups (U = 605, z = –2.15, $p < .05$). In addition, there was no statistically significant difference in the age of second- and third-born children of experimental and control groups ($p > .05$) (Table 5.9).

Those with an oldest child of a higher age have more experience in handling their relationship with their adolescents, as they may have more than one adolescent child. Such experience may affect their perception of their relationship with early adolescents. They may perceive their adolescent as less problematic. On the contrary, those with an oldest child of a lower age have less experience in handling relationship with their adolescents. In addition, their adolescents are at the time of puberty, during which a lot of conflicts may arise between adolescents and their parents. This affects their perception of their adolescents' problems as more serious than those who have more experience of having adolescent children.

Concerning the gender of participants' children, the first-born child for the majority of both groups (56.9% for experimental and 57.7% for the comparison) was a boy (Table 5.10). The second-born child was a boy for 65.2% of the experimental group families compared with 47.1% of the comparison group. The proportion of first-born boys and girls was nearly the same across the groups. A chi-square test indicated that there was no significant difference between them in terms of the gender of the first- ($p > .05$) and second-born child ($p > .05$), as indicated in Table 5.10.

The demographic data shows that more mothers than fathers took part in the experimental and comparison groups. Most were from low-income Hong Kong households with no more than two children. The majority were married and lived with their original partners. In terms of education, most were educated to Form 5 level, which means they had left school at 16. More than half of the participants in both groups were housewives, with the experimental groups containing more participants who worked full time. As noted from the statistical tests reported above, there were statistically significant differences in the age of participants, their partners and their first-born children. Members of the experimental groups had a higher mean age than those in the comparison group. In addition, the partners of the latter were younger. This is mainly because more fathers participated in the experimental than the control group, and it is common in Hong Kong for

Table 5.9 Age of children of experimental and comparison group members

	Experimental groups (n = 65)	*Comparison group* (n = 26)	*Mann-Whitney U-test / Significance*
	Mean (SD)	*Mean (SD)*	
Mean age of first-born child	13.9 (1.8)	14.8 (2.0)	$U = 605$, $z = -2.15$, $p = .03$*
Mean age of second-born child	12.2 (2.9)	11.8 (2.2)	$U = 177$, $z = -.29$, $p = .77$
Mean age of third-born child	13.5 (2.1)	5.5 (6.3)	$U = .00$, $z = -1.85$, $p = .06$
***$p < .05$**			

Table 5.10 Gender of participants' children

	Experimental groups		*Comparison group*		*Chi-square test / Significance*
	Male	*Female*	*Male*	*Female*	
First-born child	37 (56.9%)	28 (43.1%)	15 (57.7%)	11 (42.3%)	$X^2(1) = .004$, $p = .95$
Second-born child	15 (65.2%)	8 (34.8%)	8 (47.1%)	9 (52.9%)	$X^2(1) = 1.32$, $p = .26$

husbands to be older than their wives. In addition, the mean age of the first-born child was higher for the comparison than the experimental groups. Furthermore, there was also a statistically significant difference in place of birth, with a high proportion of members of the comparison group having been born in Mainland China. Nevertheless, there was no such difference when years of residence in Hong Kong were compared. Apart from these matters, there were no significant differences in other demographic variables between the two groups.

Dropouts

A total of 36 parents dropped out of the programme, having participated in at least one session. While 36 parents completed the pre-test forms, only 20 of the questionnaires could be used for analysis due to missing data, making analysis difficult. Therefore, only 20 of the 36 questionnaires were used in the analysis.

As shown in Table 5.11, there was no statistically significant difference in gender between the experimental groups and dropouts. However, there were statistically significant differences in marital status; a higher percentage of dropouts were remarried or divorced compared to the experimental groups (Table 5.12). In addition, the dropouts had more children than the parents in the experimental groups; again, this difference was statistically significant (Table 5.13).

Nevertheless, there were no statistically significant differences between the groups in terms of the age of participants and their partners, their years of residence and the ages of their children. It may be speculated that drop out from the programme may be associated with the higher proportion of parents who were not married to their partners together with having more children in the family.

Table 5.11 Gender of experimental groups and dropouts

Experimental groups (n = 65)		*Dropouts* (n = 20)	
Male	*Female*	*Male*	*Female*
13 (20%)	52 (80%)	2 (10%)	18 (90%)
X^2 (1) = 1.05, *p* = .31			

Table 5.12 Marital status of experimental groups and dropouts

	Experimental groups (n = 65)		*Dropouts* (n = 20)	
Married	58	89.2%	13	65%
Divorced	3	4.6%	4	20%
Remarried	2	3.1%	1	5%
Others	2	3.1%	2	10%
Total	65	100%	20	100%
X^2 (4) = 10.9, *p* = .03*				

Table 5.13 Differences between experimental groups and dropouts

	Experimental groups (n = 65)	*Dropouts* (n = 20)	*Mann-Whitney U-test / Significance*
	Mean (SD)	*Mean (SD)*	
Age of participants	45.6 (4.9)	44.5 (4.6)	$U = 553.5$, $z = -.91$, $p = .36$
Age of partners	47.1 (5.0)	47.6 (6.0)	$U = 452$, $z = -.45$, $p = .65$
Years of residence in Hong Kong	17.9 (15)	13.5 (9.5)	$U = 88.5$, $z = -.49$, $p = .63$
Number of children	1.6 (0.7)	2.8 (3.0)	$U = 387$, $z = -2.9$, $p = .00^*$
Age of first-born child	13.9 (1.8)	15 (2.7)	$U = 461.5$, $z = -1.7$, $p = .09$
Age of second-born child	12.2 (2.9)	13.1 (3.5)	$U = 120.5$, $z = -.42$, $p = .68$
Age of third-born child	13.5 (2.1)	10.4 (4.9)	$U = 6.5$, $z = -.86$, $p = .39$

$^*p < .05$

Table 5.14 Place of birth of experimental groups and dropouts

	Experimental groups (n = 65)	*Dropouts* (n = 20)	*Statistics*
Hong Kong	43 (66.2%)	11 (55%)	X^2 (1) = .82, $p = .43$
Mainland China	22 (33.8%)	9 (45%)	

Table 5.15 Education level of experimental groups and dropouts

	Age of leaving school	*Experimental groups*		*Dropouts*	
Primary or below	11	2	3.1%	4	20%
Secondary 1–3	12–14	15	23.1%	4	20%
Secondary 4–5	15–16	29	44.6%	10	50%
Secondary 6–7	17–18	7	10.8%	1	5%
Post-secondary	Above 18	7	10.8%	1	5%
University or above	Above 18	4	6.2%	0	0%
Others	---	1	1.5%	0	0
Total	---	65	100%	20	100%

X^2 (6) = 8.99, $p = .17$

There was no statistically significant difference in education level between the experimental groups and dropouts (X^2 (6) = 8.99, $p = .17$) (Table 5.15), nor in employment (X^2 (8) = 3.24, $p = .0.92$; Table 5.16), monthly family income (X^2 (7) = 4.4, $p = .73$) and source of income (X^2 (4) = 86.78, $p = .15$). Accordingly, there were no significant differences between the experimental groups and dropouts other than that the latter had more children and fewer lived in intact families with their partners.

Pre-programme differences between groups

Before looking at whether any changes in score between the two groups after the programme are statistically significant, it is important to check whether any such differences existed before participation. The SDQ is a 25-item behavioural screening questionnaire measuring parents' perceptions of their children's pro-social and difficult behaviour. This falls into five categories measured by the pro-social, emotional symptoms, conduct problems, peer problems and hyperactivity subscales plus an overall total score. Scores are categorised into normal, borderline and abnormal, as shown in Table 5.17.

Table 5.18 sets out the mean differences in score for the experimental and control groups before commencing the parenting programme.

The Mann-Whitney U-test was used to compare the differences in scores between the groups. Table 5.17 shows that there were significant differences in several areas. First of all, the experimental group scored significantly higher

Table 5.16 Employment of experimental groups and dropouts

	Experimental groups			*Dropouts*		
	Male (n = *13)*	*Female* (n = *52)*	*Total* **(n = 65)**	*Male* **(n = 2)**	*Female* (n = *18)*	*Total* **(n = 20)**
Manager	5	3	8	2	0	2
Professional	1	2	3	0	1	1
Paraprofessional	1	1	2	0	0	0
Clerical	2	9	11	0	5	5
Service	1	3	4	0	1	1
Salesmen	1	1	2	0	0	0
Housewife	0	32	32	0	10	10
Unemployed	2	0	2	0	1	1
Total	13	52	65	0	0	0
X^2 (8) = 8.02, *p* = .43						

Table 5.17 SDQ category scores

Category	*Normal*	*Borderline*	*Abnormal*
Emotional symptoms	0–3	4	5–10
Conduct problems	0–2	3	4–10
Hyperactivity	0–5	6	7–10
Peer problem	0–2	3	4–10
Pro-social behaviour	6–10	5	0–4
Total difficulties	0–13	14–16	17–40

Table 5.18 Pre-programme scores for comparison and experimental groups

	Experimental groups	*Comparison group*	*Mann-Whitney U-test / Significance*
	Mean	*Mean*	
PAC score	8.6	6.12	$U = 605.5$, $z = -2.1$, $p = .04$*
SDQ scores			
Emotional symptoms	2.6	2.5	$U = 792$, $z = -.36$, $p = .72$
Conduct problems	1.9	1.6	$U = 676$, $z = -1.42$, $p = .16$
Hyperactivity	3.9	3.5	$U = 686.5$, $z = -1.3$, $p = .19$
Peer problem	2.6	2.4	$U = 8.8.5$, $z = -1.2$, $p = .90$
Pro-social behaviour	6.3	7.0	$U = 617$, $z = -1.9$, $p = .05$*
Total difficulties	11.0	10.0	$U = 685.5$, $z = -1.3$, $p = .19$
PSI-SF			
Parental distress	31.7	31.0	$U = 661$, $z = -1.52$, $p = .13$
Parent–childdysfunctional interaction	31.7	29.3	$U = 662$, $z = -1.52$, $p = .13$
Difficult child	30.5	28.1	$U = 601.5$, $z = -2.1$, $p = .04$*
Total	94.0	86.7	$U = 603$, $z = -2.0$, $p = .04$*
CPBQ			
Authoritative subscale	4.6	4.6	$U = 834$, $z = -.12$, $p = .91$
Autonomy subscale	3.4	2.9	$U = 632.5$, $z = -1.9$, $p = .05$*
Shame subscale	2.4	2.4	$U = 838.5$, $z = -.06$, $p = .95$
Training subscale	3.9	3.9	$U = 824.5$, $z = -1.9$, $p = .85$

***$p < .05$**

in terms of conflict ($U = 605.5$, $z = -2.1$, $p = .04$). Secondly, the SDQ scores indicated significant differences in pro-social behaviour between the groups ($U = 617$, $z = -1.93$, $p = .05$), with the children in the comparison group scoring higher for pro-social behaviour than those in the experimental groups.

Thirdly, there were no significant differences in the PSI–SF except for the difficult child subscale and total stress score, in both of which the experimental groups had a higher mean score than the comparison group ($U = 601.5$, $z = -2.1$, $p = .04$; $U = 603$, $z = -2.04$, $p = .04$). Fourthly, there were no significant differences in CPBQ scores for the authoritative, shame and training subscales, but a significant difference was observed on the autonomy subscale ($U = 632.5$, $z = -1.94$, $p = .05$), with parents in the experimental group more willing to grant autonomy to their teenage children than those in the comparison group. The autonomy subscale measures "parents' need to encourage, protect, and nurture children's exploration, wills self-concept, expression, and autonomy" (Lieber, Fung & Leung, 2006: 144). Since enrolment in the group was voluntary, parents with fewer difficulties may have chosen to join the programme later (that is, to be part of the waiting list) than those with stronger needs. In conclusion, the experimental groups displayed higher levels of conflict with their adolescent children, although their children's behaviour was almost the same (other than higher pro-sociality scores) as that of the comparison group children. Furthermore, the parents in the experimental groups experienced more parenting stress than those in the comparison groups and gave their adolescent children more autonomy.

Pre-programme differences between experimental groups and dropouts

The Mann-Whitney U-test was run to explore the differences in scores between the experimental groups and dropouts. Table 5.19 sets out the results for the four measures used. It can be seen that there were no significant differences between groups in the total scores for the SDQ, PSI–SF, PAC and CPBQ. However, there were differences in the hyperactivity and conduct problem subscales of the SDQ, with the dropouts' children scoring higher on both. In addition, there was a statistically significant difference in the autonomy subscale of the CPBQ ($U = 287.5$, $z = -3.9$, $p = .00$), indicating that the adolescent children of dropouts were granted less autonomy. Such families may not have been able to accept the underlying principle of the programme, which stresses the value of autonomy, leading them to decide not to continue after the first session.

In summary, there were some general differences between the experimental group and dropouts. More of the dropouts were divorced, and they tended to have more children to take care of. Their children also displayed higher levels of conduct and hyperactivity problems. These may be some of the reasons why the dropouts stopped attending the programme.

Statistical testing

As noted above, the null hypothesis was that there would be no significant difference in the scores on the SDQ, PSI–SF, PAC and CPBQ before and after the parenting programme in the experimental groups.

Table 5.19 Pre-programme scores for experimental groups and dropouts

	Experimental groups	*Dropouts*	*Significance*
	Mean (SD)	*Mean (SD)*	
PAC scores	8.55 (4.9)	9.84 (4.3)	U = 528, z = –.96, p = .34
SDQ scores			
Emotional symptoms	2.61 (2.0)	2.20 (1.7)	$U = 571.5, z = -.73, p = .47$
Conduct problems	2.08 (1.6)	3.26 (2.0)	$U = 397.5, z = -2.3, p = .02$*
Hyperactivity	4.11 (2.0)	5.05 (2.0)	$U = 482, z = -1.67, p = .04$*
Peer problem	2.63 (2.0)	2.95 (1.7)	$U = 538.5, z = -1.1, p = .28$
Pro-social behaviour	6.05 (2.2)	6.40 (2.4)	$U = 568.5, z = -.76, p = .45$
Total difficulties	11.45(5.3)	13.40(4.6)	$U = 482, z = -1.67, p = .10$
PSI-SF			
Parental distress	32.3 (8.3)	34.8 (6.0)	$U = 492.5, z = -1.25, p = .21$
Parent–childdysfunctional interaction	32.3 (7.8)	35.1 (4.8)	$U = 480.5, z = -1.38, p = .17$
Difficult child	31.5 (8.2)	32.2 (5.3)	$U = 607.5, z = -.01, p = 1.0$
Total	96.1 (21.1)	102.2 (12.3)	$U = 521.5, z = -.94, p = .35$
CPBQ			
Authoritative subscale	4.6 (0.6)	4.6 (0.6)	$U = 648.5, z = -.02, p = 1.0$
Autonomy subscale	3.4 (1.1)	2.2 (1.1)	$U = 287.5, z = -3.9, p = .00$*
Shame subscale	2.4 (1.0)	2.5 (.90)	$U = 616.5, z = -.37, p = .72$
Training subscale	3.9 (1.3)	4.1 (1.2)	$U = 598, z = -.56, p = .58$

***$p < .05$**

Comparison of pre- and post-intervention score

It can be seen that most of the children of parents in both groups were within the normal range of the SDQ. Looking at the pre- and post-test scores for the experimental groups (Table 5.20), however, it can be seen that there was an increase in the percentage of adolescents in the normal and borderline ranges and a decrease

Table 5.20 Pre- and post-intervention SDQ scores for experimental groups (n = 65)

Category	*Normal*		*Borderline*		*Abnormal*	
	Before	*After*	*Before*	*After*	*Before*	*After*
Emotional symptoms	43 (67.2%)	52 (81.3%)	12 (18.8%)	3 (3.2%)	9 (14.1%)	9 (14.1%)
Conduct problems	40 (62.5%)	44 (68.8%)	10 (15.6%)	10 (15.6%)	14 (21.9%)	10 (15.6%)
Hyperactivity	50 (78.1%)	54 (84.4%)	8 (12.5%)	7 (10.9%)	6 (9.4%)	3 (4.7%)
Peer problems	34 (53.1%)	40 (62.5%)	11 (17.2%)	7 (10.9%)	19 (29.7%)	17 (26.6%)
Pro-social behaviour	34 (53.1%)	38 (59.4%)	14 (21.9%)	20 (31.3%)	16 (25%)	6 (9.4%)
Total difficulties	43 (67.2%)	45 (70.3%)	9 (14.1%)	13 (20.3%)	12 (18.7%)	6 (9.4%)

Table 5.21 Pre- and post-intervention SDQ scores for comparison group (n = 26)

Category	*Normal*		*Borderline*		*Abnormal*	
	Before	*After*	*Before*	*After*	*Before*	*After*
Emotional symptoms	19 (73%)	21 (80.8%)	2 (7.7%)	2 (7.7%)	5 (19.2%)	3 (11.5%)
Conduct problems	19 (73%)	21 (80.8%)	3 (11.5%)	2 (7.7%)	4 (15.4%)	3 (11.5%)
Hyperactivity	20 (76.9%)	21 (80.8%)	2 (7.7%)	0	4 (15.4%)	5 (19.2%)
Peer problems	15 (57.7%)	16 (61.5%)	5 (19.2%)	6 (23.1%)	6 (23.1%)	4 (15.4%)
Pro-social behaviour	21 (80.8%)	20 (76.9%)	3 (11.5%)	4 (15.4%)	2 (7.7%)	2 (7.7%)
Total difficulties	21 (80.8%)	20 (76.9%)	0	4 (15.4%)	5 (19.2%)	2 (7.7%)

in all subscale and total scores. In the comparison group, the only difference was in the peer problem subscale score. This may indicate that there were more positive changes in the experimental than the comparison groups, but this cannot be concluded without statistical examination.

This was explored using non-parametric testing for the reasons given earlier. The Wilcoxon Signed-Rank test, the non-parametric equivalent of the t-test of related samples, was used to test the significance of the pre- and post-test score changes. This test is appropriate for testing the relationship between dichotomous and continuous variables in related samples (Wuensch, 2011). Firstly, the difference between the before and after score in each pair is computed, and then the absolute values of the difference scores are ranked and the sums of the two ranks obtained. This produces two sets of information on the sum of positive and negative ranks. A negative rank means that the post-test score is smaller than the pre-test score, while positive rank means the reverse. The test statistic, *T*, is the smaller of these sums for a non-directional test. If the difference in the two scores is zero, this is ignored since it does not provide any information (Dancey & Reidy, 2002). If there are no significant differences between the two conditions, there will be a similar number of pluses or minuses.

Table 5.22 shows that the change in total SDQ score ($T = 784$, $n = 64$, $p < .05$) was statistically significant. In addition, the sum of the negative difference ranks ($\Sigma R- = 784$) was larger than the sum of the positive difference ranks ($\Sigma R+ = 344$), demonstrating that the programme had had a positive impact. A negative difference rank means that the post-test SDQ is smaller than the pre-test score and a positive difference rank means the reverse. Since the sum of the negative ranks was higher than the sum of the positive ranks, this indicates the positive impact of the programme. In addition, the effect size can also be calculated from the statistic generated.

The effect size of the SDQ total score of the experimental groups was calculated as 0.29. Cohen (1988) defines a small effect size as 0.10, medium as 0.30 and large as 0.50. The result therefore indicated a small effect size.

In addition, the Wilcoxon Signed-Rank test of the SDQ emotional problem subscale score for the experimental groups indicated that there was a significant pre- and post-test difference ($T = 649$, $n = 64$, $p < .05$). Furthermore, the sum of the negative difference ranks ($\Sigma R- = 649$) is more than the positive difference ranks ($\Sigma R+ = 254$), indicating the programme had had a positive impact. The effect size of the emotional problem score was 0.31, which indicated a medium effect size. Nevertheless, the same test performed on the other subscales of the SDQ indicated no significant pre- or post-test differences for the experimental

Table 5.22 Statistical test of pre- and post-test SDQ scores for the experimental groups

	Before	*After*	*Wilcoxon Signed-Rank test / Significance (2-tailed)*	*Effect size (d)*
	Mean (SD)	*Mean (SD)*		
SDQ total	11.45 (5.31)	10.33 (4.86)	$T = 784$, $n = 65$, $p = .02$*	0.29
SDQ pro-social subscale	6.05 (2.24)	6.09 (1.73)	$T = 448.5$, $n = 65$, $p = .76$	0.04
SDQ hyperactivity subscale	4.11 (1.99)	3.83 (1.87)	$T = 604$, $n = 65$, $p = .19$	0.16
SDQ emotional problem subscale	2.61 (1.97)	2.06 (2.05)	$T = 649$, $n = 65$, $p = .01$*	0.31
SDQ peer problems subscale	2.63 (1.96)	2.53 (1.67)	$T = 555.5$, $n = 65$, $p = .67$	0.05
SDQ conduct problems subscale	2.08 (1.60)	1.94 (1.51)	$T = 535.5$, $n = 65$, $p = .44$	0.10

$^*p < .05$

Table 5.23 Statistical test of pre- and post-test SDQ scores for the comparison group ($n = 26$)

	Before	*After*	*Wilcoxon Signed-Rank test / Significance (2-tailed)*	*Effect size (d)*
	Mean (SD)	*Mean (SD)*		
SDQ total	10.0 (5.69)	9.2 (4.65)	$T = 122.5$, $n = 26$, $p = .63$	0.09
SDQ pro-social subscale	7.0 (1.78)	9.2 (1.75)	$T = 76$, $n = 26$, $p = .67$	0.08
SDQ hyperactivity subscale	3.5 (2.61)	3.6 (2.45)	$T = 71$, $n = 26$, $p = .80$	0.05
SDQ emotional problem subscale	2.5 (2.16)	2.2 (1.59)	$T = 67.5$, $n = 26$, $p = .41$	0.16
SDQ peer problems subscale	2.4 (1.27)	2.1 (1.29)	$T = 111$, $n = 26$, $p = .61$	0.10
SDQ conduct problems subscale	1.6 (1.65)	1.4 (1.47)	$T = 53$, $n = 26$, $p = .68$	0.08

***$p < .05$**

groups. This shows that the experimental groups saw a reduction in score for the SDQ overall and the emotional problem subscale after the parenting programme.

A Wilcoxon Signed-Rank test was also performed on SDQ scores of the comparison group. As shown in Table 5.23, the results were not significant.

PSI–SF

This was used to examine the parenting stress of participants. It is a 36-item questionnaire measuring three factors: parenting distress, parent–child dysfunctional interaction and difficult child. A higher score indicates greater difficulties. Table 5.24 reports the scores categorised as indicating normal and clinically significant stress levels.

It may be observed from Table 5.25 that fewer participants reported a reduction from clinically significant levels of stress in all but the difficult child subscale scores. A Wilcoxon Signed-Rank test was used to test the significance of these changes in score. As shown in Table 5.27, the post-test total stress scores were lower than the pre-programme scores. The Wilcoxon test ($T = 590$) was converted into a z-score of -2.04 with an associated two-tailed probability of 0.04 (i.e., $p < .05$). The sum of negative difference ranks ($\sum R- = 1426$) is more than the positive difference ranks ($\sum R+ = 590$), indicating the programme had a positive impact. The effect size of the total stress score was 0.36, indicating a medium effect size. In addition, the same test performed on other subscales of the PSI–SF indicated the pre- and post-test differences in all other subscales were significant. It can therefore be concluded that the total parenting stress of participants in the experimental groups was reduced after taking part in the programme.

Table 5.24 PSI–SF category scores

Category	*Normal*	*Clinically significant*
Parental distress	20–31	33–49
Parent–child dysfunctional interaction	14–25	26–35
Difficult child	19–31	32–49
Total stress score	56–82	83–112

Table 5.25 Pre- and post-intervention PSI–SF scores for experimental groups (n = 65)

Category	*Normal*		*Clinically significant*	
	Before	*After*	*Before*	*After*
Parental distress	31 (48.4%)	34 (53.1%)	33 (51.6%)	30 (46.9%)
Parent–child dysfunctional interaction	9 (14.1%)	13 (20.3%)	55 (85.9%)	51 (79.7%)
Difficult child	41 (64.1%)	41 (64.1%)	23 (35.9%)	23 (35.9%)
Total stress score	13 (20.3%)	16 (25%)	51 (79.7%)	48 (75%)

Table 5.26 Pre- and post-intervention PSI–SF scores for comparison group (n = 26)

Category	*Normal*		*Clinically significant*	
	Before	*After*	*Before*	*After*
Parental distress	16 61.5%)	15 (57.7%)	10 (38.5%)	11 (42.3%)
Parent–child dysfunctional interaction	7 (26.9%)	6 (23.1%)	19 (73.1%)	20 (76.9%)
Difficult child	17 (65.4%)	22 (84.6%)	9 (34.6%)	4 (15.4%)
Total stress score	10 (38.5%)	10 (38.5%)	16 (61.5%)	16 (61.5%)

Table 5.27 Statistical test of pre- and post-test PSI–SF scores for the experimental groups (n = 65)

	Before	*After*	*Wilcoxon Signed-Rank test / Significance (2-tailed)*	*Effect size (d)*
	Mean (SD)	*Mean (SD)*		
Total stress score	96.1 (21.1)	89.8 (23.2)	T = 590, n = 64, p = .00*	0.36
Parental distress	32.3 (8.2)	30.4 (8.1)	T = 506, n = 64, p = .04*	0.26
Parent–child dysfunctional interaction	32.3 (7.8)	30.2 (7.7)	T = 537, n = 64, p = .01*	0.33
Difficult child	31.5 (8.2)	29.2 (9.9)	T = 529, n = 64, p = .01*	0.32

***p < .05**

Table 5.28 Statistical test of pre- and post-test PSI–SF scores for the comparison group ($n = 26$)

	Before	*After*	*Wilcoxon Signed-Rank test / Significance (2-tailed)*	*Effect size (d)*
	Mean (SD)	*Mean (SD)*		
Parental distress	30.0 (8.4)	31.0 (8.1)	$T = 122.5$, $n = 26$, $p = 0.51$	0.13
Parent–child dysfunctional interaction	30.2 (6.2)	29.3 (5.6)	$T = 98$, $n = 26$, $p = 0.22$	0.24
Difficult child	28.1 (7.9)	26.4(6.5)	$T = 94.5$, $n = 26$, $p = 0.11$	0.31
Total stress score	88.8 (19.4)	88.7 (17.4)	$T = 131.5$, $n = 26$, $p = 0.40$	0.16

$^*p < .05$

On the other hand, Table 5.26 shows that there was no change for the comparison group in the parental stress subscale and total scores. In addition, more parents reported clinically significant levels of stress on the parent–child dysfunction subscale. Nevertheless, fewer parents reported clinically significant results on the difficult child subscale.

Table 5.27 shows that there was a post-test reduction in the mean scores of all the subscales. The Wilcoxon Signed-Rank test indicated that all these reductions were significant. The effect size for the total score was 0.36, which is a medium effect. This result suggests that there had been a statistically significant reduction in the PSI–SF scores of the experimental groups after taking part in the programme with a medium effect size.

A reduction in post-test scores was also observed in the comparison group (see Table 5.28), but this was not significant according to the Wilcoxon Signed-Rank test. It can therefore be concluded that there was a statistically significant reduction in the PSI–SF score of the experimental but not the comparison groups after the programme.

PAC

This was developed by Robin and Foster (1989) based on the Conflict Behaviour Questionnaire (Prinz, 1977) and is designed to measure perceived conflict behaviours at home. It also provides a general estimate of how much conflict and negative communication there is within a family and the level of distress its members are experiencing with reference to their pattern of interaction (Robin & Foster, 1989). The version of the PAC adopted in this study was the short form of the Conflict Behaviour Questionnaire. This scale has been tested and correlates .96 or higher with the longer-form scores. The highest possible score is 20; a mean score indicating distress for mothers is 12.4, while for fathers it is 10.5. The non-distressed mean score for mothers is 2.4 and 3.2 for fathers.

Table 5.29 PAC pre- and post-test scores for the experimental and comparison groups

	Before	*After*	*Wilcoxon Signed-Rank test / Significance (2-tailed)*	*Effect Size (d)*
	Mean (SD)	*Mean (SD)*		
Experimental groups	8.6 (4.9)	6.6 (4.7)	$T = 1297$, $n = 65$, $p = .00$*	0.43
Comparison group	6.1 (4.8)	5.0 (4.2)	$T = 70.5$, $n = 26$, $p = .07$	0.36

***$p < .05$**

Table 5.29 shows that the mean post-test PAC scores were smaller than the pre-test scores for the experimental groups. The Wilcoxon Signed-Rank test ($T = 414$) was converted into a *z*-score of −3.438 with an associated two-tailed probability of 0.00 (that is, $p < .05$). The sum of the negative difference ranks ($\Sigma R- = 1297$) is more than the positive ($\Sigma R+ = 414$), indicating the programme had a positive impact. The effect size was 0.43, indicating a medium effect.

On the other hand, Table 5.29 also shows that there was a post-test reduction in mean score for the comparison group as well. Again, a Wilcoxon Signed-Rank test was performed to see if the change in scores across groups was significant. The score ($T = 182.5$) was converted into a *z*-score of −.18 with an associated two-tailed probability of 0.07 ($p > .05$), indicating that it was not.

It may therefore be concluded that there was a significant reduction in the pre- and post-test SDQ, PSI–SF and PAC scores for the experimental groups, with a medium effect size. On the other hand, there was also a non-significant decrease in all scores in the comparison group.

Repeated-measures ANOVA (RM-ANOVA)

The findings reported above suggested that there had been a statistically significant reduction in scores for the experimental groups after the programme, while the same changes for the comparison group were not significant. Nevertheless, it is necessary to undertake further analysis to determine whether the reduction in score could be attributed to the programme or may have arisen from other factors. RM-ANOVA was used to compute the between- and within-participants differences for the experimental groups. This test is used to determine whether a statistically significant change has occurred when the same subjects have been measured more than once, for example pre- and post-test (Vogt, 1999). A RM-ANOVA can identify within-group (scores pre- and post-test) and between-group (experimental and comparison) differences. This avoids the statistical difficulties involved in interpreting the data when participants have responded twice to the same instrument. There may be a strong likelihood that those who have scored higher in the first measurement will tend to be closer to the average in the second: the phenomenon known as "regression to the mean". If this happened for those participants who had scored high in the pre-test measures, the null hypothesis would be wrongly rejected (that is, a type I error) if the significant reduction in score was not attributed to the parenting programme. The RM-ANOVA was therefore used to test for any interaction and group effects between the pre- and post-test scores and between groups.

Since the data collected in the SDQ, PSI–SF and PAC were not normally distributed, they were transformed into a normal distribution by the SPSS software. The RM-ANOVA was then used to test for within-group and between-participants differences.

As can be seen from Table 5.30, there were no significant changes in the SDQ scores over time ($F(1, .03) = 2$, $p = .16$). In addition, there was a non-significant between-group difference ($F(1, .01) = .58$, $p = .58$), meaning that the experimental and comparison groups were changing in more or less the same way. In other words, the changes observed were not attributable to the parenting programme. It can be further observed from Figure 5.1 that while there was a

Table 5.30 RM-ANOVA of SDQ scores

Source	*Mean square*	*Sum of squares*	*df*	*F*	*p*
Time	.03	.03	1	2.0	.16
Time × experimental gp and control gp	.01	.01	1	.58	.58
Error (time)	.02	1.4	88		

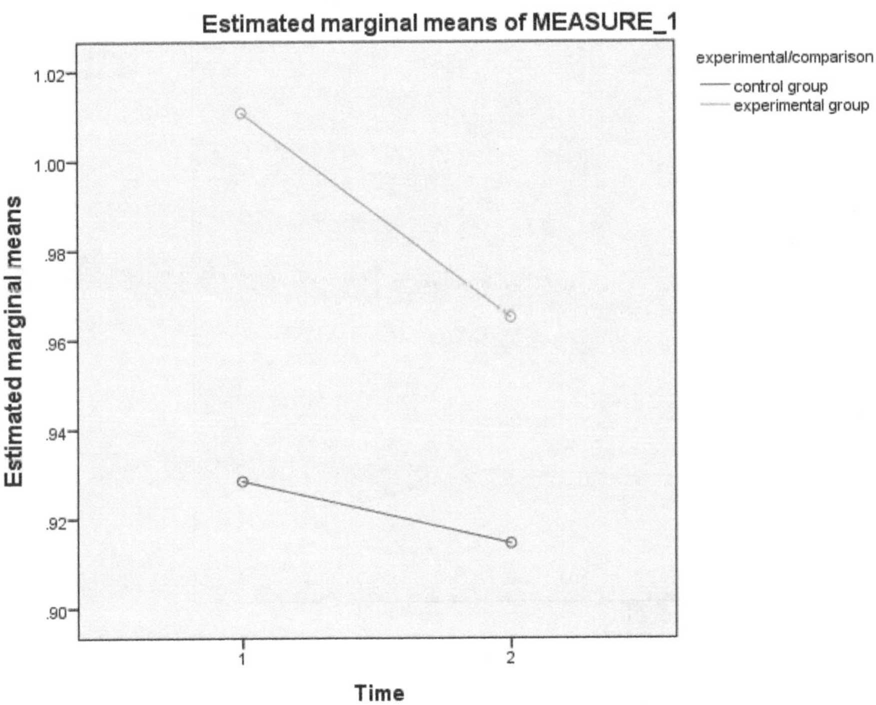

Figure 5.1 Strength and Difficulties Questionnaire

reduction in the pre- and post-test scores of both groups, the two lines are almost parallel, meaning that there was no interaction effect between time and group.

A similar RM-ANOVA test was performed on the PSI–SF scores. As shown in Table 5.31, there was a significant within-group difference for the experimental groups (F (1, .01) = 5.27, p = .02), meaning that there was a significant change in score across time. Figure 5.2 indicates that the post-test score was lower. Nevertheless, there was no between-group difference (F (1, .00) = 0.96, p = .33), suggesting that the reduction was more or less the same for the experimental and control groups and hence was not attributable to the parenting programme.

Concerning the PAC scores, Table 5.32 shows that there were significant within-group differences across time (F (1, .48) = 12.6, p = .001) and a significant reduction in scores across time (Figure 5.3). Nevertheless, there was no

Table 5.31 RM-ANOVA of PSI–SF scores

Source	*Sum of squares*	*df*	*Mean square*	*F*	*Sig.*
Time	.01	1	.01	5.27	.02
Time × experimental gp and comparison gp	.00	1	.00	.956	.33
Error (time)	.15	85	.00		

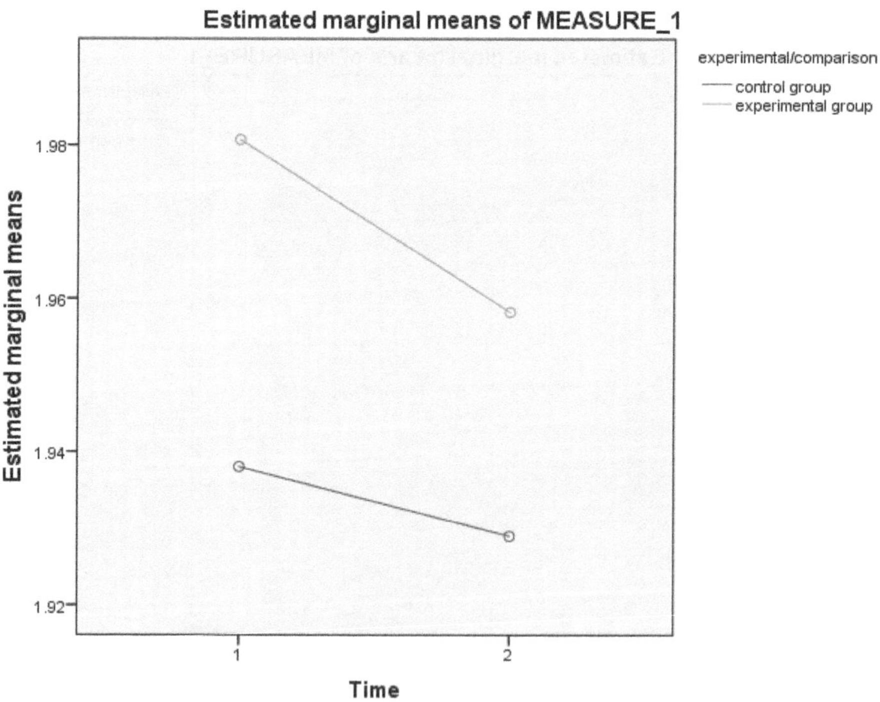

Figure 5.2 Parenting Stress Index Short Form

Table 5.32 Main effect table for PAC scores

Source	*Sum of squares*	*df*	*Mean square*	*F*	*Sig.*
Before and after scores	.478	1	.478	12.6	.001
Interaction effect of score and experimental gp and control gp	.000	1	.000	.04	.947
Error (time)	2.91	77	.038		

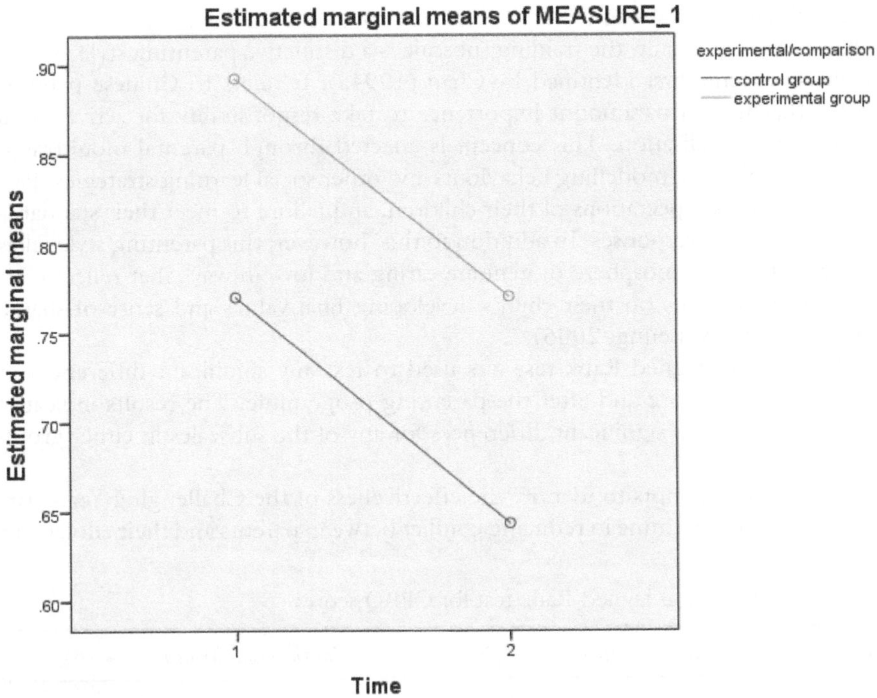

Figure 5.3 Parent–Adolescent Conflict Scale

significant between-group difference ($F(1, .00) = .04$, $p = .95$). Figure 5.3 shows that there was a reduction in post-test scores for both groups, but no between-group difference over time. Again, this suggests there was no significant treatment effect from participating in the programme.

CPBQ

A modified version of the CPBQ (Lieber, Fung & Leung, 2006) was used to measure any changes in parenting belief before and after taking part in the programme. The CPBQ consists of four subscales: authoritative, autonomy, shame and training. The authoritative subscale is considered to be consistent with similar scales developed in Western populations. This concept, when referring to Chinese populations, denotes "awareness, respect, and encouragement for children's exploration and expression of ideas and emotions, encouraging parent–child communication, and recognizing parents' and children's rights" (Lieber, Fung & Leung, 2006: 144). The autonomy subscale refers to "parents' need to encourage, protect, and nurture children's exploration, wills self-concept, expression, and autonomy" (Lieber, Fung & Leung, 2006: 144). The shame subscale denotes a distinctive characteristic of Chinese parenting in which it is important to motivate children to display and express appropriate behaviour. Shame items in the Chinese cultural context are considered to reflect the fostering of pro-social characteristics. Finally, the training subscale is a distinctive parenting style among Chinese parents first identified by Chao (1994a). It refers to Chinese parents' belief that it is of paramount importance to take responsibility for active social and moral socialisation. This concept is enacted through parental monitoring, regular reminders, modelling behaviours and other social learning strategies. Parents have high expectations of their children, and failure to meet their standards can evoke harsh responses. In addition to this, however, this parenting style takes place within an atmosphere of genuine caring and love in ways that reflect Chinese parents' focus on their child's developing filial values and sense of shame (Lieber, Fung & Leung, 2006).

A Wilcoxon Signed-Rank test was used to test any significant differences in CPBQ scores before and after the parenting programme. The results indicated that there were no significant differences for any of the subscales in either group (see Table 5.33).

This study attempts to identify the effectiveness of the Challenging Years parent training programme in reducing conflict between parents and their adolescent

Table 5.33 Wilcoxon Signed-Rank test for CPBQ scores

Category	*Experimental groups* (N = 65)				*Comparison group* (N = 26)			
	Before	*After*	*Sig*	*Effect Size*	*Before*	*After*	*Sig*	*Effect Size*
	Mean (SD)				*Mean (SD)*			
Authoritative	4.6 (0.6)	4.6 (0.7)	$T = 111$, $n = 65$, $p = .86$	0.0	4.6 (0.5)	4.7 (0.5)	$T = 13.5$, $n = 26$, $p = .48$	0.1
Autonomy	3.4 (1.1)	3.3 (1.2)	$T = 293$, $n = 65$, $p = .52$	0.1	2.9 (1.1)	2.8 (1.2)	$T = 53.5$, $n = 26$, $p = .70$	0.1
Shame	2.4 (1.0)	2.4 (1.1)	$T = 276.5$, $n = 65$, $p = .94$	0.0	2.4 (0.9)	2.3 (1.0)	$T = 45.5$, $n = 26$, $p = .65$	0.1
Training	3.9 (1.2)	3.8 (1.3)	$T = 243.5$, $n = 65$, $p = .49$	0.1	3.9 (1.3)	3.9 (1.3)	$T = 76$, $n = 26$, $p = .98$	0.0

children in Hong Kong. A mixed methodology was adopted to achieve methodological triangulation in which quantitative and qualitative data were both collected and analysed separately and then compared in the analysis process. This approach has the advantage of using the strengths of the quantitative and qualitative approaches to achieve the overall objectives of the study. In addition, precautions were taken to resolve ethical issues and to guard against extraneous variables that may affect the reliability of this study. Although the study has a number of limitations, it was hoped that it would add to the existing knowledge in delivering interventions to the parents of adolescents in Hong Kong.

The quantitative anaylsis indicated that the participants were drawn from schools in the Northern District of Hong Kong and had on average two children. Most lived with their partners and the majority were housewives educated to Form 5 level, having left school at 16. They were in the lower reaches of the income spectrum. A comparison of demographic variables between the experimental and comparison groups showed few differences; members of the former tended to be older, as were their children. In addition, the comparison group exhibited lower levels of stress and conflict than the experimental groups. Apart from these differences, the two groups were similar. A comparison between the experimental groups and dropouts indicated no significant differences other than that the dropouts had more children, reported more difficulties with them and were mostly divorced or not living with their partners. This indicated that the dropouts had more family problems or more complex difficulties and so might not have been able to benefit as much from this particular programme.

The statistical tests carried out using non-parametric equivalents to the paired sample t-test indicated that after the parenting programme had been completed, there had been statistically significant reductions in scores for all the measurement scales used. However, no significant differences in scores for the comparison group were found. A RM-ANOVA was carried out to test for any interaction effects between time and groups. This showed that there were no significant group (experimental and control group) or time (pre- and post-test measurement) effects, which means that although the reduction in scores was significant, it could not be attributed to the programme. For the CPBQ, statistical analysis indicated that there were no significant pre- and post-test differences in score for either group, which suggests that the programme had no effect on changing participants' parenting beliefs; however, this was not one of its explicit goals.

Qualitative data analysis

Sixty-five participants from the seven experimental groups participated in semi-structured group interviews after the final session of the parenting programme. A total of seven interviews took place, each lasting around an hour. The aim of the groups was firstly to augment the quantitative data by exploring the participants' reasons for joining the programme; secondly to gather views on what had been effective and ineffective; and thirdly to find out what changes participants perceived as having resulted from their involvement in the programme. The group interviews also provided an opportunity to explore whether there had been culturally specific parenting issues requiring adaptation of the programme to be more suitable for Hong Kong Chinese parents. All groups were asked similar questions, but depending on the flow of the discussion, some questions were covered in some but not all the groups.

As well as the group interviews, all participants were required to fill in a questionnaire before taking part. Participants' written comments provided rich qualitative as well as quantitative data about their reasons for joining the parenting programme, activities that they had found helpful, whether they had talked to their partners about the programme and their suggestions for improving it. In this chapter, the qualitative data from the questionnaire and group interviews are discussed, organised around three important themes: parents' outcomes, adolescents' outcomes and relationships with partners. The qualitative data from the questionnaires are used to support or elaborate further on the points made during the group interviews. In the latter sections, the reasons parents gave for joining the programme, what the facilitator did that best helped them and any culturally sensitive elements identified are further discussed.

Reasons for joining the programme

The questionnaire data indicated that most of the parents (20 of 65, or 30.8%) gave their reason for coming to the programme as a desire "to change my pattern of communication with my adolescent children" (see Table 5.34).

One parent indicated she had come to the programme because she wanted to "establish a trusting relationship [with my children] and know more about the inner thinking of today's adolescents". In addition, parents talked about their reasons for joining the programme in six of the seven group interviews. Participants in four of the groups agreed their main aim was to learn how to communicate better with their adolescent children, with 17 parents referring to this as their reason for joining. Four (23.5%) of these parents also cited "better communication with my adolescent child" as their major reason for coming to the programme.

The second theme identified from the questionnaire was the desire for parents to learn new skills. Nineteen participants (29.2%) indicated that this was their reason for joining the programme (see Table 5.34). Some of the reasons that

Table 5.34 Reasons for joining the programme taken from the questionnaire ($n = 65$)

Category	*Number of participants*
Change of communication pattern	20 (30.8%)
Learning new parenting skills	19 (29.2%)
Understanding contemporary adolescents	16 (24.6%)
Reduce conflict with adolescents	4 (6.2%)
Listen to others' experience	3 (4.6%)
To help my children	3 (4.6%)
Total	65 (100%)

participants gave in the questionnaire were "*to learn new parenting methods*", "*to [learn] how to be an effective parent*" and "*to improve my parenting skills and change my parenting style*".

Consistent with the questionnaire data, among the 17 parents who talked about their reason for joining the programme during the group interviews, four (23.5%) talked about learning new skills as their major motivation.

The third-highest number of parents, 16 (24.6%), gave their reason for joining the programme as a wish to "know more about what adolescents think nowadays" (Table 5.34). In four of the six groups where participants mentioned their reasons for joining the programme, parents also referred to a wish "to understand contemporary adolescents".

Four (6.2%) parents stated in the questionnaire that their reason for joining was "to reduce conflict with my adolescent children", but this reason was only mentioned once during the group interviews. In addition, a wish to "listen to others' experiences" was mentioned by five parents in the questionnaire (7.7%), although only one parent talked about it during the groups.

It can therefore be concluded that the main reasons participants joined the programme were to improve their communication and relationships with their adolescent children. They also wanted to know more about how the adolescents of today think, reduce conflict and learn more effective parenting skills. These answers are consistent with previous studies of programmes for ethnic minority parents, which show that such parents want to learn more about parenting and to better understand contemporary children and young people (Barlow, Shaw & Stewart-Brown, 2004).

These findings are also broadly consistent with a previous qualitative study of perceptions of parenting education in Hong Kong by Lam (2005) which indicates that parents' objectives in joining a parenting programme were to bring about internal changes (that is, to reshape their attitudes and emotional responses to their children). This study similarly indicates that these parents sought out the parenting programme to achieve personal change. The idea of such programmes as part of a process of personal development in values and behaviour is very important to Hong Kong Chinese parents. Similar findings have also emerged from previous studies showing that ethnic minority parents seek out parenting programmes to achieve personal changes such as greater self-control when communicating with their children (Thomas, 2000 quoted in Barlow, Shaw & Steward-Brown, 2004). Nevertheless, other studies indicate that some parents may be less focused on personal change and more interested in obtaining information about how to deal with adolescents' behavioural problems like drug use and violence directed against them (Clarke & Churchill, 2010). This may indicate that motivations for participating in such a programme are culturally specific.

Turning to parents' reasons for continuing with the programme, one theme emerging from the qualitative data was that they wanted to "set a positive example to their adolescent children". In other words, they wanted to demonstrate that once they had enrolled in a programme, they would try their best to complete it. This was one of the most common reasons why parents kept coming back to the programme; it was expressed in two of the interview groups and supported by a number of parents. This suggests that Hong Kong Chinese parents consider setting a positive example for their children to be an important aspect of parenting. The second reason parents kept coming back was because the topic was of interest to them. This idea was talked about by a parent in one group and the others agreed. They had looked forward to participating in the upcoming sessions and had therefore stayed in the group.

One final comment from one of the groups was what the facilitator had done in the first session determined whether parents would come back or not. This may be related to their original objectives. Since the parents were not that familiar with the group, how the facilitator addressed each individual's needs during the first session was therefore very important. In addition, it is possible that if parents are engaged early by the facilitator, they will stay in the programme. Finally, the drivers for parents' continued attendance stem from both their own motivation to set a positive example and the programme content as well as the supportive environment of the group.

Parents' outcomes

The questionnaire indicated that a large majority of the participants had found the programme very helpful (21.5%) or helpful (75.4%), with more than 90% giving a positive response (Table 5.35).

In addition, a large number of parents remarked that they had noticed a major improvement in their communication skills after the programme, with this being mentioned in 36 of the 65 questionnaire responses. Furthermore, on 22 occasions parents referred to having learned listening skills. In terms of the number of times topics were mentioned in the questionnaires, these were among the highest scoring. As an example, one parent wrote about better communication as follows:

> *We need to listen to our children. The other day I talked to my son about what he would like to do when he grows up. He said that if he has money then he can do anything he likes. I didn't comment on his idea immediately although I did not agree with him. Instead, I tried to understand his reasons for saying this and did not give my opinion immediately.*

A similar picture emerged from the group interviews. Becoming a better communicator with one's children was the most common theme in all the groups.

Table 5.35 Overall views of participants (n = 65)

Category	*Number of participants*
Very helpful	14 (21.5%)
Quite helpful	49 (75.4%)
Not very helpful	2 (3.1%)
Not at all helpful	0 (0%)
Total	65 (100%)

It is instructive to look at the examples given by some respondents about how they had learned to control their own emotions when communicating with their adolescents. One parent said:

> *When my daughter started to be emotional, I learned to calm myself down. If both of us were using a loud voice towards each other, we cannot communicate afterwards. This is very important. When my daughter was in a temper, I will calm myself first and not to be affected by her.*

It was observed that at least one participant in each group talked about how they had learned how to calm their own emotions when their adolescents had become emotional in conversation. The other participants would always agree. In one group, one participant spoke about her daughter had seen changes in her after joining the programme:

> *My daughter said "Mother, you have changed". I said to her "Yes, and it is very difficult for me. But for your benefit, I will continue the five-week course even though I have a serious neck pain".*

The programme thus had the effect of helping some participants to understand how to control their emotions when communicating with their teenage children. Indeed, the change experienced by the above participant had been acknowledged by her daughter. This theme is consistent with previous work on ethnic minority parenting programmes, in which parents reported having more self-control afterward (Barlow, Shaw & Stewart-Brown, 2004). It can therefore be seen that one of the outcomes for parents participating in the programme in this study was a greater awareness of, and ability to control, their own emotions when communicating with their adolescent children.

Another change perceived by participants was in their listening skills. For example, one participant indicated that the programme had provided her with an opportunity to learn how to listen to the feelings behind someone's words. This had led to better and more open communication between her and her daughter:

> *Before I joined this programme, I did not have the courage to ask my daughter about her dating life. After the programme, I had the courage to ask whether she is now dating a boy. But she said no.*

In general, it is very difficult for Chinese parents to talk openly with their children about dating or their sex lives. The responses here indicated that the programme had helped to encourage some participants to take a step further in communicating with their children. Another example illustrates the improvement in communication:

> *We used to have very little communication with our son, but now we talk more with each other. The facilitator said that we need to have at least 15 minutes*

> *communication each day. My son used not to respond to what I said, but now there is more communication. My husband also joins in the communication. We share our happiness as well as our difficulties. Although he [son] does not say much, it is a big improvement that at least he says something. Before, when my husband would ask my son "My son, how was your exam today?" he would only say "Umm . . ." but after the programme, he said "Not so good". This showed at least there is a difference.*

Furthermore, eight parents mentioned in the questionnaire that transactional analysis (Harris, 2004) had been helpful in their parenting practice. This supports the findings from the group interviews that communication, listening and transactional analysis skills were the major things they had learned from the programme. Transactional analysis is a concept first developed by the American psychologist Eric Berne (Berne, 1975). He observed that humans interact from three different perspectives and called them Parent, Adult and Child. The parenting programme studied here made use of these concepts to help parents understand that difficulties may arise when parents and adolescents use mismatched communication patterns. For example, when parents were in the Parent role (that is, they were ordering or instructing), their adolescent children showed no interest in communicating with them since they wanted to play an Adult role in which both parties would sit down and logically discuss the matter. Some parents found this concept helpful in their communication with their adolescent children. This suggests that another outcome of the programme for parents was that they had become better communicators.

New parenting skills

Parents also used the questionnaires to indicate that "giving more responsibility to my adolescent child" was another aspect they had found useful. Nine of the 65 questionnaires returned made this point, with comments such as "*I can help my adolescents to understand their behaviour is their choice and they need to take responsibility for their behaviour*" and "*we need to give more space for our adolescents to become independent*".

In the interviews, one group of participants talked about learning new skills, particularly in terms of giving more responsibility to their adolescent children rather than doing everything for them. They gave examples like asking the adolescent to take care of elements of the family's daily routine, like cleaning their own rooms. They found that when they gave their children more responsibility, they were able to do what was expected of them.

Another parent mentioned that the facilitator had talked about the statement "it is your choice" as one that could help adolescents to take more responsibility. She thought this was the most impressive statement the facilitator had made and gave examples of where her own children were not really taking responsibility, especially when they faced the choice of secondary schools, extracurricular activities and so on. Sometimes, parents found their adolescent children would blame them for giving them a choice. These parents found that the statement "it is your choice" could help make their children take responsibility for themselves.

In addition, 11 responses out of 65 mentioned the importance of "learning new parenting styles" through the programme. This may relate to the third session, in which the facilitators talked about different parenting styles and helped parents to establish an assertive style. Furthermore, another 11 parents mentioned 'better parenting' as the thing that they had learned from the programme, reinforcing the view from the group interviews that participants had learned better parenting skills in the programme.

Feeling supported

A few participants said that they had felt supported by the parenting programme. Three parents in two groups talked about the support they had received. One said that when she listened to other parents sharing their experiences, she felt that she was not alone and that she was being supported by the others. Another parent from a different group said that she found that her daughter's behaviour was not the worst when compared with the other participants' children. She had previously thought that she had a lot of problems with parenting but found that others shared the same problems, which made her feel supported. This suggested that the parenting programme was perceived by some parents as creating a supportive environment among the participants, which in turn could help them gain confidence in being the parents of adolescents. This is consistent with previous findings on the effectiveness of parenting programmes, which have shown that parents tend to feel supported within the programme (Wolfe & Haddy, 2001; Moran *et al.*, 2004). In addition, one study of Chinese parents' experience with Filial Therapy programmes shows that they appreciated being supported by other parents (Barlow, Shaw & Stewart-Brown, 2004).

The supportive environment of the programme was also another important reason participants stayed in the group. One father explained the importance of sharing:

> *When we share with the others, different people have different views on parenting. When other parents did not agree with me, I could think more about my own views. If I had not joined the programme and just focused on my own family, sometimes I would have lost my direction in parenting. To share with other parents helps me to think more about myself.*

This example of sharing views and ideas with other parents as a means to enhance self-awareness is similar to the findings of First and Way's (1995) study of parents' experiences with a parenting group, which found that one of the effects of the programme was to provide an opportunity for parents to meet each other to socialise and share skills and tips (First & Way, 1995).

Confidence in parenting adolescents

Most of the parents in one of the interview groups agreed that they had developed more confidence in their parenting as a result of the programme. They now understood more about the problems they were experiencing with their adolescent children and had some ideas for how to solve them. One mother explained that she had developed a better understanding of her daughter's needs which gave her more confidence as a parent. Other parents agreed and said that they also understood better how today's adolescents think, which had helped them to gain confidence.

Parent–adolescent outcomes

Two important themes emerged about parent–adolescent outcomes: the parent–adolescent relationship itself and conflict resolution.

In terms of the first of these, there were various examples of better parent–adolescent relationships after the programme as reported in the questionnaires:

> *I give more praise to my children and have changed how I communicate. Now we are happier than before and have less conflict.*
>
> *When resolving conflict, I learned that when my children get in a temper I can give them a little space.*
>
> *I used to order my adolescent daughter to take her shower before dinner. Now, I let her do this any time she likes before going to bed.*
>
> *I learned not to talk to my children in a loud voice. I also learned not to say things that hurt their self-concept like "you are foolish". Praising more can strengthen the sense of self of the child.*
>
> *Yes, because I will now focus on her feelings first, listen first and then give her instructions.*

Parents in three of the seven group interviews talked about how their relationships with their adolescent children had improved after the programme. For example, they reported spending more time talking to each other and sharing feelings, and having a better understanding of the reasons behind their children's requests. In addition, one parent talked about how she had developed a better understanding of her adolescent's thinking and was more able to see things from her perspective than before. Another mentioned that since attending the programme she and her adolescent children now talked to each other about their daily lives. Another group of parents talked about having more two-way communication with their adolescents than previously. These examples were given by participants who felt that their relationship with their children had improved as a result of the programme. One parent said that she stopped rejecting her child's requests immediately but listened to her explanation first: "*the change I observe in myself was that I now let my child talk about their ideas first to see if I can accept them*".

In terms of conflict resolution, the majority of participants (93.9%) indicated in the questionnaire that the programme had been very or quite helpful in assisting them to reduce conflict (see Table 5.36).

This was consistent with one of the themes in the group interviews, where participants said they experienced less conflict with their adolescent children after the programme. Parents in four out of the seven groups talked about how they had changed their ways of resolving conflict with their adolescent children. Some said that they had previously been very bad-tempered and had talked to their children in a very loud voice, but after joining the programme they had learned to be calmer when interacting with their children and experienced less conflict as a result.

Other parents gave examples of how they had resolved conflicts with their children. One described her daughter looking for some of her belongings and being in a bad temper about it. The participant was also angry because of her daughter's reliance on her to solve the problem. They were in conflict. However, the participant was eventually able to calm herself down and help her daughter find her things. This example illustrates two very important issues; after the programme, parents were not only better able to control their emotions but also more able to solve conflicts with their children together.

Another important theme was the dilemma of Hong Kong Chinese parents who want their adolescents to be independent (that is, not relying on others) but eventually do help their children to solve their problems. This inconsistency is common among parents in Hong Kong. Related to this is the finding from previous studies that there is a delay in the age at which adolescents in Hong Kong are expected to be autonomous compared with their Western counterparts (Feldman & Rosenthal, 1991). This means that Hong Kong Chinese adolescents do not expect to be able to spend time with their friends or on their own until they are older (Fuligni, 1998). This may imply that Hong Kong Chinese parents spend more time than their Western counterparts taking care of their teenage children.

Furthermore, one parent learned from the programme to resolve conflict by setting out boundaries of acceptable and unacceptable behaviour. Another parent said she helped her adolescent to consider the pros and cons of her decisions before making her own comments. All these examples showed that some (but

Table 5.36 Reducing conflict with adolescents ($n = 65$)

Category	*Number of participants*
Very helpful	15 (22.7%)
Quite helpful	46 (69.7%)
Not very helpful	4 (6.1%)
Not at all helpful	0
No indication	1 (1.5%)
Total	65 (100%)

not all) parents had learned some new ways to resolve conflict with their adolescent children. This is consistent with previous findings that attitudes to parenting become more positive after participating in such a programme (Moran *et al.*, 2004; Wolfe & Haddy, 2001; Barlow, Shaw & Stewart-Brown, 2004).

Changes in the adolescents

The other theme identified from the group interviews was that of changes in the adolescents themselves. An interesting, but not surprising, indicator is that most of the participants thought that their teenage children now spent more time studying, were more self-motivated to study and spent more time doing homework. All the parents in one of the groups made comments of this type. In addition, those in other groups talked about changes in their adolescents like being more obedient and going to bed earlier at night. Two parents in two different groups observed that their adolescent children were now more able to control their emotions and were more willing to talk to them than before. All of these are examples of changes observed by parents after the programme.

Another point that emerged in one of the groups was that adolescents were more aware of their attitude when talking to their parents after the programme. One parent reported that when her teenage daughter noticed that she had joined a parenting programme and wanted to change, she also changed her attitude towards her mother. The distance between them reduced and they became closer. This highlights an interesting issue about parents' concerns about their adolescents' attitude towards them, given that filial piety (meaning total and unconditional obedience and unquestioned compliance with parents' wishes) is generally highly valued in Chinese culture (Harrell, 1982, quoted in Kim & Wong, 2002).

Outcomes in relationships with partners

Nine parents indicated on their questionnaires that they had discussed what they had learned with their partners. They had done so because they recognised the importance of having a shared understanding of their parenting methods. Another point mentioned by most of the parents was that parenting is a common concern for oneself and one's partner. Furthermore, some parents indicated that they needed support from their partners. Those parents who had shared their insights with their partners had an understanding that it was very important to have their partners' support in order to parent their adolescent children properly. On the other hand, eight parents gave reasons why they had not discussed the programme with their partners. Four reported that they did not have time to talk about it with their partner and the other four said their partners would not cooperate even though they had tried and so they had chosen not to talk about this any further.

In relation to the themes emerging from the group discussions, six mothers from four of the groups talked about having an improved relationship with their partners after the programme. All of them had found that they had experienced less conflict with their partners. One of the mothers went on to explain that she had talked to her husband about what she had learned from the programme. They were now intending to find a compromise approach to parenting their adolescents. She felt better about having her husband on her side. Another mother talked about having a better relationship with her husband because he had asked her about what she had learned from the programme. A father from one of the other groups explained that after the first session he had decided that the programme was helpful and so invited his wife to join in from that point, which she did.

The majority of the parents shared their difficulties with their partners. However, most participants in the group interviewed said that their relationships had not changed as result, most commonly because they did not have enough time or had nothing to talk about with each other. As one woman explained, "*most of the time I am alone. We [her husband and her] are more distant than before. We have no time to talk about parenting*". Another woman said the reason she had not talked to her husband about the programme was because of their relationship and in particular the lack of time together:

> *When I talked to my husband, he did not reply. Talking to him about this meant nothing. I am going to solve the parenting problem alone rather than talking to my husband. He usually leaves early to go to work in the morning and comes home late at night after work.*

Another parent talked about experiencing difficulties when she wanted some assistance from her husband on parenting. Usually he would not say anything while she parented their children. As she put it, "*my husband would not say anything when I am talking to my teenage children. He would not say anything and will only let me talk to them*".

One mother talked about her difficulties in facing the conflict between her husband and her daughter.

> *My husband has very high expectations of my daughter's performance. He uses a very rude tone and gets angry when he talks to her. I have asked him one question, "do you want to settle the conflict or do you want to be the winner?" I have asked him to use some other method, but it is difficult.*

Some of the fathers also talked about their difficulties when sharing what they had learned with their partners. One explained that his wife was not able to control her own emotions when parenting their adolescents, even after he had talked to her about it. Another father talked about the difficulties he faced because after the programme he wanted his adolescent children to become more independent, while his wife wanted to look after them more and would not agree to cooperate with him.

Such examples show that many participants felt they lacked support from their partners when parenting their adolescent children, with a feeling of loneliness evident beneath the words. This suggests the importance of having both parents attend classes wherever possible. Previous work shows that fathers' involvement in parenting training is associated with longer-term improvement in their children (Eyberg & Robinson, 1982). In addition, if both parents take part they can support each other to practise the skills taught in the programme (Tiano & McNeil, 2005). There is some evidence to suggest that if fathers participate in parenting programmes with their partners the effects of the programme are enhanced (Moran & Ghate, 2005). Some authors emphasise the importance of including both parents, while the findings of other research on whether to include fathers are mixed (Lundahl *et al.*, 2008).

In addition, it is clear that when both parents come, they may develop better strategies that can help them provide more appropriate parenting to their adolescent children. The data discussed above suggest that some Hong Kong Chinese families still rely strongly on mothers to do most of the parenting, and that in some families there was little cooperation between the partners in parenting. Other studies also indicate that American men tend to participate significantly less in child-rearing activities than their wives (McBride & Rane, 1997).

The sessions most helpful to participants

In the questionnaires, parents were also asked to evaluate the sessions and elements within the programme. All the major topics covered were listed and participants were asked to indicate if each had been helpful or unhelpful. The results are summarised in Table 5.37 and Table 5.38. Since more than one session or element could be selected, the total number of responses is more than the total number of participants.

Table 5.37 Sessions that participants found helpful (total number of responses: 159)

Category	*Helpful*
Session 1 Understanding teenagers	34 (21.4%)
Session 2 Communication skills	40 (25.2%)
Session 3 Parenting style	43 (27%)
Session 4 Conflict resolution	42 (26.4%)
Total	159 (100%)

Table 5.38 Elements that participants found helpful (total number of responses: 183)

Category	*Helpful*
Understanding teenagers' development	28 (15.3%)
Listening and empathic skills	54 (29.5%)
Giving compliments	44 (24.0%)
Assertive parenting	23 (12.6%)
Conflict-resolution skills	34 (18.6%)
Total	183 (100%)

Most parents (27%) indicated that the session on assertive parenting had been useful. The other session that they had found especially helpful was the one on conflict resolution (26.4%).

It can be seen that most of the participants (29.5%) considered listening and empathic skills as particularly helpful in reducing conflict with their adolescent children, followed by the sessions on giving compliments (24.0%) and conflict-resolution skills (18.6%). These results indicate that the most important aspect of the programme was helping participants to improve their communication skills and understand more about adolescents' development. Based on these foundations, the introduction of conflict-resolution skills was also helpful to participants.

The results also showed that although participants considered communication skills and understanding teenagers as the most important elements of the programme, they enjoyed the sessions on parenting style and conflict resolution more, perhaps because these involved more role plays and sharing. In addition, by discussing different parenting styles and conflict-resolution strategies, parents were also able to learn communication skills and improve their understanding of contemporary adolescents. This could therefore be another of the reasons they preferred these sessions.

Parents in all the groups said that they found all the sessions helpful. When asked to explain their reasons, a diverse set of opinions emerged.

One father said that he had found the first session helpful because it had helped him to understand more about how adolescents think today. This was closely related to his own objective for participation. Two other members of his group agreed that the first session had been very helpful. As one of them put it:

> *The first session helped me to understand what adolescents are thinking nowadays. And we cannot always look at the children's weakness without looking at their strengths.*

Another session nominated by three groups as the most helpful was the second session on listening and communication. One parent explained that because this session made use of role play, they could try out the new skills immediately. For the same reason, two groups regarded the last session, conflict management, as the most useful. This suggests that parents will welcome sessions involving role play in which they can try out what they have learned.

One father said that the third session on parenting style was the most helpful, but there were no other specific mentions of this in the other groups. It may be concluded from the above that the favourite session for most participants in the group interviews was communication and listening, followed by the first session on understanding adolescents and then conflict management. The least favourite was the parenting style session. The reason for these choices was partly because there were opportunities for the participants to try out their new skills through role play and partly because these were the topics most parents had come to the programme to learn about.

In terms of the type of activities that participants found useful, the data from the interviews showed that parents in all seven groups favoured sharing and group discussion, in which they could share their views on parenting. In addition, the role play and interactive elements allowed them to discuss topics with the facilitator. Interestingly, a parent in one of the groups said that at the time she had not really been comfortable with the interactive nature of the programme in which parents had to role play the new skills and engage in a lot of discussion with the facilitator. Nevertheless, looking back, she had found this useful.

Importance of facilitation style

In general, participants considered the way the facilitator had led the group to be very important (37.9%) or quite important (57.6%) to the success of the programme (Table 5.39). The questionnaire also asked participants to give a view on the qualities of a facilitator that they considered to be important. Most of the respondents considered giving advice on how to handle adolescents as the most important skill for a facilitator (see Table 5.40). In other words, the participants valued a facilitator who could address their problems during the programme. The

Table 5.39 How important was the way the facilitator led the group to the success of the programme? (n = 65)

Category	*Number of participants*
Very important	25 (37.9%)
Quite important	38 (57.6%)
Not very important	2 (3%)
Not at all important	0
No indication	1 (1.5%)
Total	65 (100%)

Table 5.40 Valued qualities of a facilitator (n = 65)

Category	*Number of participants*
Giving advice on how to handle your adolescent children	57 (87.7%)
Interactive presentation skills	57 (87.7%)
Teaching of new skills	54 (81.8%)
Friendly, warm and sincere attitude	51 (78.5%)
Experience of being a parent	49 (75.4%)
Able to give empathy and understand your situation	46 (70.8%)
Able to create a supportive and trusting relationship among participants	45 (69.2%)
Providing local examples	45 (69.2%)
Good interpersonal skills	41 (63.1%)
Social work experience	41 (63.1%)
Qualification	28 (43.1%)
Not looking down on you	25 (38.5%)

next most important quality of a facilitator was being able to give an interactive presentation and teach participants new skills. Furthermore, a friendly, warm and sincere attitude; the facilitator's own experience of being a parent; and being able to display empathy and understand participants' situation were among other valued qualities.

Other areas that were less important, although still valued, included having a social work qualification and not looking down on the participants.

The surveys also showed that 11 parents thought that the facilitator's sharing of her own casework experience was useful, consistent with the data from the group interviews. Furthermore, five parents indicated that it was useful to consider participants' own personal experience as a child in relation to how these had influenced their parenting style. Participants mentioned that when the facilitator had raised this issue, it had helped them to reflect on the influence of their parents on their own parenting style. As one parent put it:

> *The facilitator helped me to think about my past experience as a child. This let me notice that my children's needs are the same as mine when I was a child. This helps me to understand how to communicate with my child now.*

In other words, helping participants to reflect on their own childhood experiences could help them to understand more about their adolescent children and therefore reflect on their parenting methods so as to improve their communication and general parenting skills.

In the group interviews, parents said they had found it useful to listen to facilitators' casework experience when working with other parents on their issues. They found that they learned a lot from each other's experiences. This was very important since the use of casework examples is intended to illustrate the points made in the programme and help parents to understand them more easily. A majority of participants in three of the interview groups highlighted this point. As one parent said,

> *I think the most important aspect was the facilitator's casework experience. The second most important is the sharing of our own experiences. The third most important thing is the programme content.*

Less useful aspects and improvements

As indicated in Table 5.41, most of the participants (34.4%) who responded to this question indicated that the second session on communication was not helpful, followed by the session on understanding contemporary adolescents (28.1%). This result was consistent with their responses on the preferred sessions.

Looking at the items participants found unhelpful in reducing conflict, the majority (36.4%) selected the session on assertive parenting, followed by understanding teenagers' development (27.3%).

Table 5.41 Sessions that participants found less helpful (total number of responses: 32)

Category	*Not helpful*
Session 1 Understanding teenagers	9 (28.1%)
Session 2 Communication skills	11(34.4%)
Session 3 Parenting style	8 (25%)
Session 4 Conflict resolution	4 (12.5%)
Total	32 (100%)

Table 5.42 Elements that participants found less helpful (total number of responses: 44)

Category	*Not helpful*
Understanding teenagers' development	12 (27.3%)
Listening and empathic skills	2 (4.5%)
Giving compliments	7 (15.9%)
Assertive parenting style	16 (36.4%)
Conflict-resolution skills	7 (15.9%)
Total	44 (100%)

In the group interviews, participants initially said that there were no parts that they had found less useful. When this was probed further, two views emerged. Firstly, a number of parents expressed concern about the first session, in which there had been very little time for discussion and no demonstration of the skills. This view was consistent with the questionnaire results, in which the first session ranked second among the unhelpful aspects of the programme. One of the reasons for these shortcomings was because participants needed to fill in all the questionnaires for this study at the first session, which took some time. This view is consistent with earlier comments from participants that they wanted more discussion, demonstration and interaction with the facilitator.

The second theme which emerged concerned communication skills. Although most of the parents commented that this session was helpful and they did make changes afterwards, one parent said she could not control her own anger and had not been able to use the skills that had been taught in the programme. Another parent admitted that she had not been able to calm herself down when she had asked her daughter to go to bed before midnight. This view was supported by other parents who explained that they needed more time to learn these skills and for them to become effective. One father said that the programme content was 'too general' and not 'concrete enough' for him to practise the skills afterwards.

In terms of possible improvements, three important themes can be identified from the qualitative data: the number of sessions, the composition of the group and the content of the programme. Three groups of parents said they would have liked to have had more than four sessions. For example, one father commented that the course had covered a lot of content and he could have understood it better if there had been more time to elaborate on this and then discuss and share parenting experiences among themselves. Nevertheless, when this issue was raised in another group, those parents said that if the programme had had more than four sessions, they would have hesitated to join in because of their jobs and family commitments. In order to allow more time for parents to share and do role plays, one group suggested a design of 'four plus four' sessions. Such a programme would have two stages, each with four sessions. After completing the first four sessions, parents could join another block of four after a break of one or two weeks. This may be a possible format for future parenting programmes.

Another theme that emerged from the data was the composition of the groups. One possible improvement suggested was to encourage both parents to attend. One group, in which only mothers had been involved, suggested that the programme organisers should encourage more fathers to participate. They wanted to know more about their views. Another parent from the same group suggested that some adolescents (not belonging to any of the participants' families) might even be asked to join one session of the programme to share their feelings about parents. This would give participants a reference point for what is in the minds of today's adolescents and is a promising idea for the design of future interventions.

The third theme that emerged from the data concerned the programme content itself. Two fathers commented that the programme was very condensed and covered a lot of material, and they needed more time to practise before they could say whether the new skills were effective or not. This suggests that the content needs to be presented more concisely or cut back altogether so that parents can more easily understand and apply it in their daily lives. In addition, parents may need more time to digest and practise what they have learned. Three questionnaire respondents suggested that more practical examples should be discussed by the facilitator to further explain the points made. This is consistent with the comments from the group interviews that more real-life examples were needed. Thus, the facilitator should use examples as much as possible to illustrate the points.

Other points made in the survey were that the facilitator should control the time for each parent to speak. Furthermore, one respondent suggested handing out written materials or self-completion questionnaires about parenting style to fill in at home which would give parents information about their own parenting style. Another suggested putting all the course materials on to a CD-ROM for them to take home and use. One final comment made by two participants was that more parents should be invited to join the programme; that is, they would have liked to be part of a bigger group. This may be because some of the groups had fewer participants than expected due to dropout. This suggests that when planning a parenting programme, enrolment should be larger so that if some drop out, there are still enough participants to enable good discussion.

While some parents perceived the conflict-resolution skills sessions as useful, others parents talked about their difficulties in using them. In two groups, some parents said that their adolescent children did not want to talk to them. One parent explained that while she was willing to talk to her adolescent children about some issues, they did not want to talk to her. Likewise, a father in another group described how his children simply shut their ears and would not talk to him, making it difficult to resolve conflicts. This probably arose because the parent–adolescent relationship in these cases was very poor before the programme started. In such cases, more time may be required to solve the problems, or it may take more than just an improvement in communication skills to tackle them.

In addition, one parent commented that it was difficult for a Chinese adult to see an adolescent as an equal and resolve conflict with him or her, and that it was hard for a parent to change. Another parent in the same group agreed, suggesting that "to keep a hierarchy with their adolescent children and have more power over them" is a deep-rooted concept in the mind of a Chinese parent. This made it difficult to use the conflict-resolution strategies covered in the programme, which assumed a non-hierarchical relationship. Similarly, another group of parents considered the conflict-resolution strategies as "lowering parents' status". According to them, these approaches were difficult to use since Chinese parents consider it important to have a hierarchy within their families. Furthermore, one father shared his view that it was important to influence adolescents' values. Once their values were closer to those of their parents, there would be no conflict, nor would conflict exist if parents and adolescents respected each other. These comments indicate that some parents could not regard the conflict-resolution strategies taught in the programme as totally acceptable.

Chinese parents normally did not want to disclose too much about their difficulties and conflicts with their adolescents. They would rather consider those conflicts with their adolescents as communication problems. As traditional parenting beliefs, discussed in Chapter 4, indicated, Chinese parents are more concerned about the hierarchy between them and their adolescents. The conflict with their adolescents thus was perceived as disobedient and a communication problem rather than a conflict situation which implied that they have a more balanced status between parents and their adolescents. In addition, the participants were not able to develop a trust and cohesive relationship that enhance their deep disclosure of their problematic relationship with their adolescents. They just shared their positive experience with their adolescents rather than disclosing their problems in a less cohesive group.

Limitation of the present study

This study adopted a non-random sampling strategy. Participants were allowed to choose themselves whether to join the experimental or the waiting-list group. It appears that parents who were more motivated and ready to change joined the experimental groups. There was, therefore, more chance of substantial differences between the groups, making comparison more difficult. Though it raises ethical issues, future studies should consider using random sampling to avoid this problem. In addition, the sample was drawn from the Northern District of Hong Kong only. The results cannot therefore be generalised to the population as a whole, but apply only to those who voluntarily join parenting programmes in the Northern District.

To minimise this problem, however, a series of measures was taken to make sure that the participants were as similar as possible, such as recruiting parents from within the same district to make sure they came from similar socio-economic backgrounds and requiring all participants to have at least some level of conflict with their adolescent children and to have received no social services within the previous three months. Nevertheless, assessment against these criteria relied solely on participants' self-reports, with no steps taken to validate them before joining the programme. This approach could be improved in future studies.

This study adopted different scales to measure adolescents' behaviour, participants' parenting stress and conflict level: the PSI (Abidin, 1995), PAC (Robin & Foster, 1989) and SDQ (Goodman, 1997). These are widely used scales which have been validated by different scholars and used in previous studies to measure parental comments on children's behaviour before and after participating in a Hong Kong parenting programme (Leung *et al.*, 2003). However, they have the disadvantage that data are gathered solely from parents, with no attempt made to collect the views of adolescents. As indicated in a review by Moran *et al.* (2004), some previous studies on parenting programmes show that parents tend to indicate a substantial improvement in their relationship with their adolescents after taking part, while their children give no such indications when interviewed. It would be better to include adolescents' views, despite the fact that difficulties would be encountered in doing so, such as the problem of how to collect such data if parents do not want their children to know that they are attending a group. In addition, the extra resources required to collect data from adolescents were beyond the scope of this study. It may be possible to get a better picture of the parent–adolescent relationship if a specific measurement scale like the Parent–Adolescent Relationship Questionnaire (Robin, Koepke & Moye, 1990) were adopted. This was not used in the present study because the focus was more on parent–adolescent conflict, and also because there is currently no validated Chinese version available for which copyright permission for use in this study could be obtained.

This study would also have been improved by using video recordings of parent–adolescent interactions to measure change before and after the programme. Though this also raises ethical dilemmas, such visual evidence can present a fuller picture, as a source of data which is not based solely on self-reports. Observing and coding such interactions, and trying to interpret the meaning behind them, may yield more information about relationships between Hong Kong Chinese parents and adolescents in the current social context, and enable behavioural changes to be observed.

It should also be noted that the return rate for the three-month post-programme follow up was very low. Most parents did not turn up to the meeting to complete the questionnaire, with only seven valid responses collected. One of the possible reasons for this was that there were no tangible or intangible rewards for parents in doing so. It might be better to offer parents a free gift or similar incentive. An even better approach might be to offer one more session of the parenting programme three months later, which might encourage more parents to attend and provide further data.

A further limitation arose from the differences in the styles of the three facilitators. Using three different group leaders was unavoidable, and the researcher participated in at least one session for each group to observe any differences in approach. Although all three facilitators were female and were registered social workers in Hong Kong, they came from different backgrounds and had diverse clinical experiences.

All facilitators used an interactive approach, where participants were encouraged to talk to each other and to respond to the facilitator's questions. One facilitator took more of a stand in addressing issues from the parent's point of view. Another focused more on explaining to participants what an adolescent would think, and the third had put in less preparation and so was unable to follow the instruction pack for the programme exactly. She spent more time on relationship building and used more of her own casework experience to explain the different issues. This indicates that even if the aim is to standardise such a programme across groups and a manual is provided for that purpose, facilitators will also still have their own style of leading the programme and may make their own modifications to the materials.

In terms of the use of local examples and personal social work experience, all facilitators used their own experiences and shared their (anonymised) casework stories with the participants to illustrate the points in the manual. One facilitator explained how adolescents tend to perceive their relationship with their parents, to help participants consider the adolescents' perspective. In contrast, the other facilitators engaged well with parents and drew more on their experience of helping families with adolescents. The differences in the way that the facilitators led the programme gave rise to more variables in the way it was perceived by different participants. Even though manuals were available, this did not guarantee that the programme was delivered in the way in which it had originally been planned and formulated (Forgatch, Patterson & DeGarmo, 2005). In future such research, more training for facilitators may be needed to try to maintain the consistency of the delivery of the programme. Another way to encourage fidelity to the programme materials is to give facilitators a checklist to complete after each session. This can ensure that the major topics within the manual have been covered.

Conclusion

The qualitative data discussed in this chapter have supplemented the quantitative data to help come to an understanding of why these Hong Kong Chinese parents joined the school-based parenting programme. Most of the participants wanted to learn how to communicate better and improve their relationship with their adolescent children. Other motivations for joining the programme were to resolve conflict with their children and to better understand contemporary adolescents. After joining the programme, they perceived that they had become better communicators, largely through being able to achieve better control of their own emotions. In addition, they had improved their relationships with their adolescent children through acquiring more understanding of their development and improving their communication skills. They also perceived their adolescents to have improved their own behaviour after they had joined the programme. Those who had had the opportunity to cooperate with their partners also found their marital relationship to have improved. Furthermore, it was clear that although these Hong Kong Chinese parents still held strong traditional beliefs, they were able to benefit from learning some new parenting and communication skills through the programme. Some culturally sensitive elements of the programme, like allowing their children more autonomy and adopting new conflict-resolution strategies, were unacceptable to some but not all of the participants. Nevertheless, the qualitative data given by the participants were perfunctory was because there was limited time in the group interview. The group interview lasted for 60 to 90 minutes and happened right after the final session of the course. Before the commencement of the group discussion, the participants were required to fill in the questionnaires that they had already spent half an hour on. Some members will be engaged in other family or job commitment after the group interview, which is why they would like to leave as early as possible and therefore give a short and brief answer. In addition, the participants were overwhelmingly positive towards the programme. They considered the programme to be very helpful and thus had very few comments on the ineffective elements. Furthermore, since the time was limited, it was not possible for all participants to express their views in detail, which became another limitation of the qualitative data. Considering the culturally sensitive aspect, it has been observed that the participants in this study in general needed more time to warm up before talking about their experience. For example, when talking about the sessions that they found useful, most of the parents said that all the sessions were good. They need more probing questions to talk about which sessions they found were good and the reasons behind their observations. This was another observation of why there were not enough rich qualitative data collected.

6 Future direction of parenting programmes for parents of adolescents

Introduction

This chapter draws conclusions from the above research findings to discuss future possible directions of parenting programmes for parents of adolescents. In addition, the discussions below are related to current policy development and evidence-based social work practice. Even though much of the research on parenting programmes has found that they are useful in reducing adolescents' negative behaviour and emotional symptoms, Hong Kong policy makers have paid very little attention (and thus have given little funding) to parenting programmes that adopt systematic strategies for helping adolescents with problems. A needs-led approach relies heavily on the initiative of parent participants to join these programmes. There is a lack of strategic policy regarding identifying those parents who need parenting programmes and encouraging them to join. This chapter discusses further policy development and looks at practices in the West to provide a comparison for policy development from an international perspective. There is also an evident lack of interest on the part of professional social workers in developing evidence-based practice. The lack of concern regarding the use of systematic evaluation tools and embedding theory-driven parenting programmes into practice is also discussed. Such a development will lead to a trend of relying heavily on professional and practical experience without any clearly outlined theory of change. In particular, the issue of culturally sensitive parenting programmes is especially important when drawing conclusions from the current research. This chapter further argues the importance of culturally sensitive practice for future parenting programmes.

Policy development

As set out above, evidence-based social work practice is becoming more and more important. However, social workers in Hong Kong have been using parenting programmes as an intervention strategy to cater for the needs of parents of children in secondary schools in Hong Kong for many years without any systematic evaluation of their effectiveness. Overall, in Hong Kong there tends to be a lack of interest in rigorously evaluating the effectiveness of parenting programmes (Cheung, 2001). Most of the evaluations that have taken place are based on participant satisfaction surveys and do not use scientific measures or control groups (Education and Manpower Bureau, 2003). In addition, not all parenting programmes in Hong Kong are theory-driven or evidence-based. Many practitioners run parenting programmes based on their practical experience, simply relying on the practical wisdom they have gained through being a social worker. The assessment of the needs of target participants also relies strongly on practitioners' observations and parents' opinions; most of the programmes, rather than focusing on children's outcomes, have been designed to address the expressed needs of their parents. There has also been limited use of scientifically verified tools to evaluate outcomes for either parents or their children, and a lack of knowledge about which elements of parenting programmes actually lead to behavioural change. The absence of knowledge and rigorous studies in these areas results in most programmes being organised in a piecemeal way, without systematic planning and evaluation (Tsang, 2004). This indicates that Hong Kong social work practice in the area of parenting programmes lacks an evidence base.

Moreover, without a clear and coherent family policy from the Hong Kong government, the development of parenting programmes has been very much reliant on individual social workers' understanding of current issues, their evaluation of the aetiology of particular problems and their experience of delivering previous programmes. As seen in previous sections, there is a lack of a coherent policy to guide the implementation of programmes for parents of adolescents in Hong Kong. There is also a lack of initiative on the part of policy makers to create an evidence base for the effective implementation of parenting programmes. Moreover, most of the studies which have been conducted have been based on interventions for parents of younger children, not adolescents. Since there are many differences in parenting adolescents compared to parenting younger children, more specific evidence about parenting programmes targeted at the former group is required. The present study set out to fill this gap by investigating the outcomes of a school-based parenting programme for parents of adolescents, using both quantitative and qualitative methods, to inform future policy development in this area.

In relation to the literature on the evaluation of parenting programmes in Hong Kong, behavioural interventions have been shown to be effective in reducing children's disruptive behaviour and increasing parents' ratings of their own performance (Ho *et al.*, 1996; Leung *et al.*, 2003). Other programme evaluations have also put more emphasis on parents' outcomes. For example, programmes based on Carl Rogers' humanistic theory, which emphasises helping parents understand how their children develop and increasing their empathy and communication skills, have been found to be effective in improving parents' knowledge of their children's development, empathic skills and parent–child communication (Cheung & Yau, 1996), as well as changing parents' parenting attitudes (Kwok, 1994). Parenting programmes have also been shown to be more effective if they are theory-driven and facilitated by more experienced and better-trained social workers (Education and Manpower Bureau, 2003).

Evaluations of parenting programmes in Hong Kong have rarely attempted to focus on interventions designed to help reduce parent–adolescent conflict, despite the evidence suggesting that such conflict is associated with adolescent anti-social behaviour in Hong Kong (Shek & Ma, 1997). A lack of attention has been paid to the experiences of adolescents' parents who have participated in such programmes. The present study also set out to fill this gap by considering such experiences.

The study also considered the views of programme participants on the effectiveness of the parenting practices that they have learned about in reducing parent–adolescent conflict. A quantitative analysis was undertaken to compare adolescent outcomes and parental sense of efficacy (that is, their confidence in their own parenting of their adolescents) before and after the training. These outcomes were also analysed to consider the usefulness of any culturally specific elements included in the programme. The implications for further development of culturally sensitive approaches to parenting programmes in Hong Kong, and implementation issues in general, are considered below.

Concerning policy implications of the present study, this research did not uncover any evidence for the effectiveness of this model of parenting programme in reducing parenting stress, decreasing problem behaviours among young people or reducing parent–adolescent conflict. Nevertheless, it has shown that the programme design has promise as an intervention for those who have fewer problems with their adolescent children as well as lower levels of parenting stress. This programme may be best thought of as developmental and preventive in nature.

Further work is needed to explore whether this is because of limitations in the study or due to the programme design itself. Given the number of programmes run in Hong Kong schools, more studies in this area should be carried out in order to give policy makers a better understanding of the effectiveness of such programmes, which could be useful when allocating future funding. The positive feedback from the participants also needs to be considered, and the reasons behind it explored, in order to improve the future design and implementation of parenting programmes.

The current needs-led approach to implementing parenting programmes in Hong Kong, with no keen interest in systematic evaluation, will lead to future parenting programmes that are not evidence-based. In addition, without government initiatives at the policy level in launching and supporting parenting programmes to help achieve their goal of preventing social problems, only a fragmented effort to support and enhance parenting practices can be expected in future. Policy makers should look at the evidence from parenting programmes and fund those programmes that show promise in reducing social problems. These parenting programmes include those that are aimed at reducing child abuse and neglect and those that reduce parent–child conflict, which is one of the risk factors contributing to adolescent suicide.

Evidence-based practice

Interest in evidence-based social work practice arises from the idea that social workers should provide services which are based on a rigorous research methodology (Webb, 2001). Evidence-based practice therefore means "treatment based on the best available science" (McNeece & Thyer, 2004). It also denotes reliance on empirical literature to guide the selection and execution of treatment, with the application of systematic hypothesis testing to each case (Persons, 1999). What distinguishes evidence-based practice from other models of social work intervention is that the practitioner of the former identifies the best available evidence, evaluates its scientific applicability to the client's situation and applies it as a treatment option (McNeece & Thyer, 2004). Practitioners of evidence-based practice consider the use of the best available evidence to select and implement their intervention strategies not simply as a choice but as a professional obligation. For example, randomised controlled trials (RCTs), quasi-experimental studies, rigorous surveys and qualitative studies have generally been considered as reliable evidence for practice. The UK Cabinet Office's Strategic Policy Making Team describes evidence in this context as

> expert knowledge; published research; existing statistics; stakeholder consultations; previous policy evaluations; the Internet; outcomes from consultations; costing of policy options; output from economic and statistical modelling.
>
> (Nutley, Davies & Walter, 2002: 2)

This view considers evidence-based practice as relying not solely on purely scientific research but also on more informal sources such as stakeholders' views. In the UK, the link between research and social policy has existed since the nineteenth century. In addition, successive governments have regarded the construction of an evidence base as one of the elements of an effective policy formulation process (Nutley, Davies & Walter, 2002). The UK government funded the establishment of the Centre for Evidence-based Practice to conduct research into the best outcomes from stakeholders' perspectives (Webb, 2001). This initiative is an example of the importance of evidence-based practice in current social work practice in the UK. All these initiatives indicate that evidence-based practice has started to shape the professional culture in health and social care in the UK.

Equally, in the US it is compulsory for all social workers to appraise and use research evidence. The custom of routinely building evaluation into programme designs and budgets has now been widely adopted (Solesbury, 2001). This indicates the importance of social workers' understanding and appraising research evidence and using it to guide their practice. There is also much emphasis on evidence-based social work practice and the importance of using it as a basis for carrying out interventions (Webb, 2001). Such an emphasis arises from critiques of the theory and practice gaps reported across many professions (Swinkels *et al.*, 2002). Nevertheless, social work knowledge has also been criticised as poorly organised, unsystematic and scientifically unsound (Light & Pillemer, 1984). For example, a review by Gambrill (2018) indicates that the majority of studies in the social work literature are not rigorous enough from either a quantitative or qualitative point of view. Some of the studies covered in the review involved surveys that did not employ probability sampling, and a small percentage involved only one case (Gambrill, 2018). This suggests that research in social work needs to become more rigorous in order to achieve an adequate evidence base.

Furthermore, contemporary concerns about audit, effectiveness, rationalism, transparency, professional accountability and consumerism have contributed to the development of evidence-based practice in the social work field. This, along with the emergence of managerialism and the prominence of the concept of value for money, has directed social welfare services towards evidence-based practice (Swinkels *et al.*, 2002). Social work research has also been criticised for failing to adequately address the needs of practitioners and for allowing gaps in the dissemination of research in an accessible form to policy makers and practitioners (Krik & Reid, 2002; Swinkels *et al.*, 2002; Shek, Lam & Tsoi, 2004).

In addition to the importance of evidence-based practice, we also need to consider which type of evidence will be considered acceptable. For example, it is widely accepted that RCTs are the gold standard, and they form the dominant source of evidence in medicine (Nutley, Davies & Walter, 2002). The Campbell tradition of using experimental and control groups is also widely accepted as the most 'scientific' way of considering the outcomes of social work practice. However, relying solely on quantitative methodology has limitations, in that it lacks the power to address the complex and multi-faceted nature of social work practice; other, qualitative methodologies may be needed to evaluate it effectively.

For example, the empiricist view that knowledge only builds on raw sensory data has been challenged by critical theorists (Habermas, 1968) who suggest that there are no certain foundations for empirical knowledge (Webb, 2001). An understanding of evidence-based practice which relies solely on quantitative data proves lacking when applied to social work practice, in which more complex issues such as the influence of cultural background and worker–client interaction in the service delivery process need to be taken into consideration when delivering services. Methodologies which use qualitative and quantitative research methods together can provide a more comprehensive picture of the outcomes of interventions.

The gap between research and practice needs to be bridged in order to improve current practice and to identify good practice which is both beneficial to service users and evidence-based. In addition, some knowledge is generated from 'practice wisdom'; while this is not systematically written down or researched, social work providers also need to consider whether the skills generated from long practice can sometimes be generalised to other, similar situations. Given this background to the development of social work interventions, more studies of the outcomes of practice are needed in order to make services more accountable to funders and users.

There is also a need for a better connection between theory and practice that will help practitioners provide helpful and cost-effective services to users. It has been documented that the conduct and dissemination of research in itself does not necessarily lead to evidence-based practice. Rosen (2003) suggests that it is necessary to develop practitioner-friendly tools for workers which are based on good-quality evidence. We also need to delineate what sorts of intervention is useful for which clients in which situations, and to weigh up carefully how such knowledge can be linked with practice wisdom and local knowledge. In addition, the treatments that social work practitioners are prepared to use must be approached systematically to fulfil the need for ongoing evaluation of whether specific interventions are achieving their goals (Rosen, 2003). The foregoing have been suggested to be the essential elements needed to achieve evidence-based practice. They require social work to be more scientific, theory-driven and grounded in evidence.

Nevertheless, the literature suggests that there are still numerous barriers to fully implementing evidence-based social work practice in Hong Kong. Shek and colleagues (2004) indicate that the lack of demand for rigorous social work services arises because clients are not aware that they have choices regarding interventions, since (influenced by traditional Chinese culture) they think they should simply be grateful to the workers for providing services to them. In addition, there is little awareness of the importance of service effectiveness among social workers in Hong Kong, because of a lack of pressure from the public. In addition, consistent funding from the government without open bidding and competition also creates less incentive to have awareness of the importance of evaluation. There is also a lack of monetary incentives for evidence-based practice in Hong Kong and limited documentation of effective practice. Furthermore, social workers in Hong Kong are more practical in their mindset and tend to lack interest in evidence-based practice (Shek, Lam & Tsoi, 2004).

An integrated approach to implementing and evaluating parenting programmes

The example illustrated in this book has demonstrated the advantage of using both quantitative and qualitative methods to evaluate the effectiveness of a parenting programme. Although the qualitative data generated many positive responses, the quantitative data helped to distinguish which of these perceived improvements actually stemmed from the parenting programme and which did not. In addition, the use of mixed methods was also helpful in combatting the disadvantage of using only quantitative methods, in which outcomes are emphasised without also considering the content of the intervention. In this way, the study could capture the complexity of social work practice, in which multiple factors and influences are at work simultaneously (Cheetham *et al.*, 1992). More inferences could be drawn as a result of using both quantitative and qualitative data, and different dimensions of the intervention could be addressed through different methods of evaluating the outcomes. The use of mixed methods in evaluating the effectiveness of social work practice seems to be an important element of research design.

Quantitative results

This example in chapter five reported on parents' experiences of a programme held in secondary schools in the Northern District of Hong Kong. All participants had at least one adolescent child aged 11–14. The majority were women who had been educated to at least Form 5 (that is, they had not left school before the age of 16). They were at the low-income end of the Hong Kong population and lived in an area mainly composed of public housing estates. Most had been born in Hong Kong, were living with their partners and had no more than two children. More than half of the participants in the experimental groups were housewives.

By comparison with the control group, the experimental groups had more parents who were working. The participants in the experimental groups, and their children, were generally older than those in the comparison group. Furthermore, parents in the experimental groups had experienced more conflict with their adolescent children than those in the comparison group. Otherwise, there were no significant demographic differences between the groups. This suggests that the experimental groups were generally comparable with the control.

On the other hand, programme dropouts tended to be participants who were not living with their partners and whose children had more difficulties, particularly in relation to conduct problems and hyperactivity. In addition, they had lower autonomy scores in relation to their parenting beliefs when compared with those in the experimental groups. This finding is similar to those of previous work, which found that most dropouts were experiencing more difficulties than those who had completed the programmes (Moran *et al.*, 2004). They may have felt after the first session that the programme was not likely to meet their needs. This finding also suggests that the parenting programme used in this study is generally suitable for preventive rather than remedial or treatment purposes. Rather than participating in group programmes, parents with more substantial difficulties may need more personalised social work services to cater to their particular needs.

This example in Chapter five compared the before and after scores of the experimental and comparison groups to consider the effects of the parenting programme on adolescents' behaviour, parenting stress and levels of conflict. The results indicate that members of the experimental groups saw improvements in their adolescents' behaviour, a reduction in parenting stress and lower levels of parent–adolescent conflict immediately after completion. Compared with the control group, these improvements were statistically significant – that is, they did not occur by chance. In addition, there were also improvements in the before and after scores of the control group, but these changes were not statistically significant.

Further statistical tests were used to explore any effects between the two groups and their before and after scores. The results indicated that the pre- and post-test differences in the experimental groups were significant for the PSI–SF and PAC scores. However, there were no interaction effects in the before and after scores or between the experimental and comparison groups. This indicates that the reduction in scores were not statistically different between the two groups. Accordingly, it is not possible to attribute the significant reduction in the PSI and PAC scores in the experimental groups to the programme. It might have occurred because those who most wanted to join the programme were enrolled in the experimental groups; in other words, they were highly motivated and prepared to change. This is also consistent with the findings for the comparison group: the children displayed fewer difficulties, the adult participants had less stress and less parent–adolescent conflict was experienced. Parents on the waiting list also showed a reduction in their scores. This might have been because they were contemplating joining the programme, because they knew other parents in the group who had shared what they had learned with them or perhaps because they had participated in similar programmes offered elsewhere.

Nonetheless, it is encouraging that at least some parents derived benefit from participating in a school-based parenting programme, even if the effect was not significant. It is necessary to delineate further the processes associated with the programme which might have helped to improve participants' parenting practice. For example, previous experience of parenting programmes might have enhanced participation and understanding of the materials, hence leading to more change. Such factors could have been identified if questions about previous experience of such programmes had been included. Another potential improvement to the study method would be to recruit participants with similar levels of difficulty, stress and conflict to both the experimental and comparison groups. It would be important to ensure that there were few differences between groups to make it easier to determine whether any improvement had come from the programme or had arisen only by chance.

A further statistical test, logistic regression, was used to consider the appropriateness of the theory of change suggested in the example. This postulated that if parents of adolescents have sufficient knowledge of their development, use effective communication skills, adopt an assertive parenting style and use conflict-resolution strategies, less parent–adolescent conflict will result. The predictor used in the logistic regression to predict reduction in the PAC scores was participants' indication that they had found understanding about teenagers' development, developing listening, empathic and conflict-resolution skills and learning how to use an assertive parenting style to be useful elements of the programme. The results show that when participants were satisfied with the parenting programme, this predicted a reduction in their PAC scores. Nevertheless, it is impossible to be sure which elements within the programme led to their satisfaction. Although participants were asked in the group interviews about the aspects that they had found helpful, this information could not be used to directly describe satisfaction overall. Future studies could include ways to delineate aspects of satisfaction with the programme, which could possibly be of help in understanding further the mechanism of change.

The correlation between satisfaction with the programme and reduction in levels of parent–adolescent conflict was the only one to emerge. No such correlation was found between other specific elements within the programme, such as participants' understanding of adolescents' development, parenting style, conflict-resolution strategies and communication skills. The results of the logistic regression suggest that further work should be done to test the relationships of all these individual elements in the programme with the overall reduction in conflict. Future research into the efficacy of a similar parenting programme using this model should collect more information by using a larger sample, with a more varied demographic background, to further consider its efficacy. Moreover, it is possible that a longer programme using these elements would result in more change (see for example Macdonald & Turner, 2005; Gordon, 1975). A longer parenting programme may benefit parents by giving them more time to practise their skills, embed their learning and share among themselves their experiences of taking care of adolescent children.

Qualitative results

This study has enhanced our understanding of the views of parents of adolescents involved in a parenting programme. Previous studies in a Hong Kong context have mostly looked at parents of children under 12. This research also adds to the literature insofar as few studies so far have elicited qualitative comments from Hong Kong Chinese parents of adolescents who have participated in a parenting programme.

The qualitative data indicate that the majority of the parents joined the parenting programme because they wanted to improve communication with their adolescent children, to understand more about contemporary adolescence and to learn new parenting skills. Most continued attending the programme after the first session because they thought it would set a good example for their children if they completed the whole course. In addition, those who stayed on valued the supportive environment and thought that the content matched their needs. Although the promotional leaflet for the programme pointed out that one of its most important elements was to help parents to handle conflict with adolescents, the data indicate that parents perceived it as more important to improve their relationships with their children, through means such as better communication, for example, than simply to resolve conflict. This may explain why parents in the group interviews indicated that the changes in their relationships with their adolescent children were the most important benefits they had gained from the programme. Future programme design may need to draw on this understanding to design programme materials and promotional literature that are better aligned with parents' concerns and aspirations.

The programme met participants' aims since most considered that they had learnt how to communicate better with their children after completing it. They achieved this through learning how to control their own emotions, having a better understanding of contemporary adolescence and learning how to resolve conflict. Furthermore, participants were more confident in their role as a parent of an adolescent once they had learnt new skills and had the opportunity to share their difficulties with other parents.

Previous studies of perceptions of parenting education in Hong Kong show that parents tend to value personal change more than the acquisition of knowledge and skills (Lam, 2005). They consider changes in attitude and thinking to be more important than demonstrating behavioural changes as a result of such education. These results build on previous findings about the factors that parents consider important in a parenting programme. Those who took part thought it was important to have a better understanding of their adolescent children, which could be considered akin to a change in attitude. They also valued learning communication and parenting skills and the experience of being in a supportive environment.

In terms of the specific elements that they found most helpful, parents considered role play and discussion, as well as facilitators' sharing of casework experience, to be equally important. Sharing and discussion among participants and the use of local case examples enhanced their self-reflection on their parenting practice. In addition, the use of examples also helped to illustrate parenting skills and ideas from the training programme, which in turn made these easier for parents to understand. It is therefore suggested that it is important to include these elements in the design of such a programme.

This study has also generated some information about how to design and implement a parenting programme for Hong Kong Chinese parents. The questionnaire findings show that parents generally saw the three most important qualities of programme facilitators as their ability to give opinions on how to handle adolescent children, to teach new parenting skills and to use interactive presentation skills. Moreover, the facilitator's ability to adopt a friendly, warm and sincere attitude which conveyed an understanding of participants' situations and to provide Hong Kong case examples were also appreciated.

After joining the programme, the majority of participants thought that they had seen some changes in the behaviour of their adolescent children, such as greater obedience, spending more time on homework and going to bed earlier at night. These behaviours align greatly with those valued in traditional Chinese parenting beliefs. It is interesting to note that participants perceived their adolescents as showing many changes after they had completed the programme, but that this was not confirmed by the quantitative data. This suggests that the programme was able to change parents' perceptions, perhaps because they had gained knowledge about adolescents' development and improved their communication with them. This is consistent with previous findings from research on parenting programmes, which have indicated that they are effective in changing parents' attitudes but that there is little evidence of actual changes in the behaviour of their young children or adolescents (Moran *et al.*, 2004).

The intervention also helped some of the participants to improve their relationship with their partners, although the majority felt that they received little support from them in relation to parenting. This may reflect the fact that most were mothers who did not work outside the home and were the main carers for the children, with little support from their husbands. Some participants talked about their difficulties in discussing parenting issues with their partners, which may simply reflect a poor marital relationship irrespective of the parenting programme. This suggests that marital relationships may affect parent–adolescent relationships as well (Montemayor, 1986; Robin & Foster, 1989).

Previous studies of parenting programmes in Hong Kong have not found similar results. For example, Leung and colleagues (2003) looked at the effectiveness of the Triple-P parenting programme in Hong Kong but did not collect any qualitative data on participants' views, nor did they identify which elements within the programme had led to the changes they reported. Another point worth mentioning concerns participants' comments about the number of sessions in the parenting programme. Most of the parents in this study thought that four sessions were not enough for them to learn through role play and discussion. Nevertheless, they also would have found it hard to commit to eight sessions because of family and work obligations. Some parents suggested that it would be helpful to use a 'four plus four' design, where they would take part in four sessions as a start and then could attend another four if they wanted to learn more. This design could hold some promise for future programmes.

From the dropout data, the inference could be drawn that the parenting programme in this study was more appropriate for parents whose problems were less complicated. The data show that dropouts had more children, that their children had higher levels of hyperactivity problems and that more of them were not living with their partners. This suggested that they may have been experiencing higher levels of stress and may also have been hampered by financial and relationship problems that might have hindered them from joining a parenting programme.

The group-based programme used in this study was more developmental in nature and may be more suitable for those with less complicated problems. Those facing more complex issues may need different interventions, such as one-on-one support or personalised social work services. Alternatively, it is possible that a similar parenting programme, designed for a small group of parents facing more challenging problems and which provides high levels of emotional support (perhaps alongside one-on-one work), might be a model worth considering.

The quantitative data show that there was an improvement in the experimental groups. However, this could not be attributed directly to the programme. In addition, the quantitative data also indicate that participants' satisfaction with the programme was related to a reduction in conflict. However, other elements (such as understanding adolescents' development) showed no correlation with a reduction in conflict scores. Accordingly, there is a need to consider other programme content and approaches to helping parents reduce conflict with their adolescent children within social work practice. Parenting programmes alone may not do enough to address the complex problem of parent–adolescent conflict.

This study has shed light on how to facilitate a parenting programme. The data indicates that parents in this programme preferred an interactive facilitation style and would have liked to have seen more illustration of the points being made by listening to the group leaders' casework experiences. Participants enjoyed having opportunities to share among themselves and listen to other parents' experiences. Furthermore, they also wanted facilitators to teach new parenting skills through role play. All of these, therefore, are elements that participants would like to see in a parenting programme. Social workers in Hong Kong could use these findings to design new parenting programmes.

Towards culturally sensitive practice

The present study also sheds light on the future of culturally sensitive parenting programme practice in Hong Kong. From the results of this study, we know that Chinese parents benefit from a parenting programme by learning active listening and communication skills like transactional analysis. They also benefit from learning to grant more autonomy to their adolescents as well as reflecting on their own childhood experiences. These new findings provide some direction for the future design of parenting programmes aimed at Chinese Hong Kong parents.

This study has shown that Hong Kong Chinese parents still hold traditional Chinese beliefs about parenting, valuing qualities like obedience, respect, filial piety, maintaining moral standards, showing politeness and having control of one's emotions. The culturally sensitive concept of training (Chao, 1994b) was frequently mentioned by participants in the group interviews. In addition, the qualitative data also indicate that parents consider it important for adolescents to carry out duties at home and set a good example to their younger siblings. In particular, some parents do not agree with the concept of 'letting go', that is, giving adolescents more autonomy. This is consistent with previous findings that Chinese parents find this difficult (Russell, Crockett & Chao, 2010). Future research could focus more on the positive and negative impacts on adolescents' development of parents holding strong traditional beliefs about parenting.

Furthermore, some parents were sceptical about the conflict-resolution strategies taught in the programme, which depended on parents and adolescents being of relatively equal status when discussing matters; parents holding a strong Chinese cultural belief in filial piety found hard this to accept. Parents who strongly expect adolescents to be obedient and maintain harmony within the family will find it difficult to allow their children to adopt a more equal status in negotiations. Future research should compare the differences in adolescent outcomes between parents who adopt traditional Chinese methods of communication and those who are prepared to allow their adolescents a more equal status in conflict resolution. The results of such investigation could further enhance the design of parenting programmes.

Nevertheless, these results suggest that although Hong Kong Chinese parents still hold strong traditional parenting beliefs, they are also generally able to benefit from attending a school-based parenting programme adapted from one used in the West. Participants benefited from learning new skills for communicating and interacting with adolescents. For example, many of them mentioned that they had enjoyed learning the techniques of transactional analysis (Berne, 1975) and developing their listening and communication skills. In addition, some parents were able to benefit from learning to let go and give their children more autonomy. Participants said that they had learned how to give more responsibility to their children, requiring them to be responsible for their personal matters and to make their own choices. Some participants also benefited from an increased understanding of how to resolve conflicts with adolescents. The quantitative data together with the qualitative feedback from participants show that the content of the programme used in this study had encouraging effects on both parents and adolescents in the Hong Kong context. In general, these Hong Kong Chinese parents were responsive to skills and ideas developed in the West. More rigorous study is recommended in future to consider further whether this is because parents in Hong Kong are genuinely open to Western-inspired parenting strategies or simply because those particular ideas happen to be congruent with Hong Kong Chinese culture. Further studies may also be required to consider how best to integrate those ideas into Chinese culture.

One of the objectives of this study was to identify culturally sensitive parenting practices or techniques in order to enhance our understanding of how to design a culturally sensitive parenting programme and find out more about parenting practices in Hong Kong Chinese families. When participants were asked about the culturally sensitive elements of the programme, the general view expressed was that it was culturally well adapted. This is consistent with the questionnaire results showing that the majority of parents thought the programme was suitable for Hong Kong parents (Table 6.1).

Table 6.1 Suitability for parents of adolescents in Hong Kong (n = 65)

Category	*Number of participants*
Very suitable	17 (25.8%)
Quite suitable	44 (66.7%)
Not very suitable	1 (1.5%)
Not at all suitable	2 (3%)
No indication	1 (1.5%)
Total	65 (100%)

As shown in Table 6.1, the majority of the participants found the programme very suitable (25.8%) or quite suitable (66.7%) for parents of adolescents in Hong Kong. Only three (4.5%) participants thought it was not suitable.

Nevertheless, further exploration of this issue in the group interviews indicated that there were three important areas where participants did not regard the programme as sufficiently culturally attuned. The first was the concept of letting go, the second (as discussed above) was conflict resolution and the third was parenting goals. One of the important concepts introduced in the Challenging Years programme is that of encouraging parents to give their adolescents more autonomy in matters such as their academic work and their belongings. Parents in most of the groups said that it was really difficult to let go of their children, particularly in relation to their academic results, friends and moral conduct. One participant in particular did not trust the idea of letting go. She was extremely sceptical about the idea and claimed that she needed some time to practise it before she would believe that it was appropriate.

In addition, some parents felt that the use of the letting go strategy was impossible, since if it was left up to their children, they would not make any changes. When their adolescent children did not take responsibility for things, parents felt they needed to take responsibility. They found it hard to let go.

This suggests that Hong Kong Chinese parents are protective, possibly even over-protective, of their adolescent children. They were not able to give their children more responsibility, rather keeping the burden on their own shoulders. They found it very hard to contemplate letting their children face their own problems because they were afraid that they would not be able to take responsibility or simply would not be able to take care of themselves. On the other hand, one parent talked about the impossibility of *not* letting go, because she was no longer able to control her adolescent child. Another parent talked about having had a good experience of letting go, as a result of which her child's academic performance had improved.

Those parents who were unwilling to let go of their children reflected the traditional Chinese idea of parenthood, in which a son or daughter is not considered to be grown up until they have married and become a parent themselves (Lam, 2005). This is also in line with the traditional saying that "if you have a child who is 100 years old, you have been worrying for at least 99 years" (Lam, 2005: 118).

Such a conception of their children's development may make it hard for parents to let go and give their adolescents more autonomy to face their own problems.

The second theme that emerged was the use of the conflict-resolution strategies introduced by the programme. As discussed above, some parents found it impossible to consider resolving conflicts with their adolescent child on an equal basis. They considered parents as occupying a position of power within the family hierarchy, making it quite impossible to discuss a solution mutually with their adolescent children. Such a view also made them feel uncomfortable about establishing equal status when discussing the issues from which conflict between them and their children had arisen. As Bond (1996) discusses, this family hierarchy is one of the characteristics of Chinese interpersonal relationships, but is particularly obvious in the parent–child interaction. Thus, the concept of a win–win situation in conflict resolution seems to be in direct conflict with the Chinese conception of parent–child relationships.

Another important theme that emerged was the goals of Hong Kong Chinese parents. They considered training children to respect their parents, a topic that is not particularly emphasised in the programme, very important in parenting adolescents. In addition to the concept of respect, another important aim of parenting for these participants was inculcating their children with obedience to their parents and the plans they had made for them. Obedience and respect are two important concepts that the majority of parents sought to achieve. This finding is generally consistent with previous findings on the parenting approach of Chinese Americans, in which children are socialised to maintain harmony with others. In order to achieve this, most parents taught their offspring to show respect and support to family members (Russell, Crockett & Chao, 2010).

The third important issue was the importance of influencing adolescents to display good behaviour inside and outside the home. One of the ways to achieve this, as more than one parent explained, is to know more about their peer groups. Another theme that was common to most of the parents centred around the concepts of filial piety, maintaining moral standards, showing politeness and keeping control of one's emotions. All the parents in one group agreed on this, suggesting that Chinese parents tend to be concerned about the personal qualities of their adolescent children as well as their behaviour. This finding is also consistent with work on the parenting of Chinese Americans which shows the importance of 'saving face', a value related to shame that shapes Chinese parenting towards emphasising conformity to social and family expectations (Russell, Crockett & Chao, 2010).

Other themes that emerged from the data were the importance of elder siblings setting a good example and the importance of parenting adolescents to become achievers in society. This finding is consistent with previous work on Chinese-American parenting which shows that parents tend to have high expectations of the adolescent's role in terms of family functions like taking care of younger siblings, cleaning the home and cooking meals (Fuligni, Yip & Tseng, 2002). Apart from these, one participant considered it very important to teach her adolescent children to have a purpose in life. Other goals mentioned by parents were to help their adolescents to differentiate right from wrong, to become more independent, to have more control over their emotions and to have high expectations of themselves. We can conclude from this section that the majority of Chinese parents consider helping their adolescents to build up good personal qualities a very important parenting objective.

These goals of parenting are generally consistent with findings from previous work with Chinese-American families looking at culturally attuned parenting patterns. Further work should be done in this area by using the same kinds of measurement those as employed in these studies to examine whether Hong Kong Chinese parents adopt similar parenting goals and patterns. In addition, further studies should also consider any impact on adolescents from the adoption of culturally sensitive parenting practices.

The present study has also given us some ideas regarding adapting a Western programme to Chinese Hong Kong culture. The challenge is to respect the cultural differences of the parents that we are serving while facilitating their learning of new skills. For example, traditional Chinese parents would not allow much autonomy for their adolescents; they are more focused on the academic results of their adolescents and are more concerned about how to make their adolescents more obedient and conform to their views. These traditional beliefs provide challenges for facilitators of parenting programmes of which they need to be aware; not all participants will fully accept Western ideas. Facilitators need to tread carefully, with an understanding of participants' culture, in the engagement process so that new parenting ideas will not become points of argument or offend the participants. This is part of the 'art' of social work practice; we need to challenge some traditional beliefs that may contribute to conflicts between parents and adolescents while showing that we understand and respect their cultural beliefs.

Concerning evidence-based social work practice in Hong Kong, this study did not provide evidence for the effectiveness of the parenting programme that was delivered in this study. Nevertheless, we were able to capture those elements that participants found useful. For example, they preferred an interactive approach to delivering the parenting programme, listening to facilitators' illustrations of cases of their social work experiences. This raises the question of whether we should continue to deliver lectures and other less interactive media in parenting programmes. We also need to keep in mind that facilitators' work experience cases did benefit the delivery of the programme. Parents also benefited from role playing and sharing among each other. Therefore, these are the elements that should be included in a parenting programme.

Considering how far the parenting programme was able to produce positive parent and adolescent outcomes, this study's results are similar to those of previous studies in the West in that there was no direct evidence of the programme's effectiveness. Nevertheless, we were able to see the promise of this kind of programme in reducing parenting stress, parent–adolescent conflict and adolescents' negative behaviour because some parents did benefit from the programme. This is reflected in the reduction in the number of adolescents in the clinically significant categories from the Strength and Difficulties Questionnaire and in the number of high-stress parents after the programme. Chinese Hong Kong parents could benefit from joining a non-labelling and supportive parenting programme, but we need to further study the effectiveness of such programmes. These could possibly prevent serious problems between parents and adolescents in the future, despite the fact that there is no evidence for this at the moment. We may need to consider whether there is a possibility of combining individual-level social work service with a parenting programme; this could reduce the labelling effect of joining a parenting programme while also addressing the individual difficulties of each parent.

To deal with the rapid changes in family structure in our society, parents need support in their parenting in order to protect our adolescents from adverse effect as well as to reduce parents' parenting stress. Despite limited evidence for its effectiveness, the present programme was able to provide new insights to parents regarding parenting adolescents and reducing their stress, as evidenced from the qualitative data provided by participants. The parenting programme was also valuable in supporting parents of adolescents in Hong Kong in facing the challenges of parenting adolescents in this rapidly changing world.

Conclusion

With the changing family structure, in which many children are brought up in fragmented families, professionals face many more challenges in providing parenting programmes. We need to take both parents and carers into consideration when delivering parenting programmes. In addition, we need to take into consideration that more and more parents are practicing over parenting, meaning that they are overly intrusive in their children's lives and give less than the appropriate level of autonomy to their children. This also presents a challenge to parenting programme facilitators. When they face a group of parents with such characteristics, it becomes more and more difficult to introduce the concept that granting autonomy to their children is important. Furthermore, we could also pay more attention to the application of positive psychology in the field of parenting programmes, as emerging research is pointing towards the relationship between the character strength of parents and their children's outcomes.

Bibliography

Abidin, R. R. (1995). Parenting stress index 3rd edition: Professional manual. *Psychological Assessment Resources, Inc, Odessa, TX.*

Adams, G.R., Gullotta, T., & Clancy, M.A. (1985) Homeless adolescents: A descriptive study of similarities and differences between runaways and throwaways. *Adolescence*, Vol. 20: 715–724.

Adler, A. (1927) *Understanding human nature.* Oxford: Greenburg.

Allan, G., Hawker, S., & Crow, G. (2001) Family diversity and change in Britain and Western Europe. *Journal of Family Issues*, Vol. 22, No. 7: 819–837.

Allison, B.N. (2000) Parent–adolescent conflict in early adolescence: Research and implications for middle school programs. *Journal of Family and Consumer Sciences Education*, Vol. 18, No. 2 (Fall/Winter).

Alvy, K.T. (1988) Parenting programs for black parents. In L.A. Bond & B.M. Wagner (Eds.) *Families in transition: Primary prevention programs that work.* Newbury Park, CA: Sage Publication Inc: 135–169.

Ambert, A. (1997) *Parents, children, and adolescents: Interactive relationships and development in context.* New York, NY: Routledge.

Aseltine Jr., R.H. (1995) A reconsideration of parental and peer influences on adolescent deviance. *Journal of Health and Social Behaviour*, Vol. 36: 103–121.

Babbie, E., & Rubin, A. (1989) *Research methods for social work.* Belmont, CA: Wadsworth.

Barber, B.K. (1996) Parental psychological control: Revisiting a neglected construct. *Child Development*, Vol. 67: 3296–3319.

Barkley, R.A., Guevremont, D.C., Anastopoulos, A.D., & Fletcher, K.E. (1992) A comparison of three family therapy programs for treating family conflicts in adolescents with attention-deficit hyperactivity disorder. *Journal of Consulting and Clinical Psychology*, Vol. 60, No. 3: 450.

Barker, C., & Pistrang, N. (2005) Quality criteria under methodological pluralism: Implications for conducting and evaluating research. *American Journal of Community Psychology*, Vo. 35, Nos. 3/4: 201–212.

Barker, C., Pistrang, N., & Elliott, R. (2002) *Research methods in clinical psychology: An introduction for students and practitioners* (2nd edition). Chichester: Wiley.

Barlow, J., Coren, E., & Stewart-Brown, S. (2002) Meta-analysis of parenting programmes in improving maternal psychosocial health. *British Journal of General Practice*, Vol. 52: 223–233.

Barlow, J., Johnston, I., Kendrick, D., Polnay, L., & Stewart-Brown, S. (2005) Individual and group-based parenting programmes for the prevention of child abuse and neglect. *(Protocol) The Cochrane Database of Systematic Reviews 2005*, No. 2. Art. No.: CD005463. DOI: 10.1002/14651858.CD005463

Barlow, J., Shaw, R., & Steward-Brown, S. (2004) *Parenting programmes and minority ethnic families experiences and outcomes.* National Children's Bureau, London: Joseph Rowntree Foundation.

Barrett, H. (2003) *Parenting programmes for families at risk: A source book.* London: National Family & Parenting Institute.

Barth, R.P., Landsverk, J., Chamberlain, P., Reid, J., Rolls, J., Hurlburt, M., & Kohl, P. (2005) Parent training in child welfare services: Planning for a more evidence based approach to serving biological parents. *Research on Social Work Practice*, Vol. 15: 353–371.

Baumrind, D. (1968) Authoritarian vs. authoritative parental control. *Adolescence*, Vol. 3: 255–272.

Baumrind, D. (1971) Current patterns of parental authority. *Developmental Psychology Monograph*, Vol. 4: 1–103.

Baumrind, D. (1973). The development of instrumental competence through socialization. In A. Pick (Ed.), *Minnesota symposia on child psychology.* Minneapolis: University of Minnesota Press: pp. 3–46.

Baumrind, D. (1991) The influence of parenting style on adolescent competence and substance use. *Journal of Early Adolescence*, Vol. 11: 56–95.

Baydar, N., Reid, M.J., & Webster-Stratton, C. (2003) The role of mental health factors and program engagement in the effectiveness of a preventive parenting program for Head Start mothers. *Child Development*, Vol. 74, No. 5: 1433–1453.

Bavolet, S.J. (1987) *Building nurturing interactions in families experiencing parent–adolescent conflict: Validation of the nurturing parenting program for parents and adolescents.* Asheville: Family Development Resources, Inc.

Beck, A.T., & Steer, R.A. (1987) *Manual for the revised Beck depression inventory.* San Antonio, TX: Psychological Corporation.

Belsky, J. (1984) The determinants of parenting: A process model. *Child Development*, Vol. 55: 83–96.

Belsky, J., & Vondra, J. (1989) Lessons from child abuse: The determinants of parenting. In D. Cicchetti & V. Carlson (Eds.) *Current research and theoretical advances in child maltreatment.* Cambridge: Cambridge University Press: 153–202.

Berndt, T.J. (1979) Developmental changes in conformity to peers and parents. *Developmental Psychology*, Vol. 15: 608–616.

Berndt, T.J., Cheung, P.C., Lau, S., Hau, K.T., & Lew, W.J.F. (1993) Perceptions of parenting in Mainland China, Taiwan, and Hong Kong: Sex differences and societal differences. *Developmental Psychology*, Vol. 29, No. 19: 154–164.

Berne, E. (1975) *Transactional analysis in psychotherapy: A systematic individual and social psychiatry.* London: Souvenir Press.

Biehal, N. (2006) Preventive services for adolescents: exploring the process of change. *British Journal of Social Work*, Vol. 38, No. 3: 444–461.

Blamey, A., & Mackenzie, M. (2007) Theories of change and realistic evaluation peas in a pod or apples and oranges? *Evaluation*, Vol. 13, No. 4: 439–455.

Blos, P. (1967) The second individuation process of adolescence. *Psychoanalytical Studies of Childhood*, Vol. 22: 183–198.

Bogenschneider, K., & Stone, M. (1997) Delivering parent education to low and high risk parents of adolescents via age-paced newsletters. *Family Relations*, Vol. 46: 123–134.

Bond, M.H. (1996) *The handbook of Chinese psychology*. Hong Kong: Oxford University Press.

Bornstein, M.H. (2002) *Handbook of parenting (Vol. 1) Children & Parenting*. Mahwah, NJ: Lawrence Erlbaum Associates Inc. Publishers.

Bornstein, M.H., & Cheah, C.S.L. (2006) The place of "Culture and Parenting" in the ecological contextual perspective on developmental science. In K.H. Rubin & O.B. Chung (Eds.) *Parenting beliefs, behaviors, and parent–child relations – a cross-cultural perspective*. Hove: Psychological Press.

Bowlby, J. (1969) *Attachment and loss: Attachment* (RUidnr.: M102591232). New York, NY: Basic Books.

Bowlby, J. (1988) Developmental psychiatry comes of age. *The American Journal of Psychiatry*, Vol. 145, No. 1: 1.

Brannen, J. (2005) Mixing methods: The entry of qualitative and quantitative approaches into the research process. *International Journal of Social Research Methodology*, Vol. 8, No. 3: 130–137.

Braun, V., & Clarke, V. (2006) Using thematic analysis in psychology. *Qualitative Research in Psychology*, Vol. 3: 77–101.

Bronfenbrenner, U. (1979) Contexts of child rearing problems and prospects. *American Psychologist*, Vol. 34, No. 108: 44–850.

Brooks, J.B. (2004) *The process of parenting* (6th edition). New York: McGrow-Hill.

Brooks-Gunn, J., Graber, J.A., & Paikoff, R.L. (1994) Studying links between hormones and negative affect: Models and measures. *Journal of Research on Adolescence*, Vol. 4: 469–486.

Brooks-Gunn, J., & Reiter, E.O. (1990) The role of pubertal processes in the early adolescent transition. In S. Feldman & G. Elliot (Eds.) *At the threshold: The developing adolescent*. Cambridge, MA: Harvard University Press: 16–53.

Caffery, T., & Erdman, P. (2000) Conceptualizing parent–adolescent conflict: Applications from systems and attachment theories. *Family Journal and Therapy for Couples and families*, Vol. 8, No. 1: 14–21.

Campbell, D.T. (1969) Reforms as experiments. *American Psychologist*, Vol. 24, No. 4: 409–429.

Canary, D.J., Cupach, W.R., & Messman, S.J. (1995) *Relationship conflict: Conflict in parent–child, friendship and romantic relationships*. London: Sage Publication Inc.

Caracelli, V.J., & Greene, J.C. (1993) Data analysis strategies for mixed-method evaluation designs. *Educational Evaluation and Policy Analysis*, Vol. 15, No. 2: 195–207.

Catalano, R.F., & Hawkins, J.D. (1996) The social development model: a theory of antisocial behavior. In J.D., Hawkins (Ed.) *Delinquency & crime current theory*. Cambridge, MA: Cambridge University Press: 149–197.

Centers for Disease Control and Prevention (CDC). (2015) *Suicide, facts at a glance*. National Center for Injury Prevention and Control. Available from http://www.cdc.gov/violenceprevention/pdf/suicide-datasheet-a.pdf

Chan, D.W. (1998) Stressful life events, cognitive appraisal, and psychological symptoms among Chinese adolescents in Hong Kong. *Journal of Youth and Adolescence*, Vol. 27, No. 4: 457–472.

Chan, S., & Leong, C.W. (1994) Chinese families in transition: Cultural conflicts and adjustment problems. *Journal of Social Distress and The Homeless*, Vol. 3: 263–281.

Chan, S., Miranda, R., & Surrence, K. (2009) Subtypes of rumination in the relationship between negative life events and suicidal ideation. *Archives of Suicide Research*, Vol. 13, No. 2: 123–135.

Chau, I. (1996) *Filial therapy with Chinese parents.* Unpublished doctoral dissertation, Denton, TX: University of North Texas.

Chang, C.Y., & Ritter, K.B. (2004) Cultural considerations of Adlerian parenting education. *Journal of Individual Psychology*, Vol. 60: 67–75.

Chang, E.C., D'Zurilla, T.J., & Sanna, L.J. (Eds.). (2004) *Social problem solving: Theory, research and training.* Washington, DC: American Psychological Association.

Chao, R.K. (1994a) Extending research on consequences of parenting style for Chinese American and European Americans. *Child Development*, Vol. 72: 1832–1843.

Chao, R.K. (1994b) Beyond parental control and authoritarian parenting style: Understanding Chinese parenting through the cultural notion of training. *Child Development*, Vol. 65: 1111–1120.

Chao, R.K. (1995) Chinese and European American cultural models of the self reflected in mothers' childrearing beliefs. *Ethos*, Vol. 23, No. 3: 328–354.

Chao, R.K. (2000) The parenting of immigrant Chinese and European American mothers: Relations between parenting styles, socialization goals, and parental practices. *Journal of Applied Developmental Psychology*, Vol. 21, No. 2: 233–248.

Chao, R.K. (2005) *The importance of Guan in describing the parental control of immigrant Chinese American.* Unpublished manuscript, University of California at Riverside.

Chao, R.K., & Sue, S. (1996) Chinese parental influence and their children's school success: A paradox in the literature on parenting styles. In S. Lau (Ed.) *Growing up the Chinese way: Chinese child and adolescent development.* Hong Kong: The Chinese University of Hong Kong Press: 93–120.

Charles, R., Martinez, J.R., & Forgatch, M.S. (2002) Adjusting to change: Linking family structure transitions with parenting and boys' adjustment. *Journal of Family Psychology*, Vol. 16, No. 2: 107–117.

Charmaz, K. (2006) *Constructing grounded theory: A practical guide through qualitative analysis.* London: Sage Publication Inc.

Cheetham, J. (1992) Evaluating social work effectiveness. *Research on Social Work Practice*, Vol. 2, No. 3: 265–287.

Chen, C., Lee, S., & Stevenson, H.W. (1996) Academic achievement and motivation of Chinese students: A cross-national perspective. In S. Lau (Ed.) *Growing up the Chinese way: Chinese child and adolescent development.* Hong Kong: The Chinese University of Hong Kong Press: 69–91.

Chen, C., & Stevenson, H.W. (1989) Homework: A cross-cultural examination. *Child Development*, Vol. 60: 551–561.

Cheng Gorman, J., & Balter, L. (1997) Culturally sensitive parent education: A critical review of quantitative research. *Review of Educational Research*, Vol. 67, No. 3 (Fall): 339–369.

Cheung, C.K., Liu, S.K., & Lee, T.Y. (2005) Parents teachers and peers and early adolescent runaway in Hong Kong. *Adolescence*, Vol. 40 (Summer): 158.

Cheung, M., & Law, C.K. (2003) A culturally relevant model for evaluating family services in Hong Kong. In I. Katz & J. Pinkerton (Eds.) *Evaluating family support: Thinking internationally, thinking critically.* London: John Wiley & Sons, Inc.

Cheung, P.C., & Lau, S. (1985) Self-esteem: Its relationship to the family and school social environments among Chinese adolescents. *Youth and Society*, Vol. 16, No. 4: 438–456.

Cheung, S.K. (2001) Parent education programmes in Hong Kong: Are they Effective? *Hong Kong Journal of Social Work*, Vol. 35, Nos. 1&2: 85–96.

Cheung, S.K., & Yau, Y.L. (1996) Parent effectiveness training for Chinese parents: Adaptation and evaluation. *Asia Pacific Journal of Social Work*, Vol. 6, No. 1: 30–42.

Chou, K.L. (1999) Social support and subjective well-being among Hong Kong Chinese young adults. *Journal of Genetic Psychology*, Vol. 160, No. 3: 319–331.

Chou, K.L. (2003) Problem behavior among Chinese adolescents. *The Journal of Genetic Psychology*, Vol. 164, No. 4: 473–480.

Clarke, A., & Dawson, R. (2005) *Evaluation research: An introduction to principles, methods, and practice.* London: Sage Publication Inc.

Clarke, K., & Churchill, H. (2010) 'A chance to stand back': Parenting programmes for parents of adolescents. *Children & Society*, Vol. 26: 316–327. DOI: 10.1111/j.1099-0860.2010.00346.x

Coffey, A., & Atkinson, P. (1996) *Making sense of qualitative data: complementary research strategies.* Thousand Oaks, CA: Sage Publications, Inc.

Cohen, J. (1988) *Statistical power analysis for the behavioural sciences.* Hillsdale, NJ: Erlbaum.

Coie, J.D., & Jacobs, M.R. (1993) The role of social context in the prevention of conduct disorder. *Development and Psychopathology*, Vol. 5: 263–275.

Cojocaru, S., & Cojocaru, D. (2011) Naturalistic evaluation of programs. *Parents' voice in parent education programs, Transylvanian Review of Administrative Sciences*, Vol. 34E: 49–62.

Cole, D.A., & McPherson, A.E. (1993) Relation of family subsystems to adolescent depression: Implementing a new family assessment strategy. *Journal of Family Psychology*, Vol. 7: 119–133.

Coleman, J. (1990) The nature of adolescence. In *Youth policies in the 1990s.* London: Taylor & Francis.

Coleman, J. (2001) The needs of parents and teenagers. In J. Coleman & D. Roker (Eds.) *Supporting parents of teenagers a handbook for professionals.* London: Jessica Kingsley Publishers.

Coleman, J., & Hendry, L.B. (1999) *The nature of adolescence* (3rd edition). London: Routledge.

Coleman, J., & Roker, D. (2001) Setting the scene: Parenting and public policy. In J. Coleman & D. Roker (Eds.) *Supporting parents of teenagers a handbook for professionals.* London: Jessica Kingsley Publishers.

Collins, W.A. (1990) Parent–child relationships in the transition to adolescence: Continuity and change in interaction, affect, and cognition In R. Montemayor, G. Adams, & T. Gullotta (Eds.) *From childhood to adolescence: A transitional period?* Newbury Park, CA: Sage Publication Inc: 85–106.

Collins, W.A. (1995) Relationships and development: Family adaptation to individual change. In S. Shulman (Ed.) *Close relationships and socioemotional development.* New York: Ablex: 129–155.

Collins, W.A., & Laursen, B. (1992) Conflict and relationships during adolescence. In C.U. Shantz & W.W. Hartup (Eds.) *Conflict in child and adolescent development.* New York: Cambridge University Press: 216–241.

Collins, W.A., & Steinberg, L. (2006) Adolescent development in interpersonal context. In N. Eisenberg, W. Damon, & R.M. Lerner (Eds.) *Handbook of child psychology: Vol. 3. Social emotional and personality development* (6th edition). Hoboke, NJ: John Wiley & Sons, Inc.

Conners, N.A., Whiteside-Mansell, L., Deere, D., Ledet, T., & Edwards, M.C. (2006) Measuring the potential for child maltreatment: the reliability and validity of the Adult Adolescent Parenting Inventory—2. *Child Abuse & Neglect*, Vol. 30, No. 1: 39–53.

Consoli, A., Peyre, H., Speranza, M., Hassler, C., Falissard, B., Touchette, E., . . . & Révah-Lévy, A. (2013) Suicidal behaviors in depressed adolescents: role of perceived relationships in the family. *Child and Adolescent Psychiatry and Mental Health*, Vol. 7, No. 1: 8.

Cook, T.D., & Campbell, D.T. (1979) *Quasi-experimentation: Design and analysis for field settings*. Skokie, IL: Rand McNally.

Corder, W.C., & Foreman, D.I. (2009) *Nonparametric statistics for non-statisticians*. Hoboke, NJ: John Wiley & Sons, Inc.

Cramer, P. (2011) Young adult narcissism: A 20 year longitudinal study of the contribution of parenting styles, preschool precursors of narcissism, and denial. *Journal of Research in Personality*, Vol. 45, No. 1: 19–28.

Creswell, J., & Plano Clark, V. (2007) *Designing and conducting mixed methods research*. Thousand Oaks, CA: Sage.

Croake, J.W., & Glover, K.E. (1977) A history and evaluation of parent education. *Family Coordinator*, Vol. 26, No. 2: 151–157.

Dancey, C.P., & Reidy, J. (2002) *Statistics without maths for psychology* (2nd edition). Hemel Hempstead, UK: Prentice-Hall.

Darling, N. (1999) *Parenting style and its correlates. ERIC digest*. Champaign, IL: ERIC Clearinghouse on Elementary and Early Childhood Education.

Darling, N., & Steinberg, L. (1993) Parenting style as context: An integrative model. *Psychological Bulletin*, Vol. 113, No. 3: 487–496.

Dekovic, M. (1999) Parent–adolescent conflict: Possible determinants and consequences. *International Journal of Behavioural Development*, Vol. 23, No. 4: 977–1000.

Dekovic, M., Groenendaal, J.H.A., & Gerrits, L.A.W. (1996) Parental personality characteristics, cognitions regarding child-rearing, and experience of parenting. In J. Rispens, J. Hermanns, & W. Meeus (Eds.) *Child-rearing in the Netherlands*, Vol. 23, No. 4: 977–1000.

Dekovic, M., Wissink, I.B., & Meijer, A.M. (2004) The role of family and peer relations in adolescent antisocial behaviour: Comparison of four ethnic groups. *Journal of Adolescence*, Vol. 27: 497–514.

Dembo, M.H., Sweitzer, M., & Lauritzen, P. (1985) An evaluation of group parent education: Behavioral, PET and Adlerian programs. *Review of Educational Research*, Vol. 55: 155–200.

Demo, D.H. (1991) A sociological perspective on parent–adolescent disagreements. In R.L. Paikoff (Ed.) *Shared views in the family during adolescence*. San Francisco, CA: Jossey-Bass: 111–118.

Dinkmeyer, D., & McKay, G. (1976) *Systematic training for effective parenting*. Circle Pines, MN: American Guidance Service.

Dishion, T.J., & Andrews, D.W. (1995) Preventing escalation in problem behaviours with high-risk young adolescents: Immediate and 1-year outcomes. *Journal of Consulting and Clinical Psychology*, Vol. 63: 538–548.

Dishion, T.J., & Kavanagh, K. (2000) A multilevel approach to family-centered prevention in schools: Process and outcome *Addictive Behaviors*, Vol. 25, No. 6: 899–911.

Dishion, T.J., & McMahon, R.J. (1998) Parental monitoring and the prevention of child and adolescent problem behaviour: A conceptual and empirical formulation. *Clinical Child and Family Psychology Review*, Vol. 1: 61–75.

Dishion, T.J., Patterson, G.R., & Kavanagh, K. (1992) An experimental test of the coercion model: Linking theory, measurement and intervention. In J. McCord & R. Trembley (Eds.) *The interaction of theory and practice: Experimental studies of interventions.* New York: Guilford Press: 253–282.

Dooley, D. (2000) *Social research methods* (4th edition). Upper Saddle River, NJ: Prentice-Hall.

Doorn, D.V., Branje, S.J.F., & Meeus, W.H.J. (2008) Conflict resolution in parent–adolescent relationships and adolescent delinquency. *Journal of Early Adolescence*, Vol. 28, No. 4: 503–527.

Dornbusch, S.M. (1989) The sociology of adolescence. *Annual Review of Sociology*, Vol. 15: 233–259.

Dornbusch, S.M., Ritter, P.L., Leiderman, P.H., Roberts, D.F., & Fraleigh, M.J. (1987) The relation of parenting style to adolescent school performance. *Child Development*, Vol. 58: 1244–1257.

Dreikurs, R., & Soltz, V. (1964) *Children: The challenge.* New York: Hawthorn.

Education and Manpower Bureau (2003) *Parent education database in Hong Kong – a pilot study.* Unpublished report of Hong Kong SAR Government.

Eisenberg, N., Fabes, R.A., Shepard, S.A., Murphy, B.C., Guthrie, I.K., Jones, S., Friedman, J., Poulin, R., & Maszk, P. (1997) Contemporaneous and longitudinal prediction of children's social functioning from regulation and emotionality. *Child Development*, Vol. 68: 642–664.

Elder, G.H. (1974) *Children of the great depression.* Chicago: University of Chicago Press.

Elliott, A. (2002) *Psychoanalytic theory: An introduction* (2nd edition). Basingstoke: Palgrave.

Elliott, D.S., Huizinga, D., & Ageton, S.S. (1985) *Explaining delinquency and drug use.* Beverly Hills, CA: Sage Publications Inc.

Elliott, D.S., & Menard, S. (1996) Delinquent friends and delinquent behavior: Temporal and developmental patterns. In J.D. Hawkins (Ed.) *Delinquency and crime: Current theories.* New York: Cambridge University Press: 28–67.

Erikson, E. (1968) *Identity: Youth and crisis.* New York: Norton.

Eyberg, S.M., & Robinson, E.A. (1982) Parent–child interaction training: Effects on family functioning. *Journal of Clinical Child Psychology*, Vol. 11, No. 2: 130–137.

Eyberg, S.M., & Ross, A.W. (1978) Assessment of child behaviour problems: The validation of a new inventory. *Journal of Clinical Psychology*, Vol. 16: 113–116.

Farrington, D.P. (1991) Childhood aggression and adult violence: Early precursors and later life outcomes. In D.J. Pepler & K.H. Rubin (Eds.) *The development and treatment of childhood aggression.* Hillsdale, NJ: Lawrence Erlbaum Associates Inc. Publishers: 5–29.

Farrington, D.P. (1994) Parental separation, adolescent psychopathology, and problem behaviours. *Journal of the American Academy of Child and Adolescent Psychiatry*, Vol. 33: 1122–1131.

Farrington, D.P. (2003) Key results from the first forty years of the Cambridge study in delinquent development. In T.P. Thornberry & M.D. Krohn (Eds.) *Taking stock of delinquency: An overview of findings from contemporary longitudinal studies.* New York: Kluwer Academic Publishers/Plenum.

Farrington, D.P., Ohlin, L.E., & Wilson, J.Q. (1986) *Understanding and controlling crime: Toward as new research strategy.* New York: Springer-Verlag.

Farrington, D.P., & West, D.J. (1990) The Cambridge study of delinquent development: A long-term follow-up of 411 London males. In H.J. Kerner & G. Kaiser (Eds.) *Criminality: Personality, behavior and life history.* New York: Springer-Verlag: 117–138.

Feldman, S.S., & Rosenthal, D.A. (1991) Age expectations of behavioral autonomy in Hong Kong, Australian and American Youth: The influence of family variables and adolescents' values. *International Journal of Psychology*, Vol. 26, No. 1: 1–23.

Feldman, S.S., Rosenthal, D.A., Mont-Reynaud, R., Leung, K., & Lau, S. (1991) Ain't misbehavin': Adolescent values and family environments as correlates of misconduct in Australia, Hong Kong, and the United States. *Journal of Research on Adolescence*, Vol. 1: 109–134.

Fine, M.J. (1980) The parent education movement: An introduction. In M.J. Fine (Ed.) *Handbook on parent education.* New York: Academic Press: 3–26.

Fine, M.J., & Henry, S.A. (1989) Professional issues in parent education. In M.J. Fine (Ed.) *The second handbook on parent education contemporary perspectives.* London: Academic Press.

First, J.A., & Way, W.L. (1995) Parent education outcomes insights into transformative learning. *Family Relations*, Vol. 44, No. 1 (January): 104–109.

Fitzpatrick, J.J., & Norbeck, J. (1997) *Annual review of nursing research*, Vol. 15. New York: Springer Publishing Company.

Forehand, R., & Long, N. (1988) Outpatient treatment of the acting-out child: Procedures, long-term follow-up data and clinical problems. *Advances in Behavior Research and Therapy*, Vol. 10: 129–177.

Forehand, R., & McMahon, R.J. (1981) *Helping the noncompliant child: A clinician's guide to parent training.* New York: Guilford Press.

Forgatch, M.S., Patterson, G.R., & DeGarmo, D.S. (2005) Evaluating fidelity: predictive validity for a measure of competent adherence to the Oregon model of parent management training. *Behavior Therapy*, Vol. 36, No. 1: 3.

Foster, S.L., Prinz, R.J., & O'Leary, K.D. (1983) Impact of problem solving communication training and generalization procedures on family conflict. *Child and Family Behavior Therapy*, Vol. 5: 1–23.

Freud, A. (1958) Adolescence. *Psychoanalytic Study of the Child*, Vol. 15: 255–278.

Fuligni, A.J. (1998) Authority, autonomy, and parent–adolescent conflict and cohesion: A study of adolescents from Mexican, Chinese, Filipino, and European Backgrounds. *Developmental Psychology*, Vol. 34, No. 4: 782–792.

Fuligni, A.J., Yip, T., & Tseng, V. (2002) The impact of family obligation on the daily activities and psychological well-being of Chinese American adolescents. *Child Development*, Vol. 73: 302–314.

Fuller, R. (1996) Evaluating social work effectiveness: A pragmatic approach. In P. Alderson, S. Brill, I. Chalmers, R. Fuller, P. Hindley-Smith, G. Macdonald,

T. Newman, A. Oakley, H. Roberts, & H. Ward (Eds.) *What works? Effective social interventions in child welfare*. Ilford, Essex: Barnardos.

Gambrill, E. (2018) Evidence based practice: An alternative to authority-based practice. *Families in society: The Journal of Contemporary Social Services*, Vol. 99, No. 3: 283–294.

Gar, N.S., & Hudson, J.L. (2008) An examination of the interactions between mothers and children with anxiety disorders. *Behaviour research and therapy*, Vol. 46, No. 12: 1266–1274.

Garbarino, J., & Gilliam, G. (1980) *Understanding abusive families*. Lexington, MA: Lexington Books.

Garbarino, J., & Kelly, A.F. (1986) An introduction to troubled youth and troubled families. In J. Garbarino, C.J. Shellenbach, & J.M. Sebes (Eds.) *Troubled youth, troubled families*. New York: Aldine Publishing Company: 3–26.

Garbarino, J., Sebes, J., & Schellenbach, C. (1984) Families at risk for destructive parent–child relations in adolescence. *Child Development*, Vol. 55: 174–183.

Ge, X., Conger, R.D., & Elder Jr., G.H. (1996) Coming of age too early: Pubertal influences on girls' vulnerability to psychological distress. *Child Development*, Vol. 67: 3386–3400.

Ghate, D., & Ramella, M. (2002) *Positive Parenting: The National Evaluation of the Youth Justice Board's Parenting Programme*, London: Policy Research Bureau of the Youth Justice Board.

Gibaud-Wallston, J., & Wandersman, L.P. (1978, August) *Development and utility of the parenting sense of competence scale*. Paper presented at the meeting of the American Psychological Association, Toronto.

Givertz, M., & Segrin, C. (2014) The association between overinvolved parenting and young adults' self-efficacy, psychological entitlement, and family communication. *Communication Research*, Vol. 41, No. 8: 1111–1136.

Glaser, B., & Strauss, A. (1967) *The discovery of grounded theory*. New York: Aldine Publishing Company.

Goemans, A., van Geel, M., Vedder, P., & Bradley, R.H. (2016) HOME in the Netherlands: Validation of the home observation for measurement of the environment inventory. *Journal of Family Issues*, Vol. 37, No. 15: 2118–2137.

Goodman, R. (1997) The strengths and difficulties questionnaire: A research note. *Journal of Child Psychology and Psychiatry*, Vol. 38: 581–586.

Goodman, R. (2001) Psychometric properties of the strengths and difficulties questionnaire. *Journal of the American Academy of Child and Adolescent Psychiatry*, Vol. 40, No. 11: 1337–1345.

Gordon, T. (1975) *P.E.T. Parent Effectiveness Training: The tested new way to raise responsible children*. New York: Plume.

Gorman, J.C. (1998) Parenting attitudes and practices of immigrant Chinese American mothers of adolescents. *Family Relations*, Vol. 47: 73–80.

Gould, M., Greenberg, Velting, D.M., & Shaffer, D. (2003) Youth suicide risk and preventive interventions: a review of the past 10 years. *Journal of American Academy of Child & Adolescent Psychiatry*, Vol. 42, No. 4, 386–405. doi:10.1097/01.CHI.0000046821.95464.CF.

Greenberger, E., Chen, C., Tally, S.R., & Dong, Q. (2000) Family, peer and individual correlates symptomatology among US and Chinese adolescents. *Journal of Consulting and Clinical Psychology*, Vol. 68, No. 2: 209–219.

Greene, J.C., Caracelli, V.J., & Graham, W.F. (1989) Toward a conceptual framework for mixed-method evaluation designs. *Educational Evaluation and Policy Analysis*, Vol. 11: 255–274.

Greer, K. (1986) Today's parents: How well are they doing? *Better Homes and Gardens*: 36–46.

Guerney, B.G., Coufal, J., & Vogelsong, E. (1981) Relationship enhancement versus a traditional approach to therapeutic/ preventative/enrichment parent–adolescent programs. *Journal of Consulting and Clinical Psychology*, Vol. 49, No. 6: 927–939.

Habermas, J. (1968) Science and technology as ideology. In B. Barnes (Ed.) *Sociology of science*. Harmondsworth: Penguin.

Hall, J.A. (1987) Parent–adolescent conflict: An empirical review. *Adolescence*, Vol. 22, No. 88: 767–789.

Hamner, T., & Turner, P. (1996) *Parenting in contemporary society*. Boston, MA: Allyn & Bacon.

Hanson, W.E., Creswell, J.W., Creswell, J.D., Plano Clark, V.L., & Petska, K.S. (2005) Mixed methods research designs in counseling psychology. *Journal of Counselling Psychology*, Vol. 52, No. 2: 224–235.

Harris, T.A. (1969) *I'm ok you're ok*. New York: Harper & Row.

Harris, T.A. (2004) I'm Ok You're Ok. London: Pan Books Ltd.

Harter, S., Whitesell, N. R., & Junkin, L. J. (1998) Similarities and differences in domain-specific and global self-evaluations of learning-disabled, behaviorally disordered, and normally achieving adolescents. *American Educational Research Journal*, Vol. 35, No. 4: 653–680. https://doi.org/10.3102/00028312035004653

Hayes, S.P. (1959) *Measuring the results of development projects*. New York: UNESCO.

Henggeler, S.W., Schoenwald, S.K., Borduin, C.M., Rowland, M.D., Cunningham, P.B. (1998) *Multisystemic treatment of antisocial behavior in children and adolescents*. New York: Guilford Press.

Henricson, C. (1997) *An evaluation of exploring parenthood's and young minds' advice line services*. London: Exploring Parenthood/Young Minds.

Henricson, C., & Roker, D. (2000) Support for the parents of adolescents: A review. *Journal of Adolescence*, 23: 763–783.

Hinton, S. & Taylor, A. (2006) *Challenging years, living with teenagers*. Brighton: Trust for the study of Adolescence.

Hirschi, T. (1969) *Causes of delinquency*. University of California Press.

Ho, D.Y.F. (1987) Fatherhood in Chinese culture. In M.E. Lam (Ed.) *The father's role: Cross-cultural perspectives*. Hillsdale, NJ: Lawrence Erlbaum Associates Inc. Publishers.

Ho, D.Y.F. (1989) Continuity and variation in Chinese patterns of socialization. *Journal of Marriage and the Family*, Vol. 51, No. 1: 149–163.

Ho, D.Y.F. (1994) Cognitive socialization in Confucian heritage cultures. In P.M. Greenfield & R.R. Cocking (Eds.) *Cross-cultural roots of minority child development*. Hillsdale, NJ: Lawrence Erlbaum Associates Inc. Publishers: 285–313.

Ho, D.Y.F., & Kang, T.K. (1984) Intergenerational comparisons of child-rearing attitudes and practices in Hong Kong. *Developmental Psychology*, Vol. 20: 1004–1006.

Ho, T.P., Chow, V., Fung, C., Leung, K., Chiu, K.Y., Yu, G., & Au, Y.W. (1999) Parent management training in a Chinese population: Application and outcome. *Journal of the American Academy of Child and Adolescent Psychiatry*, Vol. 38, No. 9: 1165–1172.

Ho, T.P., Leung, P.W.L., Luk, E.S.L., Taylor, E., Baconshone, J., & Mak, F.L. (1996) Establishing the constructs of childhood behavioral disturbances in Chinese population: A questionnaire study. *Journal of Abnormal Child Psychology*, Vol. 24, No. 4: 417–431.

Hoard, D., & Shepard, K.N. (2005) Parent education as parent-centered prevention: A review of school-related outcomes. *School Psychology Quarterly*, Vol. 20, No. 4: 434–454.

Hoghughi, M. (2004) Parenting – an introduction in handbook of parenting theory and research for practice. In M. Hoghughi & N. Long (Eds.). *Handbook of parenting: theory and research for practice.* London: Sage Publications Inc.

Holden, G.W. (2010) Parenting a dynamic perspective. London: Sage Publications Inc.

Holmbeck, G.N. (1996) A model of family relational transformations during the transition to adolescence: Parent–adolescent conflict and adaptation. In J.A. Graber, J. Brooks-Gunn, & A.C. Petersen (Eds.) *Transitions through adolescence: Interpersonal domains and context.* Mahwah, NJ: Lawrence Erlbaum Associates Inc. Publishers: 167–199.

Holmbeck, G.N., & Hill, J.P. (1986) A path-analytic approach to the relations between parental traits and acceptance and adolescent adjustment. *Sex Roles*, Vol. 14, No. 5–6: 315–334.

Holmbeck, G.N., & Hill, J.P. (1991) Conflict engagement, positive affect, and menarche in families with seventh-grade girls. *Child Development*, Vol. 62: 1030–1048.

The Hong Kong Council of Social Service (2010) *Social indicators of Hong Kong-median household family income for four.* Retrieved October 28, 2010, from www.socialindicators.org.hk/en/indicators/basic_statistics/12.7

Hong Kong Family Council (2012) *Introduction to the family council.* Retrieved March 7, 2012, from www.familycouncil.gov.hk/english/home/home_intro.htm.

Hong Kong Government (1991) *Social welfare into the 1990s and beyond.* Hong Kong: Government Printing Office.

Hosmer, D.W., & Lemeshow, S. (2000) *Applied logistic regression* (2nd edition). New York: John Wiley & Sons, Inc.

Hsu, F.L.K. (1971) *Under the ancestors' shadow: Kinship, personality and social mobility in China.* Stanford: Stanford University Press.

Jocobson, K.C., & Crockett, L.J. (2000) Parental monitoring and adolescent adjustment: An ecological perspective. *Journal of Research on Adolescence*, Vol. 10: 65–97.

Johnson, D.L., & Breckenridge, J.N. (1982) The Houston parent—child development center and the primary prevention of behavior problems in young children. *American Journal of Community Psychology*, Vol. 10, No. 3: 305–316.

Johnson, R.B., Onwuegbuzie, A.J., & Turner, L.A. (2007) Toward a definition of mixed methods research. *Journal of Mixed Methods Research*, Vol. 1, No. 2: 112–133.

Johnson, D.L., & Walker, T. (1987) Primary prevention of behaviour problems in Mexican-American children. *American Journal of Community Psychology*, Vol. 15, No. 4: 375–385.

Johnson, J.H., & McCutcheon, S.M. (1980) Assessing life stress in children and adolescents: Preliminary findings with the life events checklist. In I.G. Sarason & C.D. Spielberger (Eds.) *Stress and anxiety.* Washington, DC: Hemisphere: 111–125.

Johnson, R.B., & Onwuegbuzie, A.J. (2004) Mixed methods research: A research paradigm whose time has come. *Educational Researcher*, Vol. 33, No. 7: 14–26.

Kamerman, S.B. (2009) Families and family policies: Developing a holistic policy agenda. *Hong Kong Journal of Paediatrics (New Series)*, Vol. 14, No. 2: 15–121.

Kapadia, S., & Miller, J. (2005) Parent–adolescent relationships in the context of interpersonal disagreements: view from a collectivist culture. *Psychology and Developing Societies*, Vol. 17, No. 1: 33–50.

Kim, K, & Smith, P.K. (1998) Childhood stress, behavioural symptoms and mother-daughter development. *Journal of Adolescence*, Vol. 21: 231–240.

Kim, S.Y., & Wong, Y. (2002) Assessing Asian and Asian American parenting: A review of literature. In K. Kurasaki, S. Okazaki, & S. Sue (Eds.) *Asian American mental health: Assessment methods and theories*. Netherlands: Kluwer Academic Publishers.

Kirk, S.A., & Reid, W.J. (2002) *Science and social work: A critical appraisal*. New York: Columbia University Press.

Kumpfer, K.L., Alvarado, R, Smith, P., & Bellamy, N. (2002) Cultural sensitivity in universal family-based prevention interventions. *Prevention Science*, Vol. 3, No. 3: 241–244.

Kwok, L.Y.C. (1994) Systematic Training for Effective Parenting (STEP): Its Applicability for the Chinese parents of primary school children in Hong Kong. *Hong Kong Journal of Social Work*, Vol. 28, No. 1: 22–30.

Kwok Lai, S.Y.C., & Shek, D.T.L. (2010) Hopelessness, parent-adolescent communication, and suicidal ideation among Chinese adolescents in Hong Kong. *Suicide and Life-Threatening Behavior*, Vol. 40, No. 3: 224–233.

Lai, K.W., & McBride-Chang, C. (2001) Suicidal ideation, parenting style, and family climate among Hong Kong adolescents. *International Journal of Psychology*, Vol. 36, No. 2: 81–87.

Lam, C.M. (1997) A cultural perspective on the study of Chinese adolescent Development. *Child & Adolescent Social Work Journal*, Vol. 14, No. 2: 95–113.

Lam, C.M. (2005) In search of the meaning of parent education in the Hong Kong-Chinese context. In *Contemporary issues in parenting*. New York: Nova Science Publishers: 111–124.

Lam, C.W., Lam, W.M., & Leung, Y.K. (2005) The changing nature and ideology of marriage in Hong Kong. In P.H. Youn & A.Y.L. Lok (Eds.) *Marriage, divorce and remarriage: Professional practice in Hong Kong*. Hong Kong: The Chinese Hong Kong University Press: 243–266.

Lam, D. (1999) Parenting stress and anger: The Hong Kong experience. *Child and Family Social Work*, Vol. 4: 337–346.

Lamis, D.A., & Jahn, D.R. (2013) Parent–child conflict and suicide rumination in college students: the mediating roles of depressive symptoms and anxiety sensitivity. *Journal of American College Health*, Vol. 61, No. 2: 106–113. doi:10.1080/07448481.2012.754758

Larsen, J.J., & Juhasz, A.M. (1986) The knowledge of child development inventory. *Adolescence*, Vol. 21, No. 81: 39.

Lau, S. (1992) Collectivism's individualism: Value preference, personal control, and the desire for freedom among Chinese in Mainland China, Hong Kong and Singapore. *Personality and Individual Differences*, Vol. 13, No. 3: 361–366.

Lau, S., & Kwok, L.K. (2000) Relationship of family environment to adolescents' depression and self-concept. *Social Behavior & Personality: An International Journal*, Vol. 28, No. 1: 41–51.

Lau, S., Nicholls, J.G., Thorkildsen, T.A., & Patashnick, M. (2000) Chinese and American adolescents' perception of the purposes of education and beliefs about the world of work. *Social Behaviour and Personality*, Vol. 28: 73–90.

Lau, S., & Wong, A.K. (1992) Value and sex-role orientation of Chinese adolescents. *International Journal of Psychology*, Vol. 27, No. 1: 3–17.

Lau, S., & Yeung, P.W. (1996) Understanding Chinese child development: The role of culture in socialization. In S. Lau (Ed.) *Growing up the Chinese way: Chinese child and adolescent development.* Hong Kong: The Chinese University of Hong Kong press.

Laursen, B., & Collins, W.A. (1994) Interpersonal conflict during adolescence. *Psychological Bulletin*, Vol. 115: 197–209.

Laursen, B., Coy, K.C., & Collins, W.A. (1998) Reconsidering changes in parent–child conflict across adolescence: A meta-analysis. *Child Development*, Vol. 69: 817–832.

Leahey, E. (2007) Convergence and confidentiality? Limits to the implementation of mixed methodology. *Social Science Research*, Vol. 36: 149–158.

Lee, M.T., Wong, B.P., Chow, B.W.Y., & McBride-Chang, C. (2006) Predictors of suicide ideation and depression in Hong Kong adolescents: perceptions of academic and family climates. *Suicide and Life-Threatening Behavior*, Vol. 36, No. 1: 82–96.

Lee Duckworth, A., Steen, T.A., & Seligman, M.E. (2005) Positive psychology in clinical practice. *Annual Review of Clinical Psychology*, Vo. 1: 629–651.

Loeber, R. (1982) The stability of antisocial and delinquent and child behaviour: A review. *Child Development*, Vol. 53: 1431–1446.

Loeber, R., & Dishion, T.J. (1983) Early predictors of mal delinquency: A review. *Psychological Bulletin*, Vol. 94: 68–99.

Loeber, R., & Farrington, D. (1998) *Serious and violent juvenile offenders: Risk factors and successful interventions.* Thousand Oaks, CA: Sage Publication Inc.

Leung, C., Leung, S., Chang, R., Tso, K., & Ip, F. (2005) Child behaviour and parenting stress in Hong Kong families. *Hong Kong Medical Journal*, Vol. 11: 373–380.

Leung, C., Sanders, M., Leung, S., Mak, R., & Lau, J. (2003) An outcome evaluation of the implementation of triple P- positive parenting programme in Hong Kong. *Family Process*, Vol. 42, No. 4: 531–544.

Leung, C., & Tsang, S. (2003) *Parent education data base in Hong Kong- a pilot study.* Hong Kong: Education and Manpower Bureau, Hong Kong Special Administrative Region Government.

Leung, C.Y.W., McBride-Chang, C., & Lai, B.P.Y. (2004) Relations among maternal parenting style, academic competence, and life satisfaction in Chinese early adolescents. *Journal of Early Adolescence*, Vol. 24, No. 2: 113–143.

Leung, K., & Fan, R.M.T. (1996) Adolescent delinquent behavior in Chinese society. In S. Lau (Ed.) *Growing up the Chinese way Chinese child and adolescent development.* Hong Kong: The Chinese University of Hong Kong Press.

Lieber, E., Fung, H., & Leung, P.W.L. (2006) Chinese child-rearing beliefs: Key dimensions and contributions to the development of culture-appropriate assessment. *Asian Journal of Social Psychology*, Vol. 9: 140–147.

Lieberman, M., Doyle, A.B., & Markiewicz, D. (1999) Developmental patterns in security of attachment to mother and father in late childhood and early adolescence associations with peer relations. *Child Development*, Vol. 70: 202–213.

Light, R., & Pillemer, D.B. (1984) *Summing up: The science of reviewing research.* Cambridge, MA: Harvard University Press.

Lim, S.L., & Lim, B.K. (2005) Parenting style and child outcomes in Chinese immigrant Chinese families-current findings and cross-cultural considerations in conceptualization and research. In G.W. Peterson, S.K. Steinmetz, & S.M. Wilson (Eds.) *Parent-youth relations: Cultural and cross-cultural perspectives.* New York: The Haworth Press, Inc.

Lin, C., & Fu, V.R. (1990) A comparison of child-rearing practices among Chinese, immigrant-Chinese and Caucasian-American parents. *Child Development*, Vol. 61: 429–433.

Lin, W.Y., & Wang, C.W. (1995) The perspective of Chinese parental disciplining: A perspective of strict discipline or physical punishment? *Indigenous Psychological Research in Chinese Societies*, Vol. 3: 2–92.

Lindsay, G., Davies, H., Band, S., Cullen, M.A., Cullen, S., Strand, S., Hasluck, C., Evans, R., & Stewart-Brown, S. (2008) *Parenting early intervention pathfinder evaluation.* London: Department for Children, Schools & Families.

Loeber, R., & Stouthamer-Leober, M. (1986) Family factors as correlates and predictors of juvenile conduct problems and delinquency. In M. Tory & N. Morris (Eds.) *Crime and justice.* Chicago: University of Chicago Press: 29–149.

Long, E.S., & Adams, C.D. (2001) Mediation of parent–adolescent conflict through the combination of problem-solving communication training and behavioral exchange. *Child & Family Behavior Therapy*, Vol. 23, No. 3.

Low, Y.T. (2016) Can Hong Kong Chinese parents and their adolescent children benefit from an adapted UK parenting programme? *Journal of Social Work.* DOI: 10.1177/1468017314568860

Lundahl, B.W., Tollefson, D., Risser, H., & Lovejoy, M.C. (2008) A meta-analysis of father involvement in parent training. *Research on Social Work Practice*, Vol. 18, No. 2: 97–106.

Ma, H.K., Shek, D.T.L., Cheung, P.C., & Lam, O.B. (2000) Parental, peer, and teacher influences on the social behavior of Hong Kong Chinese Adolescents. *The Journal of Genetic Psychology*, Vol. 161, No. 1: 65–78.

Maccoby, E.E. (1992) The role of parents in the socialization of children: An historical overview. *Developmental Psychology*, Vol. 28, No. 6: 1006–1017.

Maccoby, E.E. (1998) *The two sexes: Growing up apart, coming together.* Cambridge, MA: Belknap Press.

Maccoby, E.E., & Martin, J.A. (1983) Socialization in the context of the family: Parent–child interaction. In P.H. Mussen (Series Ed.) & E.M. Hetherington (Vol. Ed.) *Handbook of child psychology: Vol. 4. Socialization, personality, and social development* (4th edition) New York: Wiley: 1–101.

Macdonald, G., & Turner, W. (2005) An experiment in helping foster-carers manage challenging behaviour. *British Journal of Social Work*, Vol. 35: 1265–1282.

Mags, J.L., & Galambos, N.L. (1993) Alternative structural models for understanding adolescent problem behavior in two-earner families. *Journal of Early Adolescence*, Vol. 13: 79–101.

Mahoney, G., Kaiser, A.P., & Girolametto, L.E. (1999) Parent education in early intervention: A call for a renewed focus. *Topics in Early Childhood Special Education*, Vol. 19, No. 3: 131–140.

Malterud, K. (2001) Qualitative research: Standards, challenges, and guidelines. *The Lancet*, Vol. 358: 483–488.

Markus, H.R., & Lin, L.R. (1999) Conflictways: Cultural diversity in the meanings and practices of conflict. In D.A. Prentice & D.T. Miller (Eds.) *Cultural divides: Understanding and overcoming group conflict.* New York: Russell Sage: 302–333.

Masten, A.A., & Coatsworth, J.D. (1998) The development of competence in favourable and unfavourable environments: Lessons from research on successful children. *American Psychologist*, Vol. 53, No. 2: 205–220.

McBride, B.A., & Rane, T.R. (1997) Role identity, role investments, and paternal involvement: Implications for parenting programs for men. *Early Childhood Research Quarterly*, Vol. 12: 173–197.

McBride-Chang, C., & Chang, L. (1998) Adolescent-parent relations in Hong Kong: Parenting style, emotional autonomy and school achievement. *The Journal of Genetic Psychology*, Vol. 159, No. 4: 421–436.

McNeece, C.A., & Thyer, B.A. (2004) Evidence-based practice and social work. *Journal of Evidence-Based Social Work*, Vol. 1, No. 1: 7–25.

Medway, F.J. (1989) Measuring the effectiveness of parent education. In M.J. Fine (Ed.) *The second handbook of parent education: Contemporary perspectives.* San Diego: Academic Press: 237–255.

Minnis, H., & Devine, C. (2001) The effect of foster carer training on the emotional and behavioural functioning of looked after children. *Adoption & Fostering Journal*, Vol. 25, No. 1: 44–54.

Minuchin, S. (1974) *Families and family therapy.* Cambridge, MA: Harvard University Press.

Moffit, T. (1983) Adolescence-limited and life-course persistent antisocial behavior: A developmental taxonomy. *Psychological Review*, Vol. 100: 674–701.

Moffit, T.E. (1993) Adolescent-limited and life course persistent antisocial behavior: a developmental taxonomy. *Psychological Review*, Vol. 100, No. 4: 674–701.

Mok, D. (1985) *The sojourn experience of Chinese visa students.* Unpublished BA (Honours) thesis, Queen's University, Kingston, ON.

Molina, M., Pastor, C., & Violant, V. (2011) Parental education as health protection factor in vulnerable childhood and adolescence. *Revista de cercetare si interventie sociala*, Vol. 34: 38–55.

Montemayor, R. (1983) Parents and adolescents in conflict: All families some of the time and some families most of the time. *The Journal of Early Adolescence*, Vol. 3, No. 1–2: 83–103.

Montemayor, R. (1986) Family Variation in Parent-Adolescent Storm and Stress. *Journal of Adolescent Research*, Vol. 1, No. 1: 15–31.

Moran, P., & Ghate, D. (2005) The effectiveness of parenting support. *Children & Society*, Vol. 19, No. 4: 329–336.

Moran, P., Ghate, D., Van Der Merwe, A., & Policy research bureau. (2004) *What works in parenting support?: a review of the international evidence.* London: Department for Education and Skills.

Moran, P., & Montemayor, R. (1986) Family variation in parent-adolescent storm and stress. *Journal of Adolescent Research*, Vol. 1, No. 1: 15–31.

Myers, H.F., Alvy, K.T., Arrington, A., Richardson, M.A., Marigna, M., Huff, R., Main, M., & Newcomb, M.D. (1992) The impact of a parent training program on inner-city African-American families. *Journal of Community Psychology*, Vol. 20: 132–147.

Nastasi, B.K., Hitchcock, J., Sarkar, S., Burkholder, G., Varjas, K., & Jayasena, A. (2007) Mixed methods in intervention research theory to adaptation. *Journal of Mixed Methods Research*, Vol. 1: 164–182.

Nelsen, J. (1996) Positive discipline. New York: Ballantine Books.

Ng, A.C.Y., Philips, D.R., & Lee, W.K.M. (2002) Persistence and challenges to filial piety and informal support of older persons in a modern Chinese society: A case study in Tuen Mun. *Hong Kong Journal of Aging Studies*, Vol. 16: 135–153.

Ng, A.M.C. (1975) *Social causes of violent crime among young offenders in Hong Kong. Unpublished research report.* Hong Kong: The Chinese University of Hong Kong Press.

Ng, A.M.C. (1980) *Family relationship and delinquent behavior.* Doctoral thesis, School of Social Work, Columbia University.

Nutley, S., Davies, H., & Walter, I. (2002) *Evidence based policy and practice: Cross sector lessons from the UK.* London: ESRC UK Centre for Evidence Based Policy and Practice/Research Unit for Research Utilisation.

Offord, D.R., Boyle, M.H., & Racine, Y.A. (1991) The epidemiology of antisocial behavior in childhood and adolescence. In D.J. Peple & K.H. Rubin (Eds.) *The development and treatment of childhood aggression.* Hillsdale, NJ: Lawrence Erlbaum Associates Inc. Publishers: 31–54.

Ogbu, J.U. (1981) Origins of human competence: A cultural-ecological perspective. *Child Development*, Vol. 52, No. 2: 413–429.

Padmawidjaja, I.A., & Chao, R.K. (2010) Parental beliefs and their relations to the parental practices of immigrant Chinese Americans and European Americans. In S.T. Russell, L.J. Crockett, & R.K. Chao (Eds.) *Asian American parenting and parent–adolescent relationships, advancing responsible adolescent development.* New York: Springer Science Business Media.

Parent Education and Support Forum (2002) *Parent education evaluation toolkits.* London: National Children's Bureau.

Patterson, G.R. (1982) *Coercive family process.* Eugene, OR: Castalia.

Patterson, G.R. (1992) Developmental changes in antisocial behavior. In R. De, V. Peters, R.J. McMahon, & V.L. Quinsey (Eds.) *Aggression and violence throughout the life span.* Newbury Park, CA: Sage Publication Inc: 52–82.

Patterson, J., Barlow, J., Mockford, C., Klimes, I., Pyper, C., & Stewart-Brown, S. (2002) Improving mental health through parenting programmes: Block randomised controlled trial. *Archives of Disease in Childhood*, Vol. 87, No. 6: 472–477.

Patterson, G.R., & Stouthamer-Loeber, M. (1984) The correlation of family management practices and delinquency. *Child Development*, Vol. 55: 1299–1307.

Patton, M.Q. (1986) *Utilization-focused evaluation.* Newbury Park, CA: Sage Publications Inc.

Pawson, R., & Tilley, N. (1997) *Realistic evaluation.* London: Sage Publications Inc.

Persons, J. (1999) Evidence-based psychotherapy: A graduate course. *Clinical Science*, Vol. 2: 12.

Petersen, A.C. (1985) Pubertal development as a cause of disturbance: Myths and realities. *Genetic, Social, and General Psychology Monographs*, Vol. 111: 205–232.

Peterson, A.C., & Taylor, B. (1980) The biological approach to adolescence. In J. Adelson (Ed.) *Handbook of adolescent psychology.* New York: Wiley: 117–155.

Peterson, C.A., Wall, S., Raikes, H.A., Kisker, E.E., Swanson, M.E., Jerald, J., Atwater, J.B., & Qiao, W. (2004) Early head start: Identifying and serving children with disabilities. *Topics in Early Childhood Special Education*, Vol. 24, No. 2: 76–88.

Phinney, J.S., Kim-Jo, T., & Vilhjalmsdottir, P. (2005) Autonomy and relatedness in adolescent-parent disagreements: Ethnic and developmental factors. *Journal of Adolescent Research*, Vol. 20, No. 1: 8–39.

Popkin, M. (1993) *Active parenting today.* Atlanta, GA: Active Parenting Publishers.

Prinz, R.J. (1977) *The assessment of parent–adolescent relations: Discriminating distressed and non-distressed dyads.* Unpublished doctoral dissertation, Stony Brook, NY: State University of New York.

Prinz, R.J., & Dumas, J.E. (2004) Prevention of oppositional defiant disorder and conduct disorder in children and adolescents. In P. A. Barrett & T. H. Ollendick (Eds.), *Handbook of interventions that work with children and adolescents: prevention and treatment.* Chichester, England: Wiley: 475–488.

Prinz, R.J., Foster, S., Kent, R.N., & O'Leary, K.D. (1979) Multivariate assessment of conflict in distressed and nondistressed mother-adolescent dyads. *Journal of Applied Behavior Analysis*, Vol. 12, No. 4: 691–700.

Prinz, R.J., & Jones, T.L. (2003) Family-based interventions. In C. A. Essau (Ed.), *Conduct and oppositional defiant disorders: Epidemiology, risk factors, and treatment.* Mahwah, NJ: Erlbaum: 279–298.

Pugh, G., De'Ath, E., & Smith, C. (1994) *Confident parents, confident children: Policy and practice in parent education and support.* London: National Children's Bureau.

Purohit, S. (2005) *Effective parenting.* Hyderabad: ICFAI University Press.

Quinton, D. (2004) *Supporting parents: Messages from research.* London: Jessica Kingsley Publishers.

Rallis, S.F., & Rossman, G.B. (2003) Mixed methods in evaluation contexts: A pragmatic framework. In A. Tashakkori & C. Teddlie (Eds.) *Handbook of mixed methods in social & behavioral research.* London: Sage Publication Inc: 491–512.

Richards, M.H., & Larson, R. (1993) Pubertal development and the daily subjective states of young adolescents. *Journal of Research on Adolescence*, Vol. 3, No. 2: 145–169.

Riggin, L.J.C. (1997) Advances in mixed-method evaluation: A synthesis and comment. *New Directions for Evaluations*, Vol. 74: 87–94.

Robin, A.L., Koepke, T., & Moye, A. (1990) Multidimensional assessment of parent-adolescent relations. *Psychological Assessment: A Journal of Consulting and Clinical Psychology*, Vol. 2, No. 4: 451.

Robin, A.L., & Foster, S.L. (1989) *Negotiating parent–adolescent conflict: A behavioral family systems approach.* New York: Guilford Press.

Robin, A.L., Kent, R., O'Leary, D., Foster, S., & Prinz, R. (1977) An approach to teaching parents and adolescents problem-solving communication skills: A preliminary report. *Behavior Therapy*, Vol. 8, No. 4: 639–643.

Roker, D., & Coleman, J. (1998) Parenting teenagers programmes: a UK perspective. *Children & Society*, Vol. 12, No. 5: 359–372.

Roker, D., & Richardson, H. (2001) Schools as a context for working with parents-the 'Living with teenagers supporting parents' Project'. In J. Coleman & D. Roker (Eds.) *Supporting parents of teenagers a handbook for professionals.* London: Jessica Kingsley Publishers.

Rosen, D.S. (2003) Eating disorders in children and young adolescents: etiology, classification, clinical features and treatment *Adolescent Medicine*, Vol. 14, No. 1: 49–59.

Rosenberg, M. (1965) *Society and the adolescent self-image.* Princeton, NJ: University Press.

Rossi, P.H., Lipsey, M.W., & Freeman, H.F. (2004) *Evaluation a systematic approach* (7th edition). London: Sage Publication Inc.

Runeson, B., & Åsberg, M. (2003). Family history of suicide among suicide victims. *American Journal of Psychiatry*, Vol. 160, No. 8: 1525–1526.

Russell, S.T., Crockett, L.J., & Chao, R.K. (2010) Introduction, Asian American parenting and parent–adolescent relationships. In S.T. Russell, L.J. Crockett, & R.K. Chao (Eds.) *Advancing responsible adolescent development*. London: Springer: 1–16.

Rutter, M., Giller, H., & Hagell, A. (1998) *Antisocial behavior by young people: a major new review*. London: Cambridge University Press.

Rutter, M., Graham, P., Chadwick, O.F.D., & Yule, W. (1976) Adolescent turmoil: Fact or fiction? *Journal of Child Psychology and Psychiatry*, Vol. 17: 35–56.

Sanders, M. (1999) Triple P – Positive parenting program: Towards an empirically validated multilevel parenting and family support strategy for the prevention of behavior and emotional problems in children. *Clinical Child and Family Psychology Review*, Vol. 2, No. 2: 71–90.

Sanders, M.R., Markie-Dadds, C., Turner, K.M.T., & Ralph, A. (2004) Using the Triple P system of intervention to prevent behavioural problems in children and adolescents. In P.A. Barrett & T.H. Ollendick (Eds.), *Handbook of interventions that work with children and adolescents: Prevention and treatment*. Chichester, England: Wiley: 489–516.

Sanders, M.R., & Woolley, M.L. (2005) The relationship between maternal self-efficacy and parenting practices: implications for parent training. *Child: Care, Health & Development*, Vol. 31, No. 1: 65–73.

Satir, V. (1983) *Conjoint family therapy* (3rd edition). Palo Alto, CA: Science and Behavior Books.

Scaramella, L.V., & Conger, R.D. (2004) Continuity versus discontinuity in parent and adolescent negative affect. In R.D. Conger, F.O. Lorenz, & K.A.S. Wickrama (Eds.) *Continuity and change in family relations theory, methods and empirical findings*. Mahwah, NJ: Lawrence Erlbaum Associates, Inc. Publishers.

Seligman, M.E. (1998) What is the good life. *APA monitor*, Vol. 29, No. 10: 2.

Segrin, C., Woszidlo, A., Givertz, M., Bauer, A., & Taylor Murphy, M. (2012) The association between overparenting, parent-child communication, and entitlement and adaptive traits in adult children. *Family Relations*, Vol. 61, No. 2: 237–252.

Segrin, C., Woszidlo, A., Givertz, M., & Montgomery, N. (2013) Parent and child traits associated with overparenting. *Journal of Social and Clinical Psychology*, Vol. 32, No. 6: 569–595.

Shantz, C.U. (1987) Conflicts between children. *Child Development*, Vol. 58: 283–305.

Sheftall, A.H., Mathias, C.W., Furr, R.M., & Dougherty, D.M. (2013) Adolescent attachment security, family functioning, and suicide attempts. *Attachment & Human Development*, Vol. 15, No. 4: 368–383. doi:10.1080/14616734.2013.782649

Shek, D.T.L. (1996) Hong Kong parents' attitude about marital quality and children. *Journal of Genetic Psychology*, Vol. 157: 123–135.

Shek, D.T.L. (1998a) A longitudinal study of Hong Kong adolescents' and parents' perceptions of family functioning and well-being. *The Journal of Genetic Psychology*, Vol. 159, No. 4: 389–403.

Shek, D.T.L. (1998b) Linkage between marital quality and parent–adolescent conflict to adolescent psychological well-being. *Journal of Youth Studies*, Vol. 1, No. 2: 195–209.

Shek, D.T.L. (1999) Perceptions of family functioning among Chinese parents and their adolescent children. *American Journal of Family Therapy*, Vol. 27: 303–314.

Shek, D.T.L. (2005) Paternal and maternal influences on the psychological well-being, substance abuse, and delinquency of Chinese adolescents experiencing economic disadvantage. *Journal of Clinical Psychology*, Vol. 61: 219–234.

Shek, D.T.L., Lam, M.C., & Tsoi, K.W. (2004) Evidence-based social work practice in Hong Kong. In B. Thyer & M. Kazi (Eds.) *International perspectives on evidence-based practice in social work*. London: Venture Press: 213–222.

Shek, D.T.L., Lee, T.Y., Ngai, N.P., Law, W.O., & Chang, L.K. (1995) Assessment of perceived parenting styles, parent–adolescent conflict, and family functioning in Chinese adolescents in Hong Kong. *Hong Kong Journal of Social Work*, Vol. 29, No. 1: 74–76.

Shek, D.T.L., & Ma, H.K. (1997) Perceptions of parental treatment styles and adolescent antisocial and prosocial behavior in Chinese context. *Psychologia*, Vol. 40: 233–240.

Shek, D.T.L., & Ma, H.K. (2001) Parent–adolescent conflict and adolescent antisocial and prosocial behavior: A longitudinal study in a Chinese context. *Adolescence*, Vol. 36, No. 143: 545–555.

Shek, D. T., & Yu, L. (2012). Internet addiction phenomenon in early adolescents in Hong Kong. *The Scientific World Journal*, Vol. 2012: 104304.

Shulruf, B. (2004) *Parent support and education programmes: a systematic review*. New Zealand: Pacific Foundation for the Parenting Council. Available at http://www.pointresearch.co.nz/parentingcouncil/library.html.

Silverberg, S.B., & Steinberg, L. (1987) Adolescent autonomy, parent-adolescent conflict, and parental well-being. *Journal of Youth and Adolescence*, Vol. 16, No. 3: 293–312.

Silverberg, S., & Steinberg, L. (1990) Psychological well-being of parents at midlife: The impact of early adolescent children. *Developmental Psychology*, Vol. 26: 658–666.

Skinner, B.F. (1965) *Science and human behavior*. New York: The Free Press.

Smetana, J.G. (1989) Adolescents' and parents' reasoning about actual family conflict. *Child Development*, Vol. 60, No. 5 (October): 1052–1067.

Smith, C., & Pugh, G. (1996) Learning to be a parent: a survey of group-based parenting programmes. *Family and parenthood: policy and practice*. London: Family Policy Studies.

Snyder, J., Dishon, T.J., & Patterson, G.R. (1986) Determinants and consequences of associating with deviant peers during preadolescence and adolescence. *Journal of Early Adolescence*, Vol. 6: 29–43.

Snyder, J., & Huntley, D. (1990) Troubled families and troubled youth: The development of antisocial behavior and depression in children. In P.E. Leone (Ed.) *Understanding troubled and troubling youth*. Newbury Park, CA: Sage Publication Inc: 194–225.

Social Issues Research Centre (2008) *Childhood and family life: Socio-demographic changes report of research conducted by the social research centre*. Oxford: Social research Centre.

Social Welfare Department. (2001) *The consultancy report on family service review*. Retrieved from https://www.swd.gov.hk/en/index/site_pubsvc/page_family/sub_listofserv/id_ifscsm/.

Social Welfare Department (2006) *Family and child care service*. Retrieved from https://www.swd.gov.hk/en/index/site_pubsvc/page_family/sub_listofserv/id_childcares/.

Solesbury, W.B. (2001) *Evidence based policy: Whence it came and where it's going.* London: ESRC Centre for Evidence Based Policy and Practice.

Sorkhabi, N. (2005) Applicability of Baumrind's parent typology to collective cultures: Analysis of cultural explanations of parent socialization effects. *International Journal of Behavioral Development*, Vol. 29, No. 6: 552–563.

Stafford, L., & Dainton, M. (1995) Parent–child communication within the family system. In T.J. Socha & G.H. Stamp (Eds.) *Parents, children, and communication: Frontiers of theory and research.* Mahwah, NJ: Lawrence Erlbaum Associates, Inc. Publishers: 3–22.

Stattin, H., & Kerr, M. (2000) Parental monitoring: A reinterpretation. *Child Development*, Vol. 71, No. 4: 1072–1085.

Steinberg, L. (1988) Reciprocal relation between parent–child distance and pubertal maturation. *Developmental Psychology*, Vol. 24: 122–128.

Steinberg, L. (1990) Autonomy, conflict and harmony in the family relationship. In S.S. Feldman & G.R. Elliott (Eds.) *At the threshold: The developing adolescent.* Harvard, MA: Harvard University Press: 255–276.

Steinberg, L. (2000) The family at adolescence: Transition and transformation. *Journal of Adolescent Health*, Vol. 27: 170–178.

Steinberg, L. (2001) We know some things: Parent–adolescent relationships in retrospect and prospect. *Journal of Research on Adolescence*, Vol. 11, No. 1: 1–19.

Steinberg, L., Lamborn, S.D., Dornbusch, S.M., & Darling, N. (1992) Impact of parenting practices on adolescent achievement: authoritative parenting, school involvement, and encouragement to succeed. *Child Development*, Vol. 63: 1266–1281.

Steinberg, L., & Morris, A.S. (2001) Adolescent development. *Annual Review of Psychology*, Vol. 52: 83–110.

Steinberg, L., & Silk, J.S. (2002) Parenting adolescents. In M.H. Bornstein (Ed.) *Handbook of parenting volume 1 children and parenting.* New Jersey: Lawrence Erlbaum Associates, Inc. Publishers.

Steinberg, L., & Silverberg, S.B. (1986) The vicissitudes of autonomy in early adolescence. *Child Development*, Vol. 57: 841–851.

Stoolmiller, M. (1994) Antisocial behavior, delinquent peer association, and unsupervised wandering for boys: Growth and change from childhood to early adolescence. *Multivariate Behavioral Research*, Vol. 29: 263–288.

Strean, H.S. (1979) *Psychoanalytic theory and social work practice.* London: Collier Macmillan.

Suchman, E.A. (1967) Preventive health behavior: A model for research on community health campaigns. *Journal of Health and Social Behavior*, Vol. 8: 197–209.

Sun, R.C.F., Hui, K.P., & Watkins, D. (2006) Towards a model of suicidal ideation for Hong Kong Chinese adolescents. *Journal of Adolescence*, Vol. 29: 209–224.

Sun, R.C., & Shek, D.T. (2010) Life satisfaction, positive youth development, and problem behaviour among Chinese adolescents in Hong Kong. *Social Indicators Research*, Vol. 95, No. 3: 455–474.

Swinkels, A., Albarran, J.W., Means, R.I., Mitchell, T., & Stewart, M.C. (2002) Evidence-based practice in health and social care: Where are we now? *Journal of Interprofessional Care*, Vol. 16, No. 4: 335–347.

Tam, K.K., Chan, Y.C., & Wong, C.K.M. (1994) Validation of the parenting stress index among Chinese mothers in Hong Kong. *Journal of Community Psychology*, Vol. 22: 211–223.

Tashakkori, A., & Teddlie, C. (2003) *Mixed methodology combining qualitative and quantitative approaches*. London: Sage Publications Inc.

Tesser, A., Pilkington, C.J., McIntosh, W. (1989) Self-evaluation maintenance and the meditational role of emotion: The perception of friends and strangers. *Journal of Personality and Social Psychology*, Vo. 57, No. 3: 442–456.

Thomas, E.M. (2000) *Parent perceptions of the effective black parenting program*. Unpublished dissertation, Minneapolis: Walden University.

Thorne, B. (2003) *Carl rogers* (2nd edition). London: Sage Publication Inc.

Tiano, J.D., & McNeil, C.B. (2005) The inclusion of fathers in behavioral parent training: A critical evaluation. *Child & Family Behavior Therapy*, Vol. 27: 1–28.

Tsang, S.K.M. (2004) Parent education in Hong Kong and implications for paediatricians. *Proceedings of Update Series, Hong Kong Journal of Paediatrics*, Vol. 9: 176–185.

Vogt, W.P. (1999) *Dictionary of statistics and methodology: A non-technical guide for the social sciences* (2nd edition). Thousand Oaks, CA: Sage Publications Inc.

Wagner, B.M., Silverman, M.A.C., & Martin, C.E. (2003) Family factors in youth suicidal behaviors. *The American Behavioral Scientist*, Vol. 46, No. 9: 1171–1191.

Wahler, R.G. (1980) The insular mother: Her problems in parent–child treatment. *Journal of Applied Behavior Analysis*, Vol. 13: 207–219.

Wallerstein, J.S. (1985) Children of divorce: Preliminary report of a ten-year follow-up of older children and adolescents. *Journal of the American Academy of Child Psychiatry*, Vol. 24, No. 5: 545–553.

Webb, S.A. (2001) Come considerations on the validity of evidence-based practice in social work. *British Journal of Social Work*, Vol. 31: 51–79.

Webster-Stratton, C. (1997) From parent training to community building. *Families in Society: The Journal of Contemporary Human Services* (March/April, 1997): 156–171.

Whittaker, K.A., & Cowley, S. (2010) An effective programme is not enough: A review of factors associated with poor attendance and engagement with parenting support programmes. *Children and Society*. DOI: 10.1111/j.1099-0860.2010.00333.x

Wilding, P. (1997) Social policy and social development in Hong Kong. *Asian Journal of Public Administration*, Vol. 19, No. 2: 244–275.

Wilson, A., Edwards, J., Allen, S., & Dasgupta, C. (2003) *Schools and family change school-based support for children experiencing divorce and separation*. London: Joseph Rowntree Foundation.

Wolfe, R.B., & Haddy, L. (2001) A qualitative examination of parents' experiences in parent education groups. *Early Child Development and Care*, Vol. 167: 77–87.

Woolfenden, S.R., Williams, K., & Peat, J.K. (2003) Family and parenting interventions in children and adolescents with conduct disorder and delinquency aged 10–17 (Cochrane Review). *The Cochrane Library*, Issue 2, 2003. Oxford7 Update Software.

Wu, D.Y.H. (1981) Child abuse in Taiwan. In J.E. Korbin (Ed.) *Child abuse and neglect: Cross-cultural perspectives*. Berkeley: University of California Press: 139–165.

Wuensch, K.L. (2011) *Binary logistic regress with PASW/SPSS*.

Yau, J., & Smetana, J.G. (1996) Adolescent-parent conflict among Chinese adolescents in Hong Kong. *Child Development*, Vol. 63, No. 3: 1262.

Yeung, K. F. (1998). The dynamics of interparental conflict and adolescent's behavior problems. (Thesis). University of Hong Kong, Pokfulam, Hong Kong SAR. Retrieved from http://dx.doi.org/10.5353/th_b2980738

Yip, K.S., Ngan, M.Y., & Lam, I. (2003) Pattern of adolescent self-cutting in Hong Kong: Reports from school social workers. *International Journal of Adolescence & Youth*, Vol. 11, No. 2: 135–155.

Youniss, J., & Smollar, J. (1985) *Adolescent relations with mothers, fathers, and friends.* Chicago: University of Chicago Press.

Yue, J.S.C. (1989) Development in family life education service: Changing objectives, changing strategies and changing demand on workers.

Index

Note: Page numbers in *italics* indicate figures and in **bold** indicate tables on the corresponding pages.

For Product Safety Concerns and Information please contact our EU representative GPSR@taylorandfrancis.com Taylor & Francis Verlag GmbH, Kaufingerstraße 24, 80331 München, Germany